PRACTICAL FORENSIC IMAGING

PRACTICAL
FORENSIC
IMAGING

Securing Digital Evidence with Linux Tools

by Bruce Nikkel

**no starch
press**

San Francisco

Printed in USA

Second printing

23 22 21 20 19 18   2 3 4 5 6 7 8 9

ISBN-10: 1-59327-793-8
ISBN-13: 978-1-59327-793-2

Publisher: William Pollock
Production Editor: Alison Law
Cover Illustration: Garry Booth
Interior Design: Octopod Studios
Technical Reviewer: Don Frick
Copyeditor: Anne Marie Walker
Compositor: Alison Law
Proofreader: Paula L. Fleming
Indexer: BIM Creatives, LLC

For information on distribution, translations, or bulk sales, please contact No Starch Press, Inc. directly:

No Starch Press, Inc.
245 8th Street, San Francisco, CA 94103
phone: 415.863.9900; info@nostarch.com
www.nostarch.com

Library of Congress Cataloging-in-Publication Data

Names: Nikkel, Bruce, author.
Title: Practical forensic imaging : securing digital evidence with Linux
    tools / Bruce Nikkel.
Description: San Francisco : No Starch Press, [2016] | Includes index.
Identifiers: LCCN 2016026449 (print) | LCCN 2016033058 (ebook) | ISBN
    9781593277932 | ISBN 1593277938 | ISBN 9781593278007 (epub) | ISBN
    1593278004 (epub) | ISBN 9781593278014 (mobi) | ISBN 1593278012 (mobi)
Subjects: LCSH: Computer crimes--Investigation. | Data recovery (Computer
    science) | Data encryption (Computer science) | Evidence, Criminal. |
    Linux.
Classification: LCC HV8079.C65 N55 2016 (print) | LCC HV8079.C65 (ebook) |
    DDC 363.25/9680285586--dc23
LC record available at https://lccn.loc.gov/2016026449

This book is dedicated to everyone who provided motivation, support, guidance, mentoring, inspiration, encouragement, critiques, wisdom, tools, techniques, and research—all of which influenced and helped with the creation of this book.

About the Author

Bruce Nikkel is the director of Cyber-Crime / IT Investigation & Forensics at UBS AG, a global financial institution based in Switzerland. He has worked for the bank's security and risk departments since 1997 and has managed the IT forensics team since 2005. Active in the digital forensics community, Bruce has published research papers on various digital forensics topics and is an editor for *Digital Investigation: The International Journal of Digital Forensics and Incident Response.* He is also on the organizing committee of DFRWS Europe. Bruce holds a PhD in network forensics from Cranfield University. His forensics website is *http://digitalforensics.ch/* and he can be reached at *nikkel@digitalforensics.ch.*

BRIEF CONTENTS

CONTENTS IN DETAIL

5
ATTACHING SUBJECT MEDIA TO AN ACQUISITION HOST 101

6
FORENSIC IMAGE ACQUISITION 141

7
FORENSIC IMAGE MANAGEMENT   187

8
SPECIAL IMAGE ACCESS TOPICS 229

9
EXTRACTING SUBSETS OF FORENSIC IMAGES 259

FOREWORD

Practical Forensic Imaging is much needed, and comes at a most opportune time. In recent years, preservation of digital evidence has become crucial in corporate governance, regulatory compliance, criminal and civil actions, and military operations. This trend is not geographically constrained but applies across the majority of continents, including developing countries.

Savvy organizations preserve pertinent computer systems when handling human resource complaints, policy violations, and employment termination. Some organizations even preserve data proactively, particularly for regulatory compliance purposes. This book provides scalable solutions that can be implemented across an enterprise for reasonable cost.

Most criminal cases involve digital evidence, and responsibility to preserve the data is increasingly falling on small law enforcement agencies with limited resources or training. *Practical Forensic Imaging* is an invaluable resource for such agencies, delivering practical solutions to their everyday problems.

Civil matters can involve large quantities of data spread across many data sources, including computers, servers, removable media, and backup tapes. Efficient and effective methods are crucial in such circumstances, and this book satisfies these requirements as well.

Given the increasing importance of preserving digital evidence in a multitude of contexts, it is critical to use proper preservation processes. Weaknesses in the preservation process can create problems in all subsequent phases of a digital investigation, whereas evidence that has been preserved using forensically sound methods and tools provides the foundation to build a solid case.

Furthermore, the growing need to preserve digital evidence increases the demand for tools that are dependable, affordable, and adaptable to different environments and use cases.

Practical Forensic Imaging addresses these requirements by concentrating on open source technology. Open source tools have these advantages: high transparency, low cost, and potential for adaptability. Transparency enables others to evaluate the reliability of open source tools more thoroughly. In addition to black box testing using known datasets, the source code can be reviewed.

Reducing the cost of forensic preservation is important both for agencies with limited resources and for organizations that have to deal with large quantities of data.

Being able to adapt open source tools to the needs of a specific environment is a major benefit. Some organizations integrate open source tools and preservation tools into automated processes within their enterprise or forensic laboratory, while others deploy these same tools on portable systems for use in the field.

There is a steep learning curve associated with all digital forensic processes and tools, particularly open source tools. Bruce Nikkel's extensive experience and knowledge is evident in the impressive clarity of the technical material in this book, making it accessible to novices while interesting to experts.

Starting with the theory and core requirements of forensic imaging, this book proceeds to delve into the technical aspects of acquiring forensic images using open source tools. The use of SquashFS is simple but quite clever and novel, providing a practical open source solution to a core aspect of forensic imaging. The book closes with discussion of the important steps of managing forensic images and preparing them for forensic examination.

Practical Forensic Imaging is an indispensable reference for anyone who is responsible for preserving digital evidence, including corporations, law enforcement, and counter-terrorism organizations.

Eoghan Casey, PhD
Professor in Cybercrime and Digital Investigations
School of Criminal Sciences
Faculty of Law, Criminal Sciences and Public Administration
University of Lausanne, Switzerland
August 2016

INTRODUCTION

Welcome to *Practical Forensic Imaging: Securing Digital Evidence with Linux Tools.* This book covers a variety of command line techniques for acquiring and managing disk images for digital evidence. Acquiring disk images is the first step in preserving digital forensic evidence in preparation for postmortem examination and analysis.

Why I Wrote This Book

Many digital forensics books are available on the market today. But the importance of forensic acquisition and evidence preservation tends to receive minimal attention. Often, the topic is only briefly covered in smaller chapters or subsections of a larger book. I thought that the topic of acquisition and evidence preservation was large enough to warrant its own book, and this book addresses this gap in the literature.

Another motivating factor to write this book was my desire to give back to the community in some way. After working professionally in a digital forensics lab for more than a decade and regularly using open source tools for various tasks (in addition to other commercial tools), I wanted to provide an additional resource for my colleagues and other professionals.

A third motivating factor was the increasing importance of preserving forensic evidence in the private sector. Investigating misconduct, fraud, malware, cyber attacks, and other abuse is becoming more common across private industry. But emphasis on the steps needed to acquire and preserve evidence is often lacking. Law enforcement agencies require properly acquired and preserved evidence to prosecute criminals. Civil cases involving e-discovery might require the sound acquisition and preservation of disk images. Large organizations with internal teams managing human resources disputes, policy violations, and whistle-blowing incidents can also benefit from following accepted procedures for collecting and preserving digital evidence.

How This Book Is Different

The book is a technical procedural guide. It explains the use of Linux as a platform for performing computer forensics, in particular, forensic image acquisition and evidence preservation of storage media. I include examples that demonstrate well-known forensic methods using free or open source computer forensic tools for acquiring a wide range of target media.

Unlike Linux forensic books covering a broad range of application and OS analysis topics, this book focuses on a single specific area within computer forensics: *forensic acquisition*, also known as *forensic imaging*, of storage media. This includes the preparation, acquisition, preservation, and management of digital evidence from various types of storage media. The sound acquisition of storage media is precisely what makes this process "forensic."

In addition to covering open source tools, this book includes examples of several proprietary command line tools that are free to use but not open source.

I discuss some newer hardware topics that have not yet been incorporated into other forensic books. For example, NVME and SATA Express, 4K-native sector drives, Hybrid SSDs, SAS, UASP/USB3x, Thunderbolt, and more. Some of these are straightforward to manage in a digital forensics context; others are more challenging.

I also introduce a new forensic technique that uses the SquashFS compressed filesystem as a simple and practical forensic evidence container. With this book, I provide the sfsimage shell script, which can preserve evidence into SquashFS forensic containers.

Why Use the Command Line?

Why is a book based on the command line even useful or relevant today? The computer command line has been around since the teletype days of the 1960s, making it more than half a century old. In computing, although age is sometimes viewed as a sign of obsolescence, it can also be a sign of maturity and dependability, which is the case with the Linux/Unix command line. Even Microsoft has recognized the value and power of the command line by introducing and promoting PowerShell as an alternative to the aging DOS prompt.

There are many reasons why the command line has retained its popularity over the years and continues to be relevant for the topics I discuss in this book. Here are some examples:

- **Easier scripting and automation possibilities:** A GUI interface is designed for human use, whereas the command line can be used by either human or machine. This makes the command line particularly useful for scripting and automating work.

- **Better understanding of how things work under the hood:** Graphical tools are often simply frontends to command line tools. Learning command line tools helps you understand what is going on under the hood when you're using the GUI frontend tools.

- **Flexibility and efficiency:** When you execute certain tasks on the command line, you have more flexibility, power, and control. For example, piping and redirection allow you to combine multiple steps into a single command line.

- **Unix philosophy:** The traditional Unix philosophy is to create simple tools that do one job well, whereas large GUI programs pack rich and complex functionality into one large monolithic program.

- **Remote access:** Command line activity is secure and easy to perform remotely using ssh. In some cases, remote shell access is your only choice, especially when you're working with virtual or cloud-based servers or systems located in other cities or countries.

- **Headless servers:** On Unix and Linux servers where an incident has occurred, the command line might be your only option, because a GUI might not have been installed.

- **Embedded systems:** The increasing popularity of embedded Unix and Linux systems, such as Raspberry Pi, Beagleboard, or other Internet-of-Things devices, might only have a command line interface available.

- **Knowledge investment:** Command line tools do not change much over time compared to GUI tools. If you invest time learning to use a command line tool, you won't need to relearn everything when the command is updated or new features are added.

- **Personal preference:** Some tech people simply prefer using the command line rather than a GUI and would use it if given the option.

This book provides you with a command line guide for performing digital forensic acquisition for investigations and incident response activities. It does not cover GUI equivalent tools or frontends.

Target Audience and Prerequisites

I wrote this book with a specific audience in mind. I had some expectations and made some assumptions when writing many sections.

Who Should Read This Book?

This book primarily benefits two groups of people. First, it helps experienced forensic investigators advance their Linux command line skills for performing forensic acquisition work. Second, it's useful for experienced Unix and Linux administrators who want to learn digital forensic acquisition techniques.

The book targets the growing number of forensic practitioners coming from a number of areas, including incident response teams; computer forensic investigators within large organizations; forensic and e-discovery technicians from legal, audit, and consulting firms; and traditional forensic practitioners from law enforcement agencies.

By the end of this book, you should have a comprehensive and complete picture of the command line tool landscape available for performing forensic acquisition of storage media and the management of forensic images.

Prerequisite Knowledge

This book assumes that you have a working knowledge of OSes, in particular, the Unix and Linux shell environment. The examples in this book use the Bash shell extensively. You should also have an understanding of how to run command line programs as well as how to do basic piping and redirecting between programs.

Additionally, you should have a basic understanding of digital forensics principles, including write-blocking technology, sector-by-sector acquisition, and preserving evidence integrity with cryptographic hashing. This foundational knowledge is assumed when applying the examples presented.

Preinstalled Platform and Software

You should have access to a functioning Linux platform with the relevant tools already installed. The book doesn't cover how to find, download, compile, or install various tools. If you have a reasonably new machine (within a year of this book's publication date) with a recent distribution of Linux, the examples should work without any issues. Some of the tools are not part of standard Linux distributions but can easily be found on github or by searching for them.

How the Book Is Organized

Rather than a chronological list of steps, this book is intended to be more of a cookbook of tasks. However, the book does follow a logical progression, from setting up a platform, planning and preparation, and acquisition to post acquisition activities. In general, the book is designed as a reference, so you don't need to read it from beginning to end. Certain sections assume some knowledge and understanding of prior sections, and appropriate cross-references to those sections are provided.

- **Chapter 0** is a general introduction to digital forensics. I also cover the history and evolution of the field, mentioning significant events that have shaped its direction. I give special emphasis to the importance of standards needed to produce digital evidence that can be used in a court of law. The overall book strives to be international and independent of regional legal jurisdictions. This is important today, because more criminal investigations span country borders and involve multiple jurisdictions. Also, due to the increase in private sector forensic capabilities, the book will be useful for private forensic labs, especially in global firms.

- **Chapter 1** provides a technical overview of mass storage media, connectors and interfaces, and the commands and protocols used to access the media. It covers the technologies a typical forensic investigator will encounter working in a professional forensic lab environment. I've made an effort to help you achieve clear understanding of the different storage media interfaces, protocol tunneling, bridging, and how storage media attach and interact with a host system.

- **Chapter 2** provides an overview of Linux as a forensic acquisition platform. It briefly touches on the advantages and disadvantages of using Linux and open source software. It describes how the Linux kernel recognizes and handles new devices being attached to the system and how you can access those devices. The chapter presents an overview of Linux distributions and shell execution. It also explains the use of piping and redirection as an important concept used throughout the book.

- **Chapter 3** covers the various raw and forensic formats commonly used in the field. These formats are the digital "evidence bags" for acquired storage media. The chapter explains raw images; describes commercial forensic formats, such as EnCase and FTK; and covers formats from the research community, such as AFF. It also introduces a simple forensic evidence container, based on SquashFS, and a tool for managing it.

- **Chapter 4** is a transitional point in the book, leaving the theoretical and entering more practical and procedural territory. It begins with examples of maintaining logs and audit trails and saving command data for use in formal forensic reports. It covers various planning and logistical issues frequently faced by forensic investigators. It ends with a section on setting up a forensically sound, write-blocked working environment to prepare for the actual acquisition process.

- **Chapter 5** progresses with attaching a suspect disk to the acquisition host and gathering data (ATA, SMART, and so on) about the disk. At this stage, media accessibility restrictions, such as HPA and DCO, are removed, and locked and self-encrypted disks are made accessible. This chapter also covers several special topics, such as Apple Target Disk Mode. At this point, the disk is prepared and ready for you to execute acquisition commands.

- **Chapter 6** executes the acquisition, demonstrating multiple forms of forensic acquisition using open source as well as proprietary tools. Emphasis is placed on preserving evidence during acquisition using hashes, signatures, and timestamping services. The chapter also covers handling various scenarios with bad blocks and errors, as well as remote acquisition over a network. Special topics include the acquisition of tapes and RAID systems.

- **Chapter 7** focuses on managing acquired disk images. This chapter assumes the forensic image has been successfully made, and typical post acquisition tasks are described. These tasks include compressing, splitting, and encrypting images; converting between forensic formats; cloning or duplicating images; transferring images to other parties; and preparing images for long-term storage. The chapter ends with a section on secure data disposal.

- **Chapter 8** covers a number of special tasks that you can do post acquisition in preparation for examination. These tasks include accessing images via loop devices, accessing virtual machine images, and accessing OS-encrypted images (BitLocker, FileVault, TrueCrypt/VeraCrypt, and so on). The chapter also covers accessing other virtual disk containers. These techniques enable you to conduct forensic analysis on the images and allow you to safely browse the filesystem using regular file managers and other programs.

- **Chapter 9** partly enters the forensic analysis realm and demonstrates extracting subsets of data from images. It includes identifying and extracting partitions (including deleted partitions), extracting inter-partition gaps, extracting slack space, and extracting previously hidden areas of the disk (DCO and HPA). The chapter shows several examples of piecewise data extraction, including the extraction of individual sectors and blocks.

Each chapter might describe several different tools used to perform the same task. Often, multiple tools will be available to you to perform the same task, and depending on the situation, one tool might be more useful than another. In such cases, I discuss the advantages and disadvantages of each tool.

Each section in a chapter follows roughly the same structure. The title provides a high-level description of the topic. An introductory paragraph describes the motivation for the section and explains why the particular task is useful for investigations, digital forensics, or incident response. In many cases, the motivation is driven by legal or industry-accepted standards. It's important to know and understand these standards, because they support the forensic soundness of the work being done. Where necessary, I provide references to the source code of tools, additional information, or other articles of interest.

Prior to introducing or demonstrating a new tool, I provide a paragraph that describes the function or purpose of the tool and its relevance to digital forensics. In some cases, the history of the tool might also be of interest to you, so I include that as well.

After a description of the task and tool(s), you'll see one or more command line examples as well as the command output (displayed in blocks of monospaced or fixed-width font). A command might be repeated to show different variations or extended forms of use. Each command example is followed by a paragraph that describes the command being executed and explains the resulting output.

A final paragraph might include potential gotchas, caveats, risks, and common problems or mistakes you might encounter that are relevant to digital forensic investigations.

The Scope of This Book

This book focuses on the forensic acquisition of common storage media and the steps required to preserve evidence. Although some triage and analysis work is shown, in general, forensic analysis of application and OS data is considered outside the scope of this book.

A number of other areas are also outside the scope of this book, including data acquisition from areas other than traditional storage media, for example, network forensic acquisition, memory acquisition from live systems, cloud data acquisition, and so on.

In various places, I mention enterprise class storage media and legacy storage media, but I don't provide practical examples. These are less commonly found in forensic lab settings. However, many of the methods presented will generally work with enterprise or legacy storage hardware.

The acquisition of proprietary devices is also beyond the scope of this book. Acquiring the latest generation of mobile phones, tablets, or Internet-of-Things devices might be possible with the tools and techniques shown in the book (if they behave as block devices in the Linux kernel), but I don't explicitly cover such devices.

Conventions and Format

Examples of code, commands, and command output are displayed in a monospace or fixed-width font, similar to what you see on a computer terminal screen. In some places, nonrelevant command output may be removed or truncated and replaced with an ellipsis (...), and when lines are too long for the book's margins, they are wrapped and indented.

Commands that you can run without root privilege use a $ prompt. Privileged commands that typically need to be run as root are prefixed with #. For brevity, the use of sudo or other privilege escalation is not always shown. Some sections provide more information about running command procedures as a non-root user.

In the computer book industry, it is common practice to change the timestamps in blocks of code and command output to a point in the future after release, giving the contents a newer appearance. I felt that writing a book about preserving evidence integrity and then manipulating the very evidence provided in the book (by forward dating timestamps) wasn't appropriate. All the command output you see in this book reflects the actual output from the testing and research, including the original dates and time-stamps. Aside from snipping out less relevant areas with ... and removing trailing blank lines, I left the command output unchanged.

A bibliography is not provided at the end of the book. All references are included as footnotes at the bottom of the page where the source is referenced.

The investigator's or examiner's workstation is referred to as the *acquisition host* or *examination host*. The disk and image that are undergoing acquisition are referred to as the *subject disk, suspect disk*, or *evidence disk*.

A number of terms are used interchangeably throughout the book. *Disk, drive, media*, and *storage* are often used interchangeably when they're used in a generic sense. *Forensic investigator, examiner*, and *analyst* are used throughout the book and refer to the person (you) using the examination host for various forensic tasks. *Imaging, acquisition*, and *acquiring* are used interchangeably, but the word *copying* is deliberately excluded to avoid confusion with regular copying outside the forensic context.

0

DIGITAL FORENSICS OVERVIEW

 Some historical background about the field of digital forensics leading up to the present day helps to explain how the field evolved and provides additional context for some of the problems and challenges faced by professionals in the forensics industry.

Digital Forensics History

Here, I discuss the development of modern digital forensics as a scientific discipline.

Pre-Y2K

The history of digital forensics is short compared to that of other scientific disciplines. The earliest computer-related forensics work began during the 1980s, when practitioners were almost exclusively from law enforcement or military organizations. During the 1980s, the growth of home computers and dial-up BBS services triggered early interest in computer forensics within law enforcement communities. In 1984, the FBI developed a pioneering program to analyze computer evidence. In addition, the increase in abuse and internet-based attacks led to the creation of the Computer Emergency Response Team (CERT) in 1988. CERT was formed by the Defense Advanced Research Projects Agency (DARPA) and is located at Carnegie Mellon University in Pittsburgh.

The 1990s saw major growth in internet access, and personal computers in the home became commonplace. During this time, computer forensics was a major topic among law enforcement agencies. In 1993, the FBI hosted the first of multiple international conferences on computer evidence for law enforcement, and in 1995, the International Organization of Computer Evidence (IOCE) was formed and began making recommendations for standards. The concept of "computer crime" had become a reality, not just in the United States but internationally. In 1999, the Association of Chief Police Officers (ACPO) created a good practice guide for UK law enforcement personnel who handled computer-based evidence. Also during the late 1990s, the first open source forensic software, The Coroner's Toolkit, was created by Dan Farmer and Wietse Venema.

2000–2010

After the turn of the millennium, a number of factors increased demand for digital forensics. The tragedy of September 11, 2001, had a tremendous impact on how the world viewed security and incident response. The Enron and Anderson accounting scandals led to the creation of the Sarbanes-Oxley Act in the United States, designed to protect investors by improving the accuracy and reliability of corporate disclosures. This act required organizations to have formal incident response and investigation processes, typically including some form of digital forensics or evidence collection capability. The growth of intellectual property (IP) concerns also had an impact on civilian organizations. Internet fraud, phishing, and other IP- and brand-related incidents created further demand for investigation and evidence gathering. Peer-to-peer file sharing (starting with Napster), along with the arrival of digital copyright legislation in the form of the Digital Millennium Copyright Act (DMCA), led to increased demand for investigating digital copyright violation.

Since 2000, the digital forensics community has made great strides in transforming itself into a scientific discipline. The 2001 DFRWS Conference provided important definitions and challenges for the forensic community, and it defined digital forensics as follows:

> The use of scientifically derived and proved methods toward the preservation, collection, validation, identification, analysis, interpretation, documentation and presentation of digital evidence derived from digital sources for the purpose of facilitating or furthering the reconstruction of events found to be criminal, or helping to anticipate unauthorized actions shown to be disruptive to planned operations.[1]

1. Gary Palmer, "A Roadmap for Digital Forensic Research." Digital Forensics Research Workshop (DFRWS), 2001. Technical report DTR-T0010-01, Utica, New York.

While the forensics community defined its scope and goal of becoming a recognized scientific research field, practitioner-level standards, guidelines, and best-practice procedures were also being formalized. The Scientific Working Group on Digital Evidence (SWGDE) specified definitions and standards, including the requirement of Standard Operating Procedures (SOPs) for law enforcement. The 2000 IOCE Conference in France worked toward formalizing procedures for law enforcement practitioners through guidelines and checklists. The 13th INTERPOL Forensic Science Symposium, also in France, outlined the requirements of groups involved in digital forensics and specified a comprehensive set of standards and principles for government and law enforcement. The US Department of Justice published a detailed first responders' guide for law enforcement (US DOJ *Electronic Crime Scene Investigation: A Guide for First Responders*) and NIST's Computer Forensics Tool Testing project (CFTT) wrote the first *Disk Imaging Tool Specification*.

During this decade several peer reviewed academic journals were introduced to publish the increasing body of knowledge. The *International Journal of Digital Evidence (IJDE)* was created in 2002 (and ceased in 2007), and *Digital Investigation: The International Journal of Digital Forensics & Incident Response* was created in 2004.

2010–Present

In the years since 2010, a number of events have shifted the focus toward investigating and collecting evidence from cyber attacks and data breaches.

WikiLeaks (*http://www.wikileaks.org/*) began publishing leaked material from the US military, including videos and diplomatic cables. Anonymous gained notoriety for distributed denial-of-service (DDoS) attacks and other hacktivist activity. LulzSec compromised and leaked data from HBGary Federal and other firms.

The investigation of Advanced Persistent Threat (APT) malware became a major topic in the industry. The extent of government espionage using malware against other governments and private industry was made public. The Stuxnet worm targeting SCADA systems, in particular, control systems in the Iranian nuclear program, was discovered. Mandiant published its investigation of APT1, the Cyber Warfare unit of the Chinese Army. Edward Snowden leaked a vast repository of documents revealing the extent of NSA hacking. The release of data from the Italian company HackingTeam revealed the professional exploit market being sold to governments, law enforcement agencies, and private sector companies.

Major data breaches became a concern for private sector companies as credit card and other data was stolen from Sony, Target, JPMorgan Chase, Anthem, and others. The global banking industry faced a major increase in banking malware (Zeus, Sinowal/Torpig, SpyEye, Gozi, Dyre, Dridex, and others), which successfully targeted banking clients for the purpose of financial fraud. More recently, attacks involving ransoms have become popular (Ransomware, DDoS for Bitcoin, and so on).

This diverse array of hacking, attacks, and abuse has broadened the focus of digital forensics to include areas of network traffic capture and analysis and the live system memory acquisition of infected systems.

Forensic Acquisition Trends and Challenges

The field of digital forensics is constantly transforming due to changes and advances in technology and criminality. In this section, I discuss recent challenges, trends, and changes that are affecting traditional forensic acquisition of storage media.

Shift in Size, Location, and Complexity of Evidence

The most obvious change affecting forensic image acquisition is disk capacity. As of this writing, consumer hard disks can store 10TB of data. The availability of easy-to-use RAID appliances has pushed logical disk capacity to even greater sizes. These large disk capacities challenge traditional forensic lab acquisition processes.

Another challenge is the multitude of storage devices that are found at crime scenes or involved in incidents. What used to be a single computer for a household has become a colorful array of computers, laptops, tablets, mobile phones, external disks, USB thumb drives, memory cards, CDs and DVDs, and other devices that store significant amounts of data. The challenge is actually finding and seizing all the relevant storage media, as well as acquiring images in a manner that makes everything simultaneously accessible to forensic analysis tools.

The shifting location of evidence into the cloud also creates a number of challenges. In some cases, only cached copies of data might remain on end user devices, with the bulk of the data residing with cloud service providers. Collecting this data can be complicated for law enforcement if it resides outside a legal jurisdiction, and difficult for private organizations when outsourced cloud providers have no forensic support provisions in their service contract.

The Internet of Things is a fast-growing trend that is poised to challenge the forensics community as well. The multitude of little internet-enabled electronic gadgets (health monitors, clocks, environmental displays, security camera devices, and so on) typically don't contain large amounts of storage. But they might contain useful telemetry data, such as timestamps, location and movement data, environmental conditions, and so forth. Identifying and accessing this data will eventually become a standard part of forensic evidence collection.

Arguably, the most difficult challenge facing forensic investigators today is the trend toward proprietary, locked-down devices. Personal computer architectures and disk devices have historically been open and well documented, allowing for the creation of standard forensic tools to access the data. However, the increased use of proprietary software and hardware makes this innovation difficult. This is especially problematic in the mobile device space, where devices may need to be *jail broken* (effectively hacked into) before lower-level filesystem block access is possible.

Multijurisdictional Aspects

The international nature of crime on the internet is another challenge facing forensic investigators. Consider a company in country A that is targeted by an attacker in country B who uses relaying proxies in country C to compromise infrastructure via an outsourcing partner in country D and exfiltrates the stolen data to a drop zone in country E. In this scenario, five different countries are involved, meaning the potential coordination of five different law enforcement agencies, engaging at least five different companies, across five different legal jurisdictions. This multiple-country scenario is not unusual today; in fact, it is rather common.

Industry, Academia, and Law Enforcement Collaboration

The increasingly complex and advanced nature of criminal activity on the internet has fostered increased cooperation and collaboration to gather intelligence and evidence and to coordinate investigations.

This collaboration among competing industry peers can be viewed as fighting a common enemy (the banking industry against banking malware, the ISP industry against DDoS and spam, and so on). Such collaboration has also crossed private and public sector boundaries: law enforcement agencies work together with industry partners to combat criminal activity in public-private partnerships (PPPs). This multifaceted cooperation creates opportunities to identify, collect, and transfer digital evidence. The challenge here is ensuring that private partners understand the nature of digital evidence and are able to satisfy the standards expected of law enforcement in the public sector. This will increase the likelihood of successful prosecution based on evidence collected by the private sector.

A third group that is collaborating with industry and law enforcement is the academic research community. This community typically consists of university forensic labs and security research departments that delve into the theoretical and highly technical aspects of computer crime and forensics. These researchers are able to spend time analyzing problems and gaining insight into new criminal methods and forensic techniques. In some cases, they're able to lend support to law enforcement where the standard forensic tools are not able to extract or analyze the evidence needed. The academic groups must also understand the needs and expectations of managing and preserving digital evidence.

Principles of Postmortem Computer Forensics

The principles of digital forensics as a scientific discipline are influenced by a number of factors, including formally defined standards, peer-reviewed research, industry regulation, and best practices.

Digital Forensic Standards

Standards for the collection and preservation of traditional physical evidence have depended heavily on the local legal jurisdiction. In contrast, digital evidence collection has matured in an international setting and interconnected environment with multiple jurisdictions contributing to the research and the development of standards. Typically hardware, software, file formats, network protocols, and other technologies are the same across the globe. For this reason, standards and processes for collecting digital evidence are more aligned across jurisdictions. A good example is the use of write blockers for attaching disks to imaging machines, a practice that is accepted nearly everywhere worldwide.

Several formal standards bodies exist that define the standards of forensic acquisition. The US National Institute of Standards and Technology (NIST) provides the Computer Forensic Tool Testing (CFTT) program. Its goal is stated here:

> The goal of the Computer Forensic Tool Testing (CFTT) project at the National Institute of Standards and Technology (NIST) is to establish a methodology for testing computer forensic software tools by development of general tool specifications, test procedures, test criteria, test sets, and test hardware.

Although NIST is a US-centric organization, many of its standards are adopted internationally or at least influence the standards bodies in other countries.

The International Organization for Standardization (ISO) also provides a number of standards pertaining to digital evidence. Relevant to forensic acquisition are the ISO Guidelines for identification, collection, acquisition, and preservation of digital evidence:

> ISO/IEC 27037:2012 provides guidelines for specific activities in the handling of digital evidence, which are identification, collection, acquisition and preservation of potential digital evidence that can be of evidential value.
>
> It provides guidance to individuals with respect to common situations encountered throughout the digital evidence handling process and assists organizations in their disciplinary procedures and in facilitating the exchange of potential digital evidence between jurisdictions.

Individual police forces may have their own standards that outline the evidence collection process. For example, in the United Kingdom, the Association of Chief Police Officers (ACPO) provides the *ACPO Good Practice Guide for Digital Evidence*. The guide states:

> This best practice guide has been produced by the ACPO Crime Business Area and was originally approved by ACPO Cabinet in December 2007. The purpose of this document is to provide guidance not only to assist law enforcement but for all that assists in

investigating cyber security incidents and crime. It will be updated according to legislative and policy changes and re-published as required.

This document references a number of other standards and documents put forth by ACPO and others.

The US Department of Justice maintains *Electronic Crime Scene Investigation: A Guide for First Responders.* The introduction to the guide states:

> This guide is intended to assist State and local law enforcement and other first responders who may be responsible for preserving an electronic crime scene and for recognizing, collecting, and safeguarding digital evidence.

A number of other international organizations contribute to the development of standards through the creation of forensic working groups, committees, and communities.

Peer-Reviewed Research

Another source of digital forensic standards and methods is peer-reviewed research and academic conferences. These resources put forward the latest advances and techniques in the digital forensics research community. Basing forensic work on peer-reviewed scientific research is especially important with newer methods and technologies because they may be untested in courts.

Several international academic research communities exist and contribute to the body of knowledge. The most prominent research journal in the field of forensics is *Digital Investigation: The International Journal of Digital Forensics & Incident Response*, which has been publishing academic research from the field for more than a decade. The stated aims and scope are described as follows:

> The *Journal of Digital Investigation* covers cutting edge developments in digital forensics and incident response from around the globe. This widely referenced publication helps digital investigators remain current on new technologies, useful tools, relevant research, investigative techniques, and methods for handling security breaches. Practitioners in corporate, criminal and military settings use this journal to share their knowledge and experiences, including current challenges and lessons learned in the following areas:
>
> Peer-reviewed research: New approaches to dealing with challenges in digital investigations, including applied research into analyzing specific technologies, and application of computer science to address problems encountered in digital forensics and incident response.
>
> Practitioner reports: Investigative case studies and reports describing how practitioners are dealing with emerging challenges in the field, including improved methods for conducting effective digital investigations. . . .

The leading digital forensics academic research conference is the Digital Forensics Research WorkShop (DFRWS). This conference began in 2001 and has remained US based, although in 2014, a separate European event was created. The stated purpose of DFRWS is as follows:[2]

- Attract new perspectives and foster exchange of ideas to advance digital forensic science

- Promote scholarly discussion related to digital forensic research and its application

- Involve experienced analysts and examiners from law enforcement, military, and civilian sectors to focus research on practitioner requirements, multiple investigative environments, and real world usability

- Define core technologies that form a focus for useful research and development

- Foster the discovery, explanation, and presentation of conclusive, persuasive evidence that will meet the heightened scrutiny of the courts and other decision-makers in civilian and military environments

- Establish and expand a common lexicon so the community speaks the same language

- Engage in regular debate and collaborative activity to ensure a sharp focus, high interest, and efficacy

- Maintain a dynamic community of experts from academia and practice

- Increase scientific rigor in digital forensic science

- Inspire the next generation to invent novel solutions

Full disclosure: I am an editor for *Digital Investigation* and participate in the organizing committee of DFRWS Europe.

Industry Regulations and Best Practice

Industry-specific regulations may place additional requirements (or restrictions) on the collection of digital evidence.

In the private sector, industry standards and best practice are developed by various organizations and industry groups. For example, the Information Assurance Advisory Council (IAAC) provides the *Directors and Corporate Advisors' Guide to Digital Investigations and Evidence.*

Other sources include standards and processes mandated by legal and regulatory bodies, for example, the requirements for evidence collection capability in the US Sarbanes-Oxley legislation.

Some digital evidence requirements might depend on the industry. For example, healthcare regulations in a region may specify requirements for data protection and include various forensic response and evidence collection processes in the event of a breach. Telecom providers may have

---

2. *http://www.dfrws.org/about-us/*

regulations covering log retention and law enforcement access to infrastructure communications. Banking regulators also specify requirements and standards for digital evidence. A good example is the Monetary Authority of Singapore (MAS), which provides detailed standards for the banking community in areas such as security and incident response (*http://www.mas.gov.sg/regulations-and-financial-stability/regulatory-and-supervisory-framework/risk-management/technology-risk.aspx*).

With the recent increase in cyber attacks targeting different sectors (finance, health, and so on), regulatory bodies may play a larger role in influencing and defining standards for evidence collection in the future.

Principles Used in This Book

This book focuses on forensic tasks that the private and public sectors have in common. The examples begin with a simplified forensic acquisition, and further examples demonstrate additional features and capabilities of the acquisition process. This includes preserving evidence using cryptographic hashing and signing, logging, performance, error handling, and securing an acquired image. I also explain several techniques for imaging over a network, as well as special topics, such as magnetic tapes and RAID systems.

To perform a forensic acquisition, there are several prerequisites:

- The subject drive is attached and recognized by the Linux kernel.
- Write blocking is established.
- The subject drive has been positively identified and documented.
- Full access to the device is possible (HPA, DCO, and ATA security are disabled).
- Time and storage capacity are available to perform the acquisition.

The forensic acquisition process and tools testing are well documented within the digital forensics community, and certain requirements are expected. A useful resource is the CFTT Program instituted by NIST. The top-level forensic-imaging requirements from NIST include the following:

- The tool shall make a bitstream duplicate or an image of an original disk or partition.
- The tool shall not alter the original disk.
- The tool shall log I/O errors.
- The tool's documentation shall be correct.

These principles, described in a paper published by NIST,[3] provide a foundation for the rest of the book. They exist to ensure that evidence integrity is preserved, and tampering is either prevented or detected.

---

3. *https://utica.edu/academic/institutes/ecii/publications/articles/A04BC142-F4C3-EB2B-462CCC0C887B3CBE.pdf*

Some research has challenged views that a complete acquisition can be achieved given the restrictions and limitations of the ATA interface used to access the physical disk.[4] A theoretically complete acquisition includes all sectors on magnetic disks and memory beneath the flash translation layer of SSDs and flash drives, and it now extends to the locked-down mobile devices that can't be imaged with traditional block device methods. It is becoming increasingly difficult to achieve "complete" acquisition of all physical storage of a device. For mobile devices, the forensics community has already made the distinction between physical and logical acquisition, with the latter referring to the copying of files and data rather than the imaging of drive sectors.

For the examples you'll see in this book, *forensic completeness* is considered to be acquiring areas of a disk that can be reliably and repeatably accessed with publicly available software tools using published interface specifications. Areas of a disk that are accessible only through nonpublic vendor proprietary tools (in-house diagnostics, development tools, and so on) or by using hardware disassembly (chip desoldering, head assembly replacement, disk platter removal, and so on) are not within the scope of this book.

This has been a brief introduction to the field of digital forensics. Chapter 1 continues with an introduction to storage media technologies and the interfaces used to attach them to an acquisition host.

---

4. "Forensic Imaging of Hard Disk Drives—What We Thought We Knew," Forensic Focus, January 27, 2012, *http://articles.forensicfocus.com/2012/01/27/forensic-imaging-of-hard-disk -drives-what-we-thought-we-knew-2/*.

1

STORAGE MEDIA OVERVIEW

This chapter serves as an overview of PC bus systems, common mass storage media, physical connectors and interfaces, and the low-level protocol commands used to communicate with attached storage devices. It also provides the background for understanding the forensic acquisition of storage media described in the rest of the book.

In general, mass storage technologies are grouped into three broad categories: magnetic media, non-volatile memory (flash), and optical media. Storage media can be built into a device or be removable. The device also contains the drive electronics needed to interface with the media. Storage devices are accessed by a system through an internal or external bus or interface.

The chapter begins with overviews of these three storage technologies and touches on key points related to digital forensics. The final two sections describe how these storage devices attach to and communicate with a Linux system, and I discuss items of particular interest to a forensic examiner.

This chapter primarily focuses on modern PC architectures and components. Former popular legacy technologies might be mentioned but not covered in depth. I've also limited this overview to computer equipment used in small server environments and by individuals (employees, home users, and so on) rather than covering large enterprise technology. Storage technologies in large enterprise environments are not always suited for traditional disk media forensic imaging; in some cases, the sheer volume of storage space makes traditional acquisition infeasible, and business-critical enterprise systems typically can't be taken offline like smaller PC-based systems.

Magnetic Storage Media

Magnetic media is the oldest of the three basic storage technologies (preceded by paper tape and punch cards) and is the current leader in capacity. The two primary magnetic storage media types in use today are hard disks and tapes; both provide high capacity and reliability for online storage and offline archival storage.

NOTE   *The capacity race between magnetic disks and solid state drives (SSDs) is heating up. During the writing of this book, a 16TB SSD was announced and, when released, could be the world's largest disk.*

Hard Disks

Hard disks have consistently provided higher capacities than other media, such as SSD or optical. As of this writing, 10TB hard disks are available on the consumer market, and higher capacities are expected.

Hard disks are built with rotating platters coated with magnetized material, as shown in Figure 1-1. Multiple platters are stacked on a spindle, and read/write heads on a movable arm (the *actuator*) can read/write encoded data from/to the magnetic surface. Currently, common hard disk form factor sizes include 3.5 inch, 2.5 inch, and 1.8 inch. Because hard disks are mechanical devices, they're sensitive to shock, dropping, dust, moisture, and other environmental factors. Typical hard disk failures involve scratched platter surfaces, stuck or damaged heads, motor failure, and failed electronic circuitry.

The real physical geometry (heads, platters, tracks, sectors per track) of the disk is abstracted from the computer and is accessible as a sequence of sectors using Logical Block Addresses (LBA). A sector is the smallest addressable disk unit for reading and writing data. Historically, the standard physical hard disk sector size was 512 bytes; however, modern disks have transitioned to 4K sector sizes. Most current drives continue to provide a 512-byte emulation of the sector size, but drives with a native 4K sector size (known as 4Kn drives) are already on the market. Using 4Kn disks has performance advantages, and it's likely they'll someday overtake traditional 512-byte emulated drives. Refer to "Advanced Format 4Kn" on page 41 for more detail about 4Kn disk drives.

Figure 1-1: Magnetic hard disk

Traditional computer forensics originated from the need to analyze hard disks, which continue to be significant evidence sources today. In particular, when an OS "deletes" a file, it simply unlinks any references to the data blocks on the disk (unlike SSDs, which use a TRIM command to clear unallocated blocks). Those blocks are not erased from the magnetic platters, remaining on the disk where forensic tools can recover them (until they're overwritten).

Magnetic Tapes

The use of magnetic tapes in the home user marketplace has nearly disappeared, but small business and enterprise environments continue to use magnetic tapes for backups and archiving. Tapes, as shown in Figure 1-2, are one of the earlier forms of digital storage and have a reputation as a mature technology, reliable for long-term offline storage. Unlike disks, SSD/flash, or optical disks, tapes can only read or write data sequentially. Randomly accessing different blocks on a tape requires the user to rewind or forward the tape to the desired location before it can be read or written. This lack of random block access prevents tapes from being used as regular filesystems. Data is stored on tapes as a sequence of tape files; each file is typically an archive containing a filesystem or group of files and directories (using archive formats, such as TAR, DUMP, and so on.). Tape drives are controlled using SCSI tape commands to read and write data, position or rewind the tape, and eject the tape.

NOTE *Newer Linear Tape-Open, or LTO, drives can simulate a regular filesystem with the Linear Tape File System (LTFS), but this is not random access and files are still sequentially read and written.*

Figure 1-2: Magnetic tapes

Here are some examples of a Fibre Channel LTO5 tape drive and a USB
DAT160 tape drive; both are attached to a Linux system. The dmesg output
of the tape drives looks like this:

```
[   11.290176] scsi 1:0:0:0: Sequential-Access TANDBERG LTO-5 HH
    Y629 PQ: 0 ANSI: 6
[   11.293554] scsi 1:0:0:0: Attached scsi generic sg5 type 1
[   11.345030] st: Version 20101219, fixed bufsize 32768, s/g segs 256
[   11.361189] st 1:0:0:0: Attached scsi tape st0
...
[ 3263.575014] usb 1-8: new high-speed USB device number 14 using xhci_hcd
[ 3263.703245] usb 1-8: New USB device found, idVendor=03f0, idProduct=0225
[ 3263.703250] usb 1-8: New USB device strings: Mfr=1, Product=2, SerialNumber=3
[ 3263.703253] usb 1-8: Product: DAT160 USB Tape
[ 3263.703255] usb 1-8: Manufacturer: Hewlett Packard
[ 3263.703257] usb 1-8: SerialNumber: 48553101234E4648
[ 3263.704156] usb-storage 1-8:1.0: USB Mass Storage device detected
[ 3263.704295] scsi host12: usb-storage 1-8:1.0
[ 3264.713397] scsi 12:0:0:0: Sequential-Access HP       DAT160
    WU8A PQ: 0 ANSI: 3
[ 3264.722279] st 12:0:0:0: Attached scsi tape st1
```

Once tape archive files have been written, an *End Of Data (EOD)* marker
is also written to the tape. This informs the drive that the end of the tape
data has arrived and prevents the drive from reading any further. From a
forensics perspective, however, any data beyond the EOD marker is of interest because it may contain data from previous tape writes. No generic SCSI
commands are available to acquire data beyond the EOD marker. Specialized tape drives and equipment are needed to complete this task.

Legacy Magnetic Storage

There are many legacy magnetic storage types, especially among removable media. Floppy diskettes evolved over several generations before becoming obsolete. A number of proprietary storage products, such as Jaz, Zip, Syquest, and so on, were popular on the market during the '80s and '90s. A large variety of magnetic tapes are no longer in use, for example, 4mm DAT, 8mm Exabyte, and QIC. The forensic acquisition of these storage types is beyond the scope of this book. However, if functioning hardware and interfaces are available, you can acquire the data on most of these older devices using the same techniques described in this book. If the Linux kernel recognizes the sector-based media and it's made available as a block device, you can acquire it. If the Linux kernel recognizes tape drives as SCSI tape devices, you can access them using standard SCSI tape commands. For proprietary storage, kernel drivers or userspace tools might be available, which can provide you with access to legacy storage products.

Non-Volatile Memory

Non-volatile memory, typically using NAND flash technology, is growing in popularity and starting to replace magnetic hard disks in situations where very large capacities are not needed. (*NAND* refers to transistors operating as a logical NAND gate.) This type of memory creates a new set of challenges for forensic investigators because it doesn't exhibit the same low-level properties as magnetic disks.[1]

SSD and flash media are typically NAND-based storage and have no moving parts. Data is stored in an array of memory cells, and a layer of abstraction, the *Flash Translation Layer (FTL)*, makes the drive behave as a linear sequence of sectors similar to a hard disk. Because non-volatile memory disks are implemented in circuitry and are not mechanical, they are silent, use less power, and do not suffer from the same risk of physical damage as hard disks do. In terms of performance, they can randomly access and write data faster because there are no physical heads seeking to locations on a disk. (This also means there's no performance advantage to defragmenting filesystems.) The memory in SSD/flash drives doesn't have the same longevity as the magnetic platters in hard disks. Certain methods, such as wear leveling and over-provisioning, are used to prolong the life of SSD media. *Wear leveling* refers to the mechanism used to distribute reads and writes across the drive, ensuring blocks are evenly used during the lifetime of the drive. As blocks deteriorate or become unwritable, they're removed from use by the FTL and replaced with blocks from a pool of reserved (over-provisioned) blocks. These "retired" blocks can be read by removing (desoldering) the physical chips and reading out the memory. Some professional forensic laboratories perform this process, sometimes called *chip-off*, for various flash-based storage. Over-provisioning of blocks

---

1. Jeff Hedlesky, "Advancements in SSD Forensics" (presentation, CEIC2014, Las Vegas, NV, May 19–22, 2014).

during manufacture can take up to 10 to 25 percent of a flash disk (which is inaccessible to the user). Currently, an open source SSD firmware project exists that is useful for learning and researching the underlying SSD technology. You can find more information about it at *http://www.openssd-project.org/wiki/The_OpenSSD_Project.*

Solid State Drives

The SSD, as shown in Figure 1-3, was designed as a drop-in replacement for regular SATA disks. (*SATA,* or *Serial AT Attachment,* is the standard interface for disks.) SSDs have standard SATA interfaces and Self-Monitoring, Analysis and Reporting Technology (SMART) capability and use regular ATA commands (with some additions). Even the physical form factor of common consumer SSDs is the same as that of magnetic hard disks. Newer SSDs pose several challenges to digital forensic examiners, partly in the possibility to recover data from unallocated sectors on the drive and partly in the inability to access over-provisioned areas. SSD devices and OSes that support the ATA TRIM command can cause the erasure of unallocated disk blocks in preparation for the next use (SSD blocks must be erased before they can be written to or modified). This reduces the potential recovery of data in unallocated blocks, which are typically a valuable source of evidence on magnetic disks.

Figure 1-3: SSD

You can use the hdparm command to determine the TRIM features supported by an SSD. For example:

```
# hdparm -I /dev/sda
...
Commands/features:
        Enabled Supported:
...
```

```
    *    Data Set Management TRIM supported (limit 1 block)
    *    Deterministic read data after TRIM
...
```

A modern generation of SSDs, based on new standards called SATA Express and NVM Express, interface directly with the PCI Express bus.

USB Flash Drives

Small, portable USB flash drives, as shown in Figure 1-4, are referred to by many names: thumb drives, USB sticks, flash dongles, or simply USB flash drives. Flash drives initially became the replacement for floppy disks and, due to their low price and high capacity, are now replacing CDs and DVDs.

Figure 1-4: USB flash drive

But the small size and large capacity of USB flash drives make them an information security risk. As a result, most vendors offer security solutions involving encryption. The most common encryption is software based and optional. The drive's owner must explicitly install the encryption software provided by the vendor (or use alternative software, such as BitLocker or TrueCrypt). Some USB sticks provide mandatory hardware-based encryption systems. However, the added work and complexity of software encryption and the significantly higher cost of hardware encryption have impeded their widespread use. Plain, unencrypted USB devices are still most commonly used.

Removable Memory Cards

The popularity of portable devices, such as mobile phones, tablets, cameras, and so on, has created a market for removable memory cards that you can swap out when they're full or when copying to a PC or another device. A variety of memory cards are shown in Figure 1-5. These are typically flash based and, when placed in a card reader, appear as a linear sequence of sectors similar to a hard disk.

Figure 1-5: Flash memory cards

The most common memory card is the Secure Digital (SD) standard, which is available in several form factors and speeds. The CompactFlash (CF) card is popular in high-end camera equipment and is essentially a PATA/IDE interface with a smaller form factor. You can access it using a PATA/IDE interface adapter. A card reader connected via USB provides access to both memory card types (see Figure 1-6).

Figure 1-6: USB card reader

NOTE   Parallel ATA (PATA) *and* Integrated Drive Electronics (IDE) *are older standards defining a parallel interface between a drive and a computer system.*

Legacy Non-Volatile Memory

Many legacy memory cards became obsolete as the market lost interest in their maximum capacity or proprietary interfaces. Some examples include Sony Memory Sticks, Panasonic P2 cards, SmartMedia cards, and other PCM-CIA/PCcard media. Typically, these memory cards attach to a Linux system as block devices with a linear sequence of sectors, and you can image them using the same techniques as for other memory cards (if a physical reader is available).

Optical Storage Media

Common optical disc storage media in use today includes CD-ROMs, DVD-ROMs, and Blu-ray discs. The different types of optical media vary in their physical and chemical properties. Their visible differences are shown in Figure 1-7.

Figure 1-7: Top to bottom: DVD-ROM, Blu-ray, CD-ROM

Optical discs are usually read-only, write-once, or read-writable. Professionally mastered discs are stamped rather than burned. Although they're slowly becoming obsolete, writable optical discs are still a common source of digital evidence. Many forensic labs still use them for transfer and storage of compressed forensic images.

An optical disc contains a single spiral track with a sequence of *pits* and *lands* on a reflective surface, which can be read by a laser and interpreted as data bits. Data is written to the surface using a laser to burn points on the surface, which affects the reflectivity and causes the burned areas to be interpreted as data bits. This sequence of bits is separated into sectors, which after encoding and error correction contain 2048 bytes of user-accessible data.

Optical discs have one similarity to magnetic tapes: data is written as a single linear string of bytes—files are not fragmented. Unlike tapes, it's possible to easily jump to random areas of the disc, making it feasible to mount the disc as a read-only filesystem. However, writing to an optical disc is still cumbersome and, as with a tape, must be done in a sequential order of bytes.

Compact Discs

The oldest of the three optical discs, CD-ROM/CDR discs, were once the most popular optical media for home user backups, personal archives, and exchanging information. But as the use of convenient, high-capacity USB flash drives has grown, the use of CDs for storage has declined.

A collection of standards called the *Rainbow Books* describes various CD specifications, and a number of common CD standards exist. (See the Philips intellectual property page at *http://www.ip.philips.com/licensing/program/16/* for more information.)

- Music CDs, or Compact Disc-Digital Audio (CD-DA), are specified in the *Red Book* and IEC 60908 standard. Data in this format is divided into multiple audio tracks.

- Data CDs, or Compact Disc-Read Only Memory (CD-ROM), are covered in the *Yellow Book*, ISO/IEC 10149, and ECMA 130 standard (*http://www.ecma-international.org/publications/files/ECMA-ST/Ecma-130.pdf*).

- Writable CDs, or Compact Disc-Recordable/ReWritable (CD-R/CD-RW), are part of the *Orange Book* standard and allow data to be written (CD-R) or rewritten (CD-RW) to a CD.

- Less common standards include Photo-CD, Video CD (VCD), and other obscure variations, extensions, and enhancements of the common standards.

Every CD has a linear stream of bits (pits and lands) that are abstracted into a linear sequence of sectors. Abstracted further, above these sectors, are *sessions*, which contain a lead-in area and a table of contents (TOC) for the session. Multisession CDs can exist, and each session has its own TOC.

Data CDs can have filesystems residing on a session, which can contain files and a directory structure. Some examples of CD-ROM filesystems include:

High Sierra   Original standard for PCs (8.3, uppercase)

ISO9660   Updated High Sierra for cross-platform

Joliet   ISO9660 extensions; from Microsoft for Win95 and later

HFS   Macintosh

Rock Ridge   Extensions to ISO9660 for POSIX

El Torito   Standard for bootable discs

From a forensics perspective, user data on the entire CD can be read. There is no equivalent to the EOD found on tapes or DCO/HPA (user-inaccessible areas of a hard disk) found on disks. But there are filesystem-specific artifacts that might require special analysis to interpret.

Forensic write blockers, which are forensic hardware designed to prevent tampering and contaminating evidence found on drives, are unnecessary for CD-ROMs, given their default read-only properties. The OS will not update timestamps or modify data on a CD simply by putting it into the CD drive and accessing it.

CDs do have some unique identifiers that are useful in a forensic context. A *Source Unique Identifier (SID)* is stamped on the disc and contains information about the optical disc production facility that produced that particular disc. This code begins with *IFPI* and is physically stamped on the inner area of the disc (which can be easily read with the human eye). The *Recorder Identification Code (RID)* is written to system sectors of a disc and links a burned CD to the drive that created it. The RID is not easily accessible without specialized hardware.

Other physical attributes, such as those indicative of piracy and counterfeit copies, are outside the scope of this book, but you can access a guide from the International Federation of the Phonographic Industry (IFPI) at *http://www.ifpi.org/content/library/manual-of-guidance-chap3-english.pdf*.

Digital Versatile Discs

DVDs have different physical attributes from but are logically similar to CDs. A DVD has a single spiral track of bits split into 2048-byte sectors.

DVDs can be single sided or double sided. They can also be single layer or double layer. Doubling a side or a layer effectively doubles the data capacity. They have similar standards as CDs but with some additions, discussed here: *http://www.ecma-international.org/publications/files/ECMA-ST/ECMA-382.pdf*. DVD-Video, DVD-ROM, DVD-R, and DVD-RW correspond to their CD equivalents, but an additional DVD-RAM standard is also available. An alternative set of standards was created with DVD+R and DVD+RW, which have the same data capacities as DVD-R and DVD-RW, but the "+" and "-" formats are incompatible (although most modern drives can read both).

The most common filesystem for DVD drives is the Universal Disk Format (UDF), which is designed as a packet-writing replacement for ISO9660.

Blu-ray Discs

Blu-ray discs (BDs) use new physical manufacturing processes to further increase the data capacity of the discs. BD is still similar to CD and DVD in that it uses the spiral track of data split into 2048-byte sectors.

Its standards have close counterparts to CD and DVD and include BD-ROM (Read only), BD-R (Recordable), BD-RE (ReWritable), BD-XL (double capacity ReWritable).

DVD and BD allow for content protection using encryption, which can potentially cause difficulties when acquiring a protected disc during a forensic investigation. Tools and methods to decrypt DRM-protected content exist but are left outside the scope of this book.

Legacy Optical Storage

A number of legacy optical drives exist, in particular, the cartridge-based Write Once, Read Many (WORM) times drive. The legacy optical drives were more commonly used in enterprise environments, typically used SCSI interfaces, and were accessible as a linear sequence of sectors. If the drive and a compatible controller card are still available, and the Linux kernel recognizes the media, you can read and analyze the media in the same manner as other optical discs.

Interfaces and Physical Connectors

In this section, I'll provide an overview of common drive interfaces from the perspective of a forensic examiner. A forensic examiner working in a well-equipped forensics laboratory can acquire and analyze storage media using a variety of device interfaces.

A general trend in computing (especially with storage interfaces) is the shift from parallel and shared buses to serial point-to-point connections. PATA/IDE, a once-popular parallel interface with two disks sharing a single cable, has been replaced by SATA, which has one disk on a serial cable. SCSI was a parallel shared bus that supported multiple disks and has now been replaced by SAS with individual serial connectors for each disk. The original PCI bus was parallel and shared by multiple interface cards but has been replaced by PCI Express, a serial bus with dedicated lanes per interface (also used to attach SATA Express and NVM Express drives). The parallel printer interface has been replaced by USB (a serial protocol, but using a shared bus). As transmission speeds increased, the timing of parallel electrical signals became difficult to manage. Performing serialization/deserialization of data over dedicated serial lines enabled faster transmission speeds than managing the coordination of multiple parallel data lines.

Serial ATA

The most popular internal storage media interface in use today is SATA. Inside PCs, most hard disks, SSDs, and optical drives connect to SATA interfaces on the mainboard or add-on host bus adapters. The serial architecture of SATA has replaced parallel ATA (PATA or IDE), which used to be the dominant consumer disk interface.

The SATA standard is managed by The Serial ATA International Organization (*http://www.sata-io.org/*). Currently in revision 3, SATA provides speeds of up to 6Gbps (revisions 1 and 2 had speeds of 1.5Gbps and 3.0Gbps, respectively). In addition to the internal interface, an external interface (eSATA) exists that allows you to directly attach external SATA disks. Figure 1-8 shows the SATA interface.

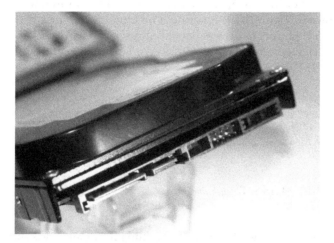

Figure 1-8: SATA disk interface

A smaller form factor, mini-SATA (mSATA), was designed for small portable devices. mSATA, shown in Figure 1-9, allows small SSD SATA drives to attach directly to a mainboard without separate SATA cabling.

Figure 1-9: mSATA disk interface

Mainboards typically allow you to install SATA disks in either Advanced Host Controller Interface (AHCI) mode or IDE mode. AHCI defines a standard SATA adapter interface here: *http://www.intel.com/content/dam/www/ public/us/en/documents/technical-specifications/serial-ata-ahci-spec-rev1-3-1.pdf*. IDE mode provides a legacy disk interface for older OSes that don't support the AHCI standard (old versions of Windows XP, for example). The mode you use doesn't affect the cryptographic hash of a forensic image. You can remove a disk from a subject PC in IDE mode, attach it to an examiner machine in AHCI mode, and acquire it without data loss or modification.

Another interface, micro SATA (not to be confused with mSATA), is shown in Figure 1-10. It was designed for 1.8-inch disk drives and slim CD/DVD players but is less commonly used today. You can combine regular SATA write blockers with various adapters to acquire mSATA and micro SATA drives.

Figure 1-10: Micro SATA disk interface

A more advanced form factor gaining in popularity is the M.2 interface, shown in Figure 4-4. Introduced with the SATA 3.2 specification, M.2 provides two standards in one interface. An M.2 card can use either AHCI/SATA or NVMHCI/NVME interfaces, depending on compatibility requirements. When you're using M.2 cards, be sure to confirm which interface the card uses (as of this writing, most M.2 cards on the market use ACHI/SATA mode).

Figure 1-11: M.2 disk interface

The SATA Express disk interface, shown in Figure 1-12, eliminates several layers of the SATA protocol stack, allowing storage (primarily SSDs) to attach directly to the PCI Express bus. These drives continue to use the AHCI standard and are different from NVME.

Figure 1-12: SATA Express disk interface

The SATA 3.2 specification supports two PCI Express lanes for 16Gbps SATA Express speeds. Write blockers exist for PCI- and M.2-based SATA Express drives.

Serial Attached SCSI and Fibre Channel

The parallel SCSI interface has largely disappeared in both consumer and enterprise markets. SATA has replaced it in the consumer market, and *Serial Attached SCSI (SAS)* and *Fibre Channel (FC)* have replaced it in the enterprise market. The physical connector of the SAS interface, shown in Figure 1-13, allows both SAS and SATA disks to be attached and accessed on a SAS backplane. The physical connector on SAS disk drives is slightly different from that on SATA disks, and various fan-out connectors are available for attaching multiple disks to the host bus adapter. The current speed of SAS-3 disks is 12Gbps, twice that of SATA-3. SAS-4 will provide speeds of 22.5Gbps.

Figure 1-13: SAS disk interface

A Mini-SAS HD 4i receptacle connector is shown in Figure 1-14.

Figure 1-14: SFF-8632/Mini-SAS HD interface

The SAS standard is maintained by the T10 technical committee of the International Committee for Information Technology Standards (INCITS). The current standards document is "Serial Attached SCSI -3 (SAS-3) INCITS 519-2014." More information, including drafts of upcoming standards, is available at *http://t10.org/*.

SAS drives cannot be connected to SATA host bus adapters, and separate SAS write blockers are needed to image SAS disks.

The Fibre Channel interface is often used to connect enterprise storage arrays. Shown in Figure 1-15 are copper and optical-based Fibre Channel connectors.

Figure 1-15: Fibre Channel interfaces

Hard disks with integrated Fibre Channel interfaces are becoming legacy and have largely been replaced with SAS drives. As of this writing, no hardware write blockers for Fibre Channel disk interfaces are available on the market.

Non-Volatile Memory Express

Non-Volatile Memory Express (NVME) was designed from the ground up as an alternative to the AHCI-based SATA drive interface. It was designed to attach directly to the PCI Express bus, eliminating the need for an AHCI/SATA host bus adapter and the associated SATA physical interfaces and protocol layers. The NVME architecture focuses specifically on SSD storage, and a simpler, more efficient command set was created. NVME devices can attach either directly to a mainboard in a PCIE slot, using the PCIE NVMe mode of an M.2 interface, or with a U.2 (SFF-8639) interface.

The physical interface is directly attached to the PCIE bus, as shown in Figure 1-16.

Figure 1-16: NVME SSD with a PCIE interface

An M.2 or Next Generation Form Factor (NGFF) version is also available. These are either directly inserted into mainboard M.2 slots or using PCIE slot adapter cards, both with NVME mode (not AHCI/SATA mode). Currently, most M.2 SSD disks are AHCI/SATA, not NVME, but this may change because the performance benefits of NVME are compelling. Figure 1-17 shows an NVME M.2 disk.

Figure 1-17: NVME SSD with an M.2 interface

The NVME U.2 interface (see Figure 1-18) allows drives with traditional 2.5-inch physical form factors to connect via cable or backplane. The U.2 (SFF-8639) interface and cable (mechanically similar to SAS but with additional pins for PCIE lanes) connect the drive enclosure to a mini-SAS HD plug on an M.2 adapter, which is attached to the mainboard.

Figure 1-18: A 2.5-inch SSD with a U.2 interface, a U.2 to mini-SAS HD cable, and a mini-SAS HD to M.2 adapter for a mainboard

NVME disks are not visible using typical SCSI or SATA command tools because they don't use SCSI or SATA commands. Linux tools designed to interact with ATA or SCSI disk interfaces will generally not work with NVME disks and require added support for compatibility. The device names for NVME disks are not the familiar */dev/sd** files but */dev/nvme*n**. An NVME device is created with an additional `namespace` number. The namespace, denoted with *n*, is a lower layer (below the OS) allocation of space on an NVME drive. The */dev/nvme*n** disk devices are block devices and should function normally when applied to the Linux device file. For example, here is the Sleuth Kit `mmls` command operating on an NVME disk:

```
# mmls /dev/nvme0n1
DOS Partition Table
Offset Sector: 0
Units are in 512-byte sectors

     Slot    Start        End           Length       Description
00:  Meta    0000000000   0000000000    0000000001   Primary Table (#0)
01:  -----   0000000000   0000002047    0000002048   Unallocated
02:  00:00   0000002048   0781422767    0781420720   Linux (0x83)
#
```

As of this writing, the use of NVME is relatively new, and Tableau has just created the first PCI Express forensic hardware write blocker with NVME support. The difficulty intercepting NVME commands on the PCIE bus makes write blockers expensive and complex to implement. For more information, see my paper "NVM Express Drives and Digital Forensics," which discusses this challenge in more detail.[2]

Universal Serial Bus

USB was created to consolidate and replace aging external peripheral interfaces, such as RS-232, the parallel printer interface, PS/2 keyboard and mouse, and other proprietary PC interfaces. It was designed to accommodate multipurpose functionality, such as disks, keyboards, mice, sound, network connections, printers and scanners, and connected small devices (mobile phones and so on). A growing number of Internet-of-Things (IoT) devices can be attached to a PC via USB and may contain data useful as forensic evidence. Because the focus of this book is on the forensic acquisition of mass storage devices, I'll limit this discussion to USB mass storage devices.

Flash drives, optical drives, some tape drives, and even magnetic hard disks (see Figure 1-19) may have a USB interface directly integrated into the drive electronics. The most common uses of the USB mass storage class are the consumer USB stick, or thumb drive, and external hard disk enclosures.

Figure 1-19: A 1.8-inch magnetic hard disk with integrated USB interface

The original USB protocol for the mass storage class of devices is known as Bulk-Only Transport (BOT). BOT is currently the most common USB transport protocol; however, with increasing disk speeds and the arrival of USB3, the BOT protocol is becoming a bottleneck and may be replaced by the USB Attached SCSI Protocol (UASP). Similar to AHCI for SATA, USB also has a defined standard for the host controller interface. The Extensible Host Controller Interface (xHCI) replaces several older USB standards (in particular, OHCI, UHCI, and EHCI). Its specification can be

---

2. Bruce Nikkel, *Digital Investigation* 16 (2016): 38–45, doi:10.1016/j.diin.2016.01.001.

found at *http://www.intel.com/content/dam/www/public/us/en/documents/technical-specifications/extensible-host-controler-interface-usb-xhci.pdf*.

The latest USB interface for USB 3.1 is Type C, shown in Figure 1-20. The Type C interface is multifunctional and can be used for USB 3.1 devices and Thunderbolt 3 devices, and as a power supply. The physical plug is reversible, meaning it does not have a top or bottom to align when plugging in to a system.

Figure 1-20: USB Type C interface

External USB disk enclosures typically contain one or more SATA drives. If feasible, you should remove SATA disks to gain direct access to the ATA interface. This allows you to directly query the drive interface and may have performance advantages in some cases (for example, USB 2.0 enclosures containing a SATA disk).

Forensic write blockers designed specifically for imaging USB devices exist and can be used for drives (flash or otherwise) that have integrated USB interfaces.

Thunderbolt

Thunderbolt was developed jointly by Apple and Intel as a high-speed external interface to connect disks, video displays, and PCI Express devices using a single interface (see Figure 1-21). Using the code name Light Peak, it was originally intended to be a fiber optic connection. The physical interface uses Mini DisplayPort for Thunderbolt 1 and Thunderbolt 2, and it transitions to the USB Type C cable and connector for Thunderbolt 3. Apple is largely responsible for the popularity of Thunderbolt (primarily among Apple users), promoting it with Apple hardware. The Thunderbolt 3 interface combines PCI Express, DisplayPort, and USB3 into a single interface. Thunderbolt 1, 2, and 3 offer speeds of 10, 20, and 40Gbps, respectively.

Figure 1-21: Thunderbolt interface

For Apple computer systems, you can use *Target Disk Mode (TDM)* with Thunderbolt (as with FireWire) to make the system behave as an external disk enclosure to another connected system. TDM instructs the Apple firmware to make the internal disks available as block devices, which can be accessed as external SCSI drives (useful when using forensic tools). I'll demonstrate the forensic acquisition of an Apple computer using TDM in "Apple Target Disk Mode" on page 137.

Thunderbolt external disks typically contain one or more SATA drives. In large thunderbolt RAID enclosures, the interface may use a SAS controller together with multiple SATA or SAS disks.

The Linux dmesg output of an external disk attached with a Thunderbolt interface looks like this:

```
[   53.408619] thunderbolt 0000:05:00.0: 0:1: hotplug: scanning
[   53.408792] thunderbolt 0000:05:00.0: 0:1: is connected, link is up (state: 2)
[   53.408969] thunderbolt 0000:05:00.0: initializing Switch at 0x1 (depth: 1,
up port: 1)
...
[   53.601118] thunderbolt 0000:05:00.0: 1: hotplug: activating pcie devices
[   53.601646] thunderbolt 0000:05:00.0: 0:6 <-> 1:2 (PCI): activating
...
[   53.602444] thunderbolt 0000:05:00.0: path activation complete
[   53.602679] pciehp 0000:04:03.0:pcie24: Card present on Slot(3-1)
[   53.609205] pciehp 0000:04:03.0:pcie24: slot(3-1): Link Up event
...
[   56.375626] ata7: SATA link up 6.0 Gbps (SStatus 133 SControl 300)
[   56.382070] ata7.00: ATA-8: ST1000LM024 HN-M101MBB, 2BA30003, max UDMA/133
[   56.382074] ata7.00: 1953525168 sectors, multi 0: LBA48 NCQ (depth 31/32), AA
[   56.388597] ata7.00: configured for UDMA/133
[   56.388820] scsi 7:0:0:0: Direct-Access     ATA      ST1000LM024 HN-M 0003 PQ: 0
ANSI: 5
```

```
[   56.389341] sd 7:0:0:0: Attached scsi generic sg2 type 0
[   56.389342] sd 7:0:0:0: [sdc] 1953525168 512-byte logical blocks:
   (1.00 TB/931 GiB)
[   56.389345] sd 7:0:0:0: [sdc] 4096-byte physical blocks
[   56.389408] sd 7:0:0:0: [sdc] Write Protect is off
[   56.389413] sd 7:0:0:0: [sdc] Mode Sense: 00 3a 00 00
[   56.389449] sd 7:0:0:0: [sdc] Write cache: enabled, read cache: enabled, doesn't
   support DPO or FUA
[   56.403702]  sdc: [mac] sdc1 sdc2
[   56.404166] sd 7:0:0:0: [sdc] Attached SCSI disk
```

At the time of this writing, the Linux kernel supports Thunderbolt interfaces on Apple computers. Add-in cards for PC mainboards, such as ASUS ThunderboltEX II, do not support the hot plugging of devices. However, booting the PC with the Thunderbolt disk attached allows the PC's BIOS/firmware to initialize the Thunderbolt adapter before the OS loads, making external disks visible to the kernel.

As of this writing, no write blockers are on the market for Thunderbolt interfaces. Also, no disks are currently available with directly integrated Thunderbolt interfaces (enclosures only).

Legacy Interfaces

This section does not discuss the long history of computer disk interfaces; instead, it briefly covers the recently obsoleted IDE, parallel SCSI, and FireWire technologies. These interfaces may still be relevant in the context of a forensic investigation as older hardware is discovered or seized as evidence.

The IDE interface (see Figure 1-22) and Enhanced version (EIDE) typically used for 3.5-inch disks were popular interfaces until they were replaced by SATA.

Figure 1-22: IDE disk interface

The mini IDE interface (see Figure 1-23) was developed for 2.5-inch disks for use in notebook computers until it was replaced by SATA.

Figure 1-23: Mini IDE disk interface

The micro IDE ZIF interface (see Figure 1-24) was developed for 1.8-inch hard disks in sub-notebooks and other small electronic devices until it was replaced by mSATA and M.2 interfaces.

Figure 1-24: Micro IDE ZIF interface

The FireWire, or IEEE1394, interface (see Figure 1-25) was developed by Apple to provide a high-speed external bus to connect video equipment and disk drives. This interface has largely been replaced by Thunderbolt and USB3.

Figure 1-25: Firewire interfaces

The parallel SCSI interface (see Figure 1-26) has largely disappeared from the consumer market and has been replaced primarily by SATA (or SAS in the enterprise market).

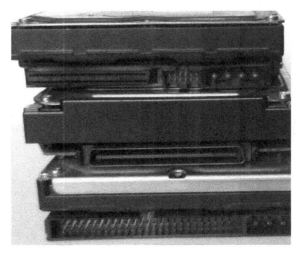

Figure 1-26: SCSI interfaces

Forensic write blockers for IDE, SCSI, and FireWire are common and also function with adapters for mini IDE, micro IDE ZIF, and various SCSI interface adapters.

Commands, Protocols, and Bridges

The communication between storage devices and computer systems has some conceptual similarities to LAN/WAN layered networking.[3] The communication between storage devices and computer systems can be similarly organized into several layers of abstraction. There is a physical layer consisting of cables, wires, and electrical signals. Above that, there is a link layer where digital bits and bytes are transmitted in an organized manner using frames or link layer packets. On top of the link layer, protocols and commands are exchanged between a sender and receiver to request and receive data. In previous sections, I described the physical connections and disk interfaces. Here, I'll describe the higher-layer command sets for ATA, SCSI, and NVME. Figure 1-27 puts the different layers of abstraction into better perspective.

ATA Commands

The current Advanced Technology Attachment (ATA) commands originally evolved from the American National Standards Institute (ANSI) standard, which defined the AT Attachment interface for disk drives.[4] The original standard described the physical interface (cables, pins, and so on), electrical

---

3. LAN/WAN layered networking is described by the Open Systems Interconnect (OSI) model's seven layers of abstraction in network communication.
4. AT Attachment Interface for Disk Drives, ANSI X3.221-199x, Revision 4c, X3T10, 1994.

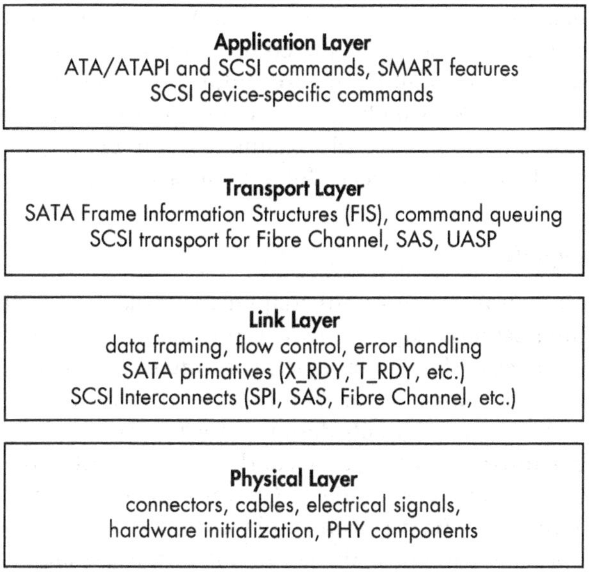

```
┌──────────────────────────────────────────────────┐
│                 Application Layer                  │
│   ATA/ATAPI and SCSI commands, SMART features      │
│         SCSI device-specific commands              │
└──────────────────────────────────────────────────┘

┌──────────────────────────────────────────────────┐
│                 Transport Layer                    │
│ SATA Frame Information Structures (FIS), command   │
│                   queuing                          │
│   SCSI transport for Fibre Channel, SAS, UASP      │
└──────────────────────────────────────────────────┘

┌──────────────────────────────────────────────────┐
│                    Link Layer                      │
│      data framing, flow control, error handling    │
│       SATA primatives (X_RDY, T_RDY, etc.)         │
│  SCSI Interconnects (SPI, SAS, Fibre Channel, etc.)│
└──────────────────────────────────────────────────┘

┌──────────────────────────────────────────────────┐
│                  Physical Layer                    │
│      connectors, cables, electrical signals,       │
│      hardware initialization, PHY components       │
└──────────────────────────────────────────────────┘
```

Figure 1-27: Abstraction layers as applied to disk interfaces

signals, and logical commands that could be issued. The current standard[5] describes feature sets that drives may have and the ATA commands available to control each drive. The ATA Packet Interface (ATAPI) adds a packet command feature set to the ATA standard, allowing additional commands not specific to disk drive functionality (for example, ejecting media, encapsulating SCSI commands, and so on).

The ATA Command Set (ACS) defines a set of commands and parameters that can be loaded into ATA registers and sent to a drive for execution. Some common ATA commands are shown in Table 1-1.

Table 1-1: Common ATA Commands

Command	Command code
DEVICE RESET	08h
READ SECTOR(S)	20h
WRITE SECTOR(S)	30h
SEEK	70h
DOWNLOAD MICROCODE	92h
MEDIA EJECT	EDh
SECURITY UNLOCK	F2h

A number of ATA and ATAPI commands can be issued using the hdparm and smartctls utilities. T13 (*http://t13.org/*) publishes the standard that defines the full set of commands. You can find additional resources at *http://sata-io.org/*.

---

5. ATA/ATAPI Command Set - 2 (ACS-2), Revision 2.

Understanding the basic operation of ATA/ATAPI commands provides the background knowledge you need to understand how SATA and IDE forensic write blockers function (preventing ATA/ATAPI commands from modifying disks). Knowing how these commands operate also improves your understanding of how a forensic examiner can query the attributes of a disk and ultimately perform a successful forensic acquisition.

SCSI Commands

SCSI commands from a host bus adapter to a disk follow a client/server model. The host bus adapter (HBA) is the client, or *initiator*, and the disk is the server, or *target*. The initiator sends commands (possibly together with data) to the target, and the target returns a response (possibly together with data). SCSI was originally designed for use with a variety of devices, including scanners, tapes, printers, and so on, not just hard disks. Therefore, SCSI has a rich command set. Commands are sent from the initiator (HBA) to the target (drive) using a *command descriptor block (CDB)*, which is a block of data containing the command and its parameters. The target receives the CDB, carries out the request, and returns a response. The interaction is somewhat similar to a UDP-based request/response in a TCP/IP client/server architecture.

SCSI commands exist to read and write blocks of data from/to a disk, control hardware (ejecting CDs or changing tapes), report status and diagnostic information, and so on. These commands are generally hidden from the end user, but various utilities are available to issue SCSI commands from user space. It's even possible to submit arbitrary commands from the Linux command line using tools from the sg3_utils software package. For example, the following command submits a low-level SCSI command to read the first sector of a SCSI disk:

```
# sg_raw -r 512 /dev/sda 08 00 00 00 01 00
SCSI Status: Good

Received 512 bytes of data:
00     00 00 00 00 00 00 00 00  00 00 00 00 00 00 00 00    ................
10     00 00 00 00 00 00 00 00  00 00 00 00 00 00 00 00    ................
...
1a0    00 00 00 00 00 00 00 00  00 00 00 00 00 00 00 00    ................
1b0    00 00 00 00 00 00 00 00  00 00 00 00 00 00 00 00    ................
1c0    02 00 ee ff ff ff 01 00  00 00 ff ff ff ff 00 00    ................
1d0    00 00 00 00 00 00 00 00  00 00 00 00 00 00 00 00    ................
1e0    00 00 00 00 00 00 00 00  00 00 00 00 00 00 00 00    ................
1f0    00 00 00 00 00 00 00 00  00 00 00 00 00 00 55 aa    ..............U.
```

In this example sg_raw is given a CDB command to be sent to */dev/sda*, a SAS disk. The first byte, 0x08, specifies the 6-byte long SCSI READ command. The subsequent zeros specify the LUN and starting sector. The 0x01 specifies the number of sectors to read, and -r 512 tells sg_raw how many bytes to display. This example should also work on SAS-, SATA-, and USB-attached drives.

Technical standards for SCSI and SAS commands are maintained by the Technical Committee T10 of INCITS (InterNational Committee for Information Technology Standards). You can find these standards at *http://t10.org/*. Books on SCSI programming are useful to better understand the SCSI command protocol.

Understanding the basic operation of SAS/SCSI commands is relevant to this book. It provides the background knowledge to understand how SAS/SCSI forensic write blockers function (preventing SAS/SCSI commands from modifying disks). Knowing how SAS/SCSI commands operate improves your understanding of how a forensic examiner can query the attributes of a disk and ultimately perform a forensic acquisition.

SCSI commands are also used to control tapes and optical devices.

NVME Commands

The NVME command set was created from scratch without providing backward compatibility for existing SCSI or ATA command sets. It was designed to support SSD media directly attached to the PCI express bus and to take advantage of parallelization with multiple CPUs and instant SSD seek times (no latency overhead from moving disk heads). The standard's developers also recognized that with the drive connected directly to the PCIE bus, much of the protocol overhead in ATA or SCSI could be eliminated. A new minimal command set was created, free of legacy commands or backward compatibility requirements. The performance and efficiency of NVME drives is a significant improvement over SATA or SAS. An extensive command queuing system provides up to 64k queues able to hold 64k commands each (in contrast, SATA had 32 queues with one command each).

A translation reference between SCSI and NVME commands is available at *http://nvmexpress.org/*. Table 1-2 shows the more common examples.

Table 1-2: SCSI and NVME Command Comparison

SCSI	NVME
COMPARE AND WRITE	Compare and Write
READ	Read
WRITE	Write
WRITE BUFFER	Firmware Image Download, Firmware Image Activate
INQUIRY	Identify
READ CAPACITY	Identify
REPORT LUNS	Identify
MODE SENSE	Identify, Get Features
LOG SENSE	Get Features, Get Log Page
SYNCHRONIZE CACHE	Flush
FORMAT UNIT	Format NVM

Disk devices can be attached to a PC system through various bus systems and bridges. Performance can be increased by attaching the drive as close as possible to the CPU and memory. Today, the closest a drive can get to the CPU and memory is through dedicated lanes of the PCI express 3.0 bus using the NVME interface (RAM disks are faster and more efficient, but they are created by the OS and are not non-volatile storage media devices). An NVME device can be directly attached to the CPU without using a southbridge chipset or any traditional disk protocol overhead, such as ATA or SCSI.

Bridging, Tunneling, and Pass-Through

ATA and SCSI are the two most common protocols for interacting with storage media. The commands can be sent over a variety of physical layer buses or transport layers, or even tunneled or encapsulated within other protocols. This complexity is hidden from the user, and attached devices can simply be accessed through standard block devices that the Linux kernel makes available.

To illustrate, consider a SATA hard disk plugged into a stand-alone USB docking station, which is plugged into an external port of a USB3 PCI express card installed in a PC. The communication between the disk interface and the dock is a lower-layer SATA protocol, using SATA Frame Information Structures (FIS) packets. The communication between the dock and the USB3 card is a lower-layer USB protocol, using BOT or USAP. The communication between the USB3 card and the PC is a lower-layer PCI express protocol, using PCIE Transaction Layer Packets (TLP) and Data Link Layer Packets (DLLP). Finally, the disk is accessed across all these bridges using the SCSI command protocol. In this example, multiple physical and link layers are used to connect the disk. To the user, the disk appears directly accessible, and the lower protocol layers are hidden or abstracted from view.

NOTE *FIS are part of the SATA protocol. PCI Express has its own set of protocols, which include TLP and DLLP.*

For each of the different physical buses, a device called a *PHY* (for *physical*) facilitates communication between devices connected to a bus (the PHYs on a bus work a bit like two modems communicating over a WAN cable). The PHY converts the digital ones and zeros into compliant electrical signals expected for that bus. After the PHY has taken care of the physical layer, a link layer protocol manages the stream of bits/bytes that is being transferred back and forth on the bus. This link layer organizes the data stream into frames or discrete packets of information that upper layers can process.

There are physical and link layer descriptions for USB, PCIE, Thunderbolt, SAS, SATA, Fibre Channel, and so on. Typically, standards exist that allow generic OS drivers to use the physical hardware in a device-independent way. For example, USB adapters are defined by the xHCI standard, SATA adapters are defined by the AHCI standard, NVME devices are defined by the NVMHCI standard (now simply called the NVME standard), and so on. Compliance with these standards allows hardware to be supported without the need for additional proprietary drivers.

Although ATA/ATAPI and SCSI are distinct command sets, they both support some degree of tunneling and pass-through of each other's commands. ATA uses the ATAPI interface to encapsulate SCSI commands for communication with devices, such as optical drives, tape drives, and other devices that understand SCSI commands for ejecting media and other commands not found in the ATA protocol. SCSI supports ATA pass-through, which allows ATA commands to be sent over the SCSI protocol. SAT (SCSI-ATA Translation) creates a bilateral translation between SCSI and ATA commands where the commands interact with storage media. This translation is implemented as a Linux kernel API within the libata library. (The libata library, sometimes spelled *libATA*, provides a number of features for interfacing with ATA controllers and devices.)

Bridges play an important role in forensic acquisition because they're the basis for implementing hardware write blockers. A hardware write blocker is typically a bridge capable of intercepting ATA or SCSI commands sent to the disk, preventing commands from modifying sectors on a disk.

Special Topics

This section covers a number of special topics related to mass storage and digital forensics. Some areas, such as UASP and SSHD, are briefly commented on regarding their relevance to digital forensics. Other areas, such as DCO, HPA, and NVME drives, are introduced here and discussed in more detail later in the book.

DCO and HPA Drive Areas

As the ATA/ATAPI standards evolved, certain features were created to benefit system vendors. The *Host Protected Area (HPA)* was introduced in the ATA/ATAPI-4 standard and allowed system vendors to reserve portions of the disk for use outside the normal OS. For example, the HPA can be used to store persistent data, system recovery data, hibernation data, and so on. Access to this data is controlled by the system firmware rather than the installed OS. The *Device Configuration Overlay (DCO)* feature was introduced in the ATA/ATAPI-6 standard and provided the ability to control reported disk features and capacity. This allowed system vendors to ship disks from multiple manufacturers while maintaining identical numbers of user-accessible sectors and features across the disks. This facilitated easier support and drive replacement. Both the HPA and DCO can coexist; however, the DCO must be created first, followed by the HPA.

The HPA and DCO have been misused by criminals and malicious actors to hide illicit files and malware code. I describe how to detect and remove the HPA and DCO, revealing sectors hidden from normal user view, in "Enable Access to Hidden Sectors" on page 118. You'll find a more detailed description of the HPA and DCO related to forensics in the paper "Hidden Disk Areas: HPA and DCO."[6] Information is also available about nation state exploitation using the HPA at *https://www.schneier.com/blog/archives/2014/02/swap_nsa_exploi.html* and *https://leaksource.files.wordpress.com/2013/12/nsa-ant-swap.jpg*.

Drive Service and Maintenance Areas

Certain maintenance areas of a hard disk are generally not accessible using standard Linux tools. These areas contain bad sectors lists and vendor service sectors (sometimes referred to as negative sectors). To access these areas of the disk, you'll need specialized disk diagnostic software and hardware. I show an example of accessing the service area of a disk and provide some additional resources in "Drive Service Area Access" on page 122. Don't confuse the service area of a disk with the HPA or DCO. You can easily access HPA and DCO areas using standard ATA commands and methods, but not the service areas of a disk.

USB Attached SCSI Protocol

USB provides two modes for accessing mass storage class devices: the more common BOT and the newer UASP. With the increased speeds of USB3 and USB3.1, a new and more efficient USB mass storage class transport protocol was developed called *USB Attached SCSI Protocol (UASP)*. This new protocol is also referred to as *UAS* and the product-marketing nicknames USB3 Boost, USB3 Turbo, or USB3 Extreme are sometimes used. You'll find more information at *http://usb.org/* and *http://t10.org/*, the organizations that jointly developed the standard. UASP improves performance by providing command queuing and asynchronous processing and by improving task and command control capability.

The dmesg output of an attached UASP-enabled USB disk uses the uas protocol for operation:

```
[15655.838498] usb 2-6.2: new SuperSpeed USB device number 6 using xhci_hcd
...
[15655.952172] scsi host14: uas
...
[15666.978291] sd 14:0:0:0: [sdk] 3907029168 512-byte logical blocks:
    (2.00 TB/1.81 TiB)
...
[15667.033750] sd 14:0:0:0: [sdk] Attached SCSI disk
```

---

6. Mayank R. Gupta, Michael D. Hoeschele, and Marcus K. Rogers, "Hidden Disk Areas: HPA and DCO," *International Journal of Digital Evidence* 5, no. 1 (2006), *https://www.utica.edu/academic/institutes/ecii/publications/articles/EFE36584-D13F-2962-67BEB146864A2671.pdf*.

In contrast, the same disk connected with a traditional BOT USB interface loads the usb-storage protocol for operation:

```
[15767.853288] usb 2-6.2: new SuperSpeed USB device number 7 using xhci_hcd
...
[15767.918079] usb-storage 2-6.2:1.0: USB Mass Storage device detected
[15767.918195] usb-storage 2-6.2:1.0: Quirks match for vid 174c pid 55aa: 400000
[15767.918222] scsi host15: usb-storage 2-6.2:1.0
...
[15777.728944] sd 15:0:0:0: [sdk] 3907029168 512-byte logical blocks:
    (2.00 TB/1.81 TiB)
...
[15777.820171] sd 15:0:0:0: [sdk] Attached SCSI disk
```

From a forensics perspective, it's important to note that the transport protocol used does not affect the contents of the USB disk and has no effect on the cryptographic hash of the forensic image. In fact, it is advantageous to use UAS-based write blockers for the performance benefits (Tableau USB3 write blockers use UAS, for example).

NOTE *One word of advice: when you're using the higher speeds of USB3, the quality of the USB cables becomes an issue. Longer, lower-quality USB3 cables can produce read errors during acquisition. For those working in a professional forensic laboratory, it's worth investing in short, high-quality USB3 cables.*

Advanced Format 4Kn

As disk capacities increased, the industry discovered that it could improve disk efficiency by switching from 512-byte sectors to 4096-byte sectors. The International Disk Drive Equipment and Materials Association (IDEMA) developed the Advanced Format standard for 4096-byte physcial sectors (see *http://www.idema.org/?page_id=2369*). Since 2009, hard disk manufacturers have committed to using IDEMA's Advanced Format standard to produce 4K sector disks. Even with 4K physical sectors, most disks today emulate 512-byte sectors and are called *Advanced Format 512e* disks. Disks that provide the host system and OS with native 4K-sized sectors are called *Advanced Format 4Kn* disks. Advanced Format 4Kn disks are still rare in the low-end marketplace but are used in enterprise environments. For higher-capacity enterprise disks, most enterprise disk manufacturers offer two models: 512e and 4Kn. Figure 1-28 shows the official logo for 4Kn disks.

You'll find a good overview of Advanced Format and 4K sectors on YouTube at *https://www.youtube.com/watch?v=TmH3iRLhZ-A/*.

Figure 1-28: Advanced Format 4Kn logo

When the Linux kernel detects an attached disk, it displays the number of sectors and the logical sector size (in some cases, it may also explicitly display the physical size). The following partial dmesg output shows two equal-sized disks, one with Advanced Format 512e and the other with 4Kn. Dividing the number of 512-byte sectors by 8 or multiplying the number of 4K sectors by 8 shows the disks are equal in capacity but have different sector counts.

```
...
[   13.605000] scsi 1:0:1:0: Direct-Access     TOSHIBA  MG03SCA300      0108 PQ: 0
   ANSI: 5
...
[   16.621880] sd 1:0:1:0: [sdb] 5860533168 512-byte logical blocks: (3.00 TB/2.73
   TiB)
...
[   14.355068] scsi 1:0:2:0: Direct-Access     ATA      TOSHIBA MG04ACA3 FP2A PQ: 0
   ANSI: 6
...
[   16.608179] sd 1:0:2:0: [sdc] 732566646 4096-byte logical blocks: (3.00 TB/2.73
   TiB)
```

On a Linux system, you can use the */sys* pseudo filesystem to find the logical and physical sector sizes of a disk. For example, you can determine the physical and logical sector sizes of the attached disk */dev/sda* as follows:

```
# dmesg
...
[   16.606585] sd 1:0:0:0: [sda] 7814037168 512-byte logical blocks: (4.00 TB/3.64
   TiB)
...
```

```
# cat /sys/block/sda/queue/logical_block_size
512
# cat /sys/block/sda/queue/physical_block_size
4096
# blockdev --getpbsz /dev/sda
4096
# blockdev --getss /dev/sda
512
```

These two methods show reading from the */sys* pseudo filesystem (which you can also do as a non-root user) and using the blockdev command.

Some SSDs allow you to choose the physical sector size with a firmware tool. For example, some recent Intel SSDs can change sector size between 512 and 4096 using a command line tool provided by Intel (*https://downloadcenter.intel.com/download/23931/*).

Several aspects of 4K disks are of interest to the digital forensics community and are discussed in the rest of this section. Some early Western Digital Advanced Format 512e disks had a jumper setting (jumpers 7 and 8) to internally offset the sectors to align the beginning of default XP partitions with the start of a 4K sector. This jumper setting to realign the disk greatly improved performance. Changing such sector alignment jumpers will affect forensic acquisition hash and potentially affect the analysis of a disk. When forensically imaging or verifying a disk, it is crucial to use the same jumper settings as when the drive was first seized.

The use of 4Kn disks will affect the value of *slack space*. RAM slack or memory slack is the unused part of the last sector of a file (not to be confused with *file slack*, which is the unused part of the last filesystem block of a file). When you're using 4Kn disks with filesystems that use 4K blocks, the RAM slack and file slack are the same. OSes that pad the unused portion of a 4K sector with zeros before writing will eliminate the possibility of any useful data in file slack on filesystems with 4K blocks.

Forensic software that assumes a 512-byte sector size may fail or, worse, produce incorrect results. When you're using 4Kn disks, it's important to confirm that the forensic software recognizes and uses 4Kn sectors. Sleuth Kit will default to 512-byte sectors and must be explicitly told to use 4K sectors for 4Kn disks. The following example shows mmls producing incorrect results by default and correct results when specifying the correct sector size.

```
# mmls /dev/sde
DOS Partition Table
Offset Sector: 0
Units are in 512-byte sectors

      Slot    Start        End          Length       Description
00:   Meta    0000000000   0000000000   0000000001   Primary Table (#0)
01:   -----   0000000000   0000000255   0000000256   Unallocated
02:   00:00   0000000256   0732566645   0732566390   Linux (0x83)
03:   -----   0732566646   5860533167   5127966522   Unallocated
```

```
...
# mmls -b 4096 /dev/sde
DOS Partition Table
Offset Sector: 0
Units are in 4096-byte sectors

      Slot    Start        End          Length       Description
00:   Meta    0000000000   0000000000   0000000001   Primary Table (#0)
01:   -----   0000000000   0000000255   0000000256   Unallocated
02:   00:00   0000000256   0732566645   0732566390   Linux (0x83)
#
```

After specifying the 4096-byte sector size with the -b flag, the sectors of the Linux partition are represented as 4K units, and there is no unallocated area at the end of the drive. An example of successfully acquiring a native 4K sector disk is shown in "The dcfldd and dc3dd Tools" on page 144.

The use of Advanced Format 4Kn disks is still uncommon. It's unclear how 4Kn sector disks will impact existing forensic acquisition and analysis software currently on the market, in particular where forensic tools fundamentally assume a 512-byte sector size. This is an area where more research by the digital forensics community is needed.

NVME Namespaces

The NVME specification introduces the concept of *namespaces*, which allow you to partition a drive at a lower layer, abstracted from the normal OS. Forensic imaging of a drive with multiple namespaces must be done separately for each namespace. You can determine the number of namespaces in several ways.

By sending an identify controller admin command using the nvme-cli tool, you can check the number of namespaces supported and used. The following example shows various information about namespace support:

```
# nvme id-ctrl /dev/nvme1 -H
NVME Identify Controller:
vid     : 0x144d
ssvid   : 0x144d
sn      : S2GLNCAGA04891H
mn      : Samsung SSD 950 PRO 256GB
fr      : 1B0QBXX7
...
oacs    : 0x7
  [3:3] : 0      NS Management and Attachment Not Supported
...
  [0:0] : 0x1    SMART/Health Log Page per NS Supported
...
nn      : 1
...
```

Here, Optional Admin Command Support (OACS) indicates that namespace management is not supported on this particular drive. The Number of Namespaces field (nn) shows the number of namespaces on the controller—one on this particular device.

You can also check the size of the namespace by using nvme-cli and compare it with the manufacturer's specifications, as follows:

```
# nvme id-ns  /dev/nvme0n1
NVME Identify Namespace 1:
nsze    : 0x2e9390b0
ncap    : 0x2e9390b0
nuse    : 0x2e9390b0
...
```

Here, nsze refers to the namespace size, ncap is the namespace capacity, and nuse is the namespace utilization. If these values match the vendor's documented drive size, they confirm that a single namespace is being used.

A third check for the existence of multiple namespace devices can be to simply list the devices (*/dev/nvme0n2**, */dev/nvme0n3**, and so on) detected by the OS.

As of this writing, there were no consumer drives available for testing that supported multiple namespaces. The information in this section is derived from the NVME specification and tool documentation.

Solid State Hybrid Disks

A hybrid of a solid state and traditional magnetic disk was developed to provide larger disk capacities, with performance comparable to SSDs, at an affordable price.

These hybrid drives, known as *Solid State Hybrid Disks (SSHDs)*, provide additional solid state caching of frequently used sectors. SSHDs can operate fully independently of the OS or accept "hints" from the OS to help decide which blocks to cache.

As of SATA 3.2, a hybrid information feature has been added to allow a host to communicate caching information to a hybrid drive using ATA commands.

To date, little research has been done on the forensics of SSHDs, and the implications for acquisition are unclear. SSHDs contain a small SSD disk that must perform wear leveling. A hybrid drive that does not support TRIM commands is not likely to erase data in unallocated filesystem blocks.

The hybrid systems described here are built into the electronics of a single drive. It is also possible to have a hybrid system with two separate drives: a smaller SSD and a larger magnetic hard drive. Using OS drivers or proprietary systems such as Intel's Smart Response Technology, equivalent hybrid caching is achieved.

Closing Thoughts

In this chapter, I reviewed the various types of storage media—magnetic, non-volatile, and optical—and I examined different drive types. I described internal and external interfaces for attaching storage devices to a examiner host system. I also explained the protocols used to access the drives and covered a number of less common specialty topics. I presented the material in this chapter from the perspective of a forensic examiner. You should now have a solid foundation for understanding the next chapter on using Linux as a forensic acquisition platform.

2

LINUX AS A FORENSIC ACQUISITION PLATFORM

This chapter describes Linux as a platform for performing digital forensic acquisition and discusses its various advantages and drawbacks. I also examine the acceptance of Linux and open source software within the digital forensics community, and the final section provides an overview of the relevant Linux fundamentals you'll need to understand subsequent sections of this book.

The examples shown in this book primarily use Ubuntu Linux Server version 16.04 LTS (supported until April 2021) with the Bourne Again shell (Bash), version 4.3.*x*. The examples should also work on other Linux distributions and other OSes, such as OS X or Windows, as long as you use the same or newer tool versions and adjust the device names. Throughout this book, the words *command line*, *shell*, and *Bash* are used interchangeably.

Linux and OSS in a Forensic Context

The growing popularity of *open source software (OSS)* like Linux has made it important as a platform for performing digital forensics. Many researchers have discussed the advantages of using OSS for satisfying the Daubert guidelines for evidential reliability.[1] Brian Carrier, author of Sleuth Kit, explored the legal arguments for using open source forensic tools and suggested that parts of forensic software (but not necessarily all) should be made open source.[2]

The primary advantage of using OSS in a forensic context is transparency. Unlike proprietary commercial software, the source code can be reviewed and openly validated. In addition, academic researchers can study it and build on the work of others in the community. Open source forensic software applications have become the tools and building blocks of forensic science research. There are also disadvantages to using OSS and situations where its use doesn't make sense. In particular, the openness of the open source community may in some cases conflict with the confidential nature of ongoing forensic investigations. Both the advantages and disadvantages of Linux and OSS are discussed in the following sections.

Advantages of Linux and OSS in Forensics Labs

The public availability of OSS means it is accessible to everyone. It is not restricted to those who have purchased licenses or signed nondisclosure agreements. OSS is freely available for download, use, examination, and modification by anyone interested, and no licensing fees or usage costs are involved.

Having access to the source code allows you to customize and facilitate integration with other software, hardware, and processes in a forensic lab. This source-level access increases the possibilities for automating and scripting workloads. Automation reduces the amount of human interaction needed, which limits the risk of human error and frees up these human resources so they can be used elsewhere.

Automation is essential in labs with high volumes of casework to foster optimization and process streamlining. Because you can freely modify the source code, OSS can be customized to meet the requirements of a particular forensic lab. Command line software especially allows you to link multiple tasks and jobs in pipelines with shell scripts to complete an end-to-end process.

Support for OSS has several advantages. The ad hoc community support can be excellent, and mailing lists and chat forums can answer calls for help within minutes. In some cases, quick implementation of patches, bug fixes, and feature requests can occur.

---

1. Erin Kenneally, "Gatekeeping Out of the Box: Open Source Software as a Mechanism to Assess Reliability for Digital Evidence," *Virginia Journal of Law and Technology* 6, no. 13 (2001).
2. Brian Carrier, "Open Source Digital Forensic Tools: The Legal Argument" [technical report] (Atstake Inc., October 2002).

Linux and OSS are ideal for an academic forensic lab setting, because they use open, published standards rather than closed or proprietary standards. OSS development communities work *with* competing groups instead of against them. Learning from others, copying code and ideas from others (with due attribution), and building on the work of others are encouraged and are the basis for learning and gaining knowledge.

The vendor independence that OSS offers prevents vendor product lock-in and fosters interoperability and compatibility between technologies and organizations. This makes it easier to change the software over time, because individual components can be swapped out with new or alternative technologies without affecting the systems and processes as a whole.

Disadvantages of Linux and OSS in Forensics Labs

The disadvantages of Linux and OSS provide arguments in support of closed proprietary software. Commercial tool implementations often provide benefits and advantages in this area.

The open source community support model is not guaranteed to be reliable, accurate, or trustworthy. The quality of the answers provided by the community can vary greatly; some answers are excellent, whereas others might be wrong or even dangerous. Often no formal support organization exists to help. In situations in which 24/7 support must be guaranteed, commercial providers have an advantage.

Support in the open source world is as transparent as the software, visible for all to see. However, in a forensic lab setting, casework and investigations may be sensitive or confidential. Reaching out to the public for support could reveal or compromise details of an ongoing investigation. Therefore, information security and privacy are issues in the open source support model.

Interoperability with proprietary technology poses difficulties with open source interfaces and APIs. Proprietary technologies that are not public are often reverse engineered, not licensed. Reverse engineering efforts are often incomplete, are at risk of incorrectly implementing a particular technology, and may take a long time to implement.

Free OSS is often a volunteer development effort, and software may be in a perpetual state of development. Some projects may be abandoned or die from neglect. Other projects may experience *forks* in the code where some developers decide to copy an existing code base and take it in a different direction from the original developers.

Free OSS can be rough around the edges. It may be buggy or difficult to learn or use. It may be poorly documented (the source code might be the only documentation). Unlike with commercial software, usually no training is provided with the software product. It takes time and effort to learn Unix/Linux; in particular, the command line is not as intuitive as an all-GUI environment. Many experience a learning curve when they first enter the free, open source world, not just for the software but also for the general attitude and mind-set of the surrounding community.

Commercial software vendors in the forensics community provide a certain degree of defensibility and guarantees for the proper functioning of their software. Some forensic companies have even offered to testify in court to defend the results provided by their software products. In the free, open source community, no one is accountable or will take responsibility for the software produced. It is provided "as is" and "use at your own risk."

Clearly, OSS is not appropriate for every situation, and that is not implied in this book. In many of the examples throughout, OSS is more useful for educational purposes and to show how things work than it is a viable alternative to professional commercial forensic software.

Linux Kernel and Storage Devices

Traditional Unix systems, from which Linux inherits its philosophy, were designed in a way that everything on them is a file. Each file is designated as a specific type, which includes regular files and directories, block devices, character devices, named pipes, hard links, and soft/symbolic links (similar to LNK files in Windows). On the examiner workstation, files of interest to forensic investigators are the block device files of attached subject disks that potentially contain forensic evidence. This section describes Linux devices—in particular, block devices for storage media.

Kernel Device Detection

Unix and Linux systems have a special directory called /dev, which stores special files that correspond to devices understood by the kernel. Original Unix and Linux systems required manual creation of device files in the /dev directory (using the mknod command) or had scripts (MAKEDEV) to create devices on boot or when required. With the arrival of plug-and-play hardware, a more dynamic approach was needed, and devfs was created to automatically detect new hardware and create device files. The requirement to interact better with userspace scripts and programs led to the development of udev, which replaced devfs. Today, udev has been merged into systemd and runs a daemon called systemd-udevd.

When a new device is attached to (or removed from) a host, an interrupt notifies the kernel of a hardware change. The kernel informs the udev system, which creates appropriate devices with proper permissions, executes setup (or removal) scripts and programs, and sends messages to other daemons (via dbus, for example).

To observe udev in action, use the udevadm tool in monitor mode:

```
# udevadm monitor
monitor will print the received events for:
UDEV - the event that udev sends out after rule processing
KERNEL - the kernel uevent

KERNEL[7661.685727] add       /devices/pci0000:00/0000:00:14.0/usb1/1-14 (usb)
KERNEL[7661.686030] add       /devices/pci0000:00/0000:00:14.0/usb1/1-14/1-14:1.0
```

```
(usb)
KERNEL[7661.686236] add       /devices/pci0000:00/0000:00:14.0/usb1/1-14/1-14:1.0/
   host9 (scsi)
KERNEL[7661.686286] add       /devices/pci0000:00/0000:00:14.0/usb1/1-14/1-14:1.0/
   host9/scsi_host/host9 (scsi_host)
...
KERNEL[7671.797640] add       /devices/pci0000:00/0000:00:14.0/usb1/1-14/1-14:1.0/
   host9/target9:0:0/9:0:0:0/block/sdf (block)
KERNEL[7671.797721] add       /devices/pci0000:00/0000:00:14.0/usb1/1-14/1-14:1.0/
   host9/target9:0:0/9:0:0:0/block/sdf/sdf1 (block)
...
```

Here a disk has been plugged into a USB port, and udev has managed
the setup of all the appropriate device files and links.

The udevadm command can also be used to determine a list of the associated files and paths for attached devices. For example:

```
# udevadm info /dev/sdf
P: /devices/pci0000:00/0000:00:14.0/usb1/1-14/1-14:1.0/host9/target9:0:0/9:0:0:0/
   block/sdf
N: sdf
S: disk/by-id/ata-ST2000DL003-9VT166_5YD83QVW
S: disk/by-id/wwn-0x5000c50048d79a82
S: disk/by-path/pci-0000:00:14.0-usb-0:14:1.0-scsi-0:0:0:0
E: DEVLINKS=/dev/disk/by-path/pci-0000:00:14.0-usb-0:14:1.0-scsi-0:0:0:0 /dev/disk/
   by-id/wwn-0x5000c50048d79a82 /dev/disk/by-id/ata-ST2000DL003-9VT166_5YD83QVW
E: DEVNAME=/dev/sdf
E: DEVPATH=/devices/pci0000:00/0000:00:14.0/usb1/1-14/1-14:1.0/host9/target9:0:0/
   9:0:0:0/block/sdf
E: DEVTYPE=disk
E: ID_ATA=1
...
```

Understanding the Linux device tree is important when you're performing forensic acquisition and analysis activities. Knowing which devices are
part of a local investigator's machine, which devices are the suspect drives,
which device is the write blocker, and so on is crucial when you're running
forensic commands and collecting information from a device.

Storage Devices in /dev

Attached drives will appear as block devices in the */dev* directory when
they're detected by the kernel. Raw disk device files have a specific naming convention: *sd** for SCSI and SATA, *hd** for IDE, *md** for RAID arrays,
nvme*n* for NVME drives, and other names for less common or proprietary
disk device drivers.

Individual partitions discovered by the kernel are represented by
numbered raw devices (for example, *hda1, hda2, sda1, sda2,* and so forth).

Partition block devices represent entire partitions as a contiguous sequence of disk sectors. A partition typically contains a filesystem, which can be mounted by the kernel and made available to users as a normal part of the directory tree. Most forensic tools can (and should) examine raw devices and partition devices without having to mount the filesystem.

Other Special Devices

Several other devices are useful to know for the examples in this book. The bit bucket, */dev/null*, discards any data written to it. A steady stream of zeros is provided when accessing */dev/zero*. The random number generator, */dev/random*, provides a stream of random data when accessed. Tape drives typically start with */dev/st*, and you can access other external media via */dev/cdrom* or */dev/dvd* (these are often symbolic links to */dev/sr**). In some cases, devices are accessed through the generic SCSI device driver interface */dev/sg**.

Other special pseudo devices include */dev/loop** and */dev/mapper/** devices. These devices are discussed in more detail throughout the book.

Linux Kernel and Filesystems

Filesystems organize storage into a hierarchical structure of directories (folders) and files. They provide a layer of abstraction above the block devices.

Kernel Filesystem Support

The Linux kernel supports a large number of filesystems (for a list, see *https://en.wikipedia.org/wiki/Category:Linux_kernel-supported_file_systems*), which can be useful when performing some forensics tasks. However, filesystem support is not necessary when performing forensic acquisition, because the imaging process is operating on the block device below the filesystem and partition scheme.

To provide a consistent interface for different types of filesystems, the Linux kernel implements a Virtual File System (VFS) abstraction layer. This allows mounting of regular storage media filesystems (EXT*, NTFS, FAT, and so on), network-based filesystems (nfs, sambafs/smbfs, and so on), userspace filesystems based on FUSE,[3] stackable filesystems (encryptfs, unionfs, and so on), and other special pseudo filesystems (sysfs, proc, and so on).

The Linux Storage Stack Diagram, shown in Figure 2-1, helps you understand the relationship among filesystems, devices, device drivers, and hardware devices within the Linux kernel.

---

3. FUSE is a userspace filesystem implementation (see *https://en.wikipedia.org/wiki/Filesystem_in_Userspace*).

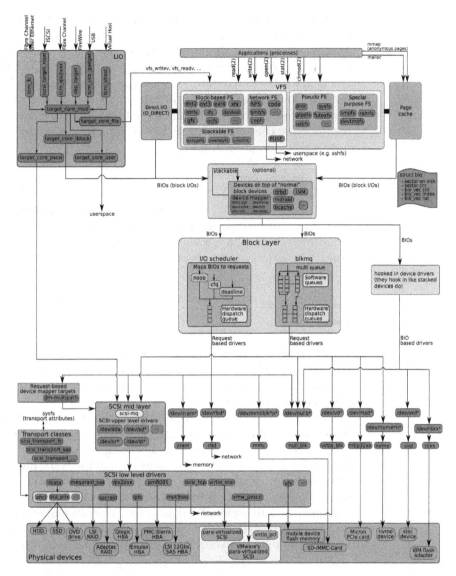

Figure 2-1: The Linux Storage Stack Diagram (https://www.thomas-krenn.com/en/wiki/
Linux_Storage_Stack_Diagram, used under CC Attribution-ShareAlike 3.0 Unported)

Mounting Filesystems in Linux

An often-misunderstood concept is the difference between an attached disk
device and a mounted disk device. A device does not need to be mounted to
acquire it or even to access it with forensic analysis tools. Forensic tools that
operate directly on block devices will have access to attached disks without
mounting them through the OS.

Filesystems that reside on disk devices in Unix and Linux require explicit mounting before being accessible as a regular directory structure. *Mounting* a filesystem simply means it is made available to use with standard file access tools (file managers, applications, and so on), similar to drive letters in the DOS/Windows world. Linux doesn't use drive letters; mounted disks become part of the local filesystem and are attached to any chosen part of the filesystem tree. This is called the filesystem's *mount point*. For example, the following command mounts a USB stick on an investigator system using (*/mnt*) as the mount point:

```
# mount /dev/sdb1 /mnt
```

To physically remove a mounted disk in Linux, unmount the filesystem first to prevent corruption of the filesystem. You can use the umount command (that is umount, not unmount) with either the device name or the mount point. These two commands perform the same action to unmount a disk filesystem:

```
# umount /dev/sdb1
# umount /mnt
```

After the filesystem is unmounted, the raw disk is still visible to the kernel and accessible by block device tools, even though the filesystem is not mounted. An unmounted disk is safe to physically detach from an investigator's acquisition system.

Don't attach or mount suspect drives without a write blocker. There is a high risk of modifying, damaging, and destroying digital evidence. Modern OSes will update the last-accessed timestamps as the files and directories are accessed. Any userspace daemons (search indexers, thumbnail generators, and so on) might write to the disk and overwrite evidence, filesystems might attempt repairs, journaling filesystems might write out journal data, and other human accidents might occur. You can mount a filesystem while using a write blocker, and it will be accessible in the same way as a regular filesystem but in a read-only state, ensuring digital evidence is protected.

Accessing Filesystems with Forensic Tools

When you're using forensic tools, such as Sleuth Kit, dcfldd, foremost, and others, you can access the filesystem (without mounting) by using the correct block device representing the partition where the filesystem resides. In most cases, this will be a numbered device, such as */dev/sda1*, */dev/sda2*, or */dev/sdb1*, and so on, as detected by the Linux kernel.

In cases where the Linux kernel does not detect the filesystem, you may need to explicitly specify it. A filesystem will not be correctly detected for any of the following reasons:

- The filesystem is not supported by the host system (missing kernel module or unsupported filesystem).
- The partition table is corrupted or missing.
- The partition has been deleted.
- The filesystem offset on the disk is unknown.
- The filesystem needs to be made accessible (unlock device, decrypt partition, and so on).

In later sections of the book, I'll explain techniques that use loop devices to access partitions and filesystems that are not automatically detected by the Linux kernel or various forensic tools.

Linux Distributions and Shells

When you're creating an investigator workstation to perform digital forensic acquisition or analysis work, it's useful to understand the basic construction or composition of a Linux system.

Linux Distributions

The term *Linux* technically refers only to the *kernel*, which is the actual OS.[4] The graphical interface, tools and utilities, and even the command line shell are not Linux but parts of a Linux *distribution*. A distribution is a functional package that typically contains the Linux kernel, installers and package managers (usually unique to the distribution), and various additional programs and utilities (including standard applications, such as Office suites, web browsers, or email/chat clients). There is only one official Linux kernel, but there are many Linux distributions—for example, Red Hat, SUSE, Arch, and Debian, among others. There are also many derivative distributions. For example, Ubuntu is a derivative based on Debian, CentOS is based on Red Hat, and Manjaro is based on Arch. For a comprehensive list of distributions (and other non-Linux, open source OSes), visit *http://distrowatch.com/*.

Multiple components make up the graphic interface of various Linux distributions and are useful to understand. The X11 window system is a display server that interacts with the graphics hardware and provides an interface to the X11 graphics primitives (Wayland is a newer alternative to X11). A window manager controls movement, resizing, placement, and other windows management on a system. Some examples of window managers

---

4. There is some naming controversy regarding the inclusion of *GNU* with *Linux*, see *https://en.wikipedia.org/wiki/GNU/Linux_naming_controversy*.

include Compiz, Mutter, and OpenBox, and you can use them without a desktop environment. Desktop environments provide the look and feel of a distribution and operate on top of the window manager. Examples of popular desktops are Gnome, KDE, Xfce, and Mate. The graphics environment you choose for your forensic investigator's workstation can be based on your personal preference; it doesn't have any impact on the evidence you collect or analyze. The examples shown in this book were performed on a system without a GUI (Ubuntu Server version).

The Shell

The shell is a command prompt that humans and/or machines use to submit commands to instruct and control an OS. The shell starts or stops programs, installs software, shuts down a system, and performs other work. Arguably, the command shell offers more powerful features and possibilities than graphical environments.

The examples in this book use the command line environment. Some GUI equivalents or GUI frontends to the command line tools may exist, but they are not covered in this book.

The most common shell in use today, and the default in most Linux distributions, is Bash. The examples in this book use Bash but may also work on other shells (zsh, csh, and so on).

Command Execution

The shell is simply another program that runs on a system. Human users interface with it in the form of typed commands, and machines interface with it in the form of executed shell scripts.

When human users enter commands, they usually type them into the prompt and then press ENTER or RETURN. There may or may not be any output, depending on the program run and the configuration of the shell.

Piping and Redirection

A useful feature of the Unix/Linux command line is the ability to pass streams of data to programs and files using piping and redirection. This is somewhat similar to drag-and-drop and copy/paste in graphical environments, but with much more flexibility.

A program can receive data from the output of other programs or from files on the filesystem. A program can also output data to the input of another program or send it to a file on the filesystem.

The following examples illustrate *tool.sh* redirecting output into *file.txt*, receiving input from *file.txt*, and piping output from *tool.sh* to the input of *othertool.sh*:

```
$ tool.sh > file.txt
$ tool.sh < file.txt
$ tool.sh | othertool.sh
```

This piping and redirection mechanism is not limited to single commands or files and can be chained in a sequence with multiple programs:

```
$ tool.sh < file.txt | othertool.sh | lasttool.sh > lastfile.txt
```

Pipelines and redirection are used extensively throughout this book. They allow you to complete multiple tasks using a single line of commands, and they facilitate scripting and automation, eliminating the need for human interaction. The examples in this book use piping and redirection to acquire images of storage media, move data between forensic programs, and save evidential information of interest in files.

Closing Thoughts

In this chapter, I discussed the use of Linux as a viable platform to perform forensic acquisition tasks and covered both its advantages and disadvantages. I provided a review of Linux distributions and how the Linux kernel works. I showed the concept of devices and filesystems and the use of shells, piping, and redirection from the perspective of the forensic examiner. You now have the Linux knowledge needed to understand the examples in the rest of the book.

3

FORENSIC IMAGE FORMATS

This chapter provides an overview of the various acquisition tools, evidence containers, and forensic image formats commonly used today. Forensic image formats and evidence containers are the structures that store the forensically acquired image together with additional case data, such as the time and duration of the acquisition, how the image was acquired, size, errors, hashes, and so on. Additional features of forensic formats typically include compressed files and encryption. This chapter demonstrates command line forensic tasks using several forensic formats.

You'll find an informative introductory paper describing various forensic formats on the Digital Forensic Research Workshop (DFRWS) website at *http://www.dfrws.org/CDESF/survey-dfrws-cdesf-diskimg-01.pdf*.

You can identify the commonly used forensic formats described in this chapter by using the Sleuth Kit command img_stat:

```
# img_stat -i list
Supported image format types:
        raw (Single or split raw file (dd))
        aff (Advanced Forensic Format)
```

```
afd (AFF Multiple File)
afm (AFF with external metadata)
afflib (All AFFLIB image formats (including beta ones))
ewf (Expert Witness format (encase))
```

In addition to these formats, this chapter introduces an ad hoc method using SquashFS as a practical forensic container for use with standard forensic tools.

NOTE   *An important concept regarding forensic images is that they do not copy files; they copy disk sectors, from sector 0 to the last accessible sector on the disk. The raw image size will always equal the full disk size independent of the number of files residing on the disk's filesystem.*

Raw Images

Raw images are not a format per se but a chunk of raw data imaged from an evidence source. Raw images contain no additional metadata aside from the information about the image file itself (name, size, timestamps, and other information in the image's own inode).

Extracting a raw image is technically straightforward: it is simply the transfer of a sequence of bytes from a source device to a destination file. This is normally done without any transformation or translation.

Disk block copying tools, such as dd and variants, are most commonly used to extract raw images. These are discussed in the following sections.

Traditional dd

To create raw images, the simplest tool available, as well as the oldest, is the original Unix dd utility. It was not designed for evidence collection, but its simple byte-by-byte transfer is useful for imaging disk devices, because it makes a complete low-level copy of individual sectors of a disk (preserving the filesystem structure, files, directories, and metadata). However, features such as logging, error handling, and hashing are either inadequate or nonexistent; dd can be used when a better alternative isn't available. The Computer Forensic Tool Testing (CFTT) Project has tested several standard dd versions. You'll find the test results on the CFTT website at *http://www.cftt.nist.gov/disk_imaging.htm.*

The dd utility was created in the 1970s on early UNIX systems for byte-order conversion and block copying. It was initially developed to convert EBCDIC-encoded data from the mainframe world into ASCII encoding, which was preferable in the UNIX environment. The program simply takes blocks of data from a source, optionally performs a conversion or transformation, and then places the blocks in a specified destination (on another device or in a file). Modern versions of dd have enhancements that make it useful for performing forensic acquisition of data from devices, such as disks and tapes.

Forensic dd Variants

Because the original dd tool was not designed for use in a forensic context, certain features are missing. Subsequently, tools based on dd were developed to include desired forensic features, such as:

- Cryptographic hashing
- Improved error handling
- Logging
- Performance enhancements
- Verification checking
- Progress monitoring (forensic imaging can take many hours)

The two most commonly used variants of the dd utility are dcfldd, created by Nicholas Harbour at the US Department of Defense Computer Forensics Lab (DCFL) in 2002, and dc3dd, created in 2007 by Jesse Kornblum while he was at the US Department of Defense Cyber Crime Center (DC3).

The dcfldd tool is based on GNU dd and included additional features, such as hashing, improved logging, and splitting output files, among others. Although there have been no updates since 2006, the tool is still used today. Alexandre Dulaunoy created a patched version of dcfldd that included some Debian bug fixes, which you'll find at *https://github.com/adulau/*.

The more recent dc3dd tool is implemented as a patch and can more easily follow code changes to GNU dd. The tool is currently maintained, and recent updates have been made. It includes similar forensic features as dcfldd and implements improved logging and error handling.

Both dcfldd and dc3dd originated from traditional dd and have similar features. Although neither tool has built-in support for writing to forensic formats (FTK, Encase, AFF), compression, or image encryption, you can use command piping and redirection for these tasks. Examples of both tools are shown throughout this book. Test reports from CFTT exist for dcfldd and dc3dd.

Data Recovery Tools

Several data recovery tools are worth mentioning because of their robust error handling and aggressive recovery methods. Although these tools were not written with forensics in mind, they can be useful in situations where all other forensic tools have failed to recover data from severely damaged media.

GNU ddrescue and dd_rescue have similar names but are different tools, developed independently. As of this writing, both tools were under active development, each with different useful features. Although they both reference dd in their names, neither tool uses the dd command syntax.

GNU ddrescue was created in 2004 by Antonio Diaz Diaz and is packaged under Debian using the package name *gddrescue*. It uses aggressive and persistent methods to attempt the recovery of bad areas of a disk.

The dd_rescue tool was created in 1999 by Kurt Garloff and has an elaborate plugin system that supports compression, encryption, hashing, and other plugins.

Other similar storage media recovery tools include myrescue and safecopy. Some of these tools will be demonstrated in Chapters 6 and 7.

Forensic Formats

Several issues with raw images have led to the creation of forensic file formats. When imaging storage media as evidence, there is metadata about the investigation, the investigator, the drive details, logs/timestamps, cryptographic hashes, and so on. In addition to metadata, there is often a need to compress or encrypt an acquired image. Specialized forensic formats facilitate the implementation of these features, and the most common formats are described here.

Forensic file formats are sometimes called *evidence containers.* Some research work has also outlined the concept of digital evidence bags.[1] Tools to perform acquisition into forensic formats are demonstrated in Chapter 6.

EnCase EWF

Guidance Software, one of the oldest forensic software companies, produces its flagship EnCase forensic software suite, which uses the Expert Witness Format (EWF). The EWF format supports metadata, compression, encryption, hashing, split files, and more. A reverse engineered, open source library and tools, libewf was created in 2006 by Joachim Metz and support can be compiled into Sleuth Kit.

FTK SMART

AccessData's FTK SMART format is a direct competitor to EnCase EWF. It's a proprietary format that also includes metadata, compression, encryption, hashing, split files, and more. The command line ftkimager tool (which is free but not open source) is available from AccessData and is demonstrated in Chapters 6 and 7.

AFF

The Advanced Forensic Format (AFF) was created by Simson Garfinkel as an open, peer-reviewed, published format. It includes all the expected features of a forensic format and also includes additional encryption and signing features using standard X.509 certificates. The AFFlib software package contains a number of tools for converting and managing the AFF format.

---

1. Philip Turner, "Unification of Digital Evidence from Disparate Sources (Digital Evidence Bags)" (paper presented at Digital Forensic Research Workshop [DFRWS], New Orleans, Louisiana, August 18, 2005). *http://dfrws.org/2005/proceedings/turner_evidencebags.pdf*.

AFF version 3 is separately maintained at *http://github.com/sshock/AFFLIBv3/*. In 2009, a paper on AFF version 4 was published.[2] The Current AFF version 4 website can be found at *http://www.aff4.org/*. The Advanced Forensic Format 4 Working Group (AFF4 WG) was announced in summer 2016 with the first meeting held at the DFRWS conference in Seattle.

SquashFS as a Forensic Evidence Container

Throughout this book, I'll demonstrate a technique for creating a hybrid forensic container that combines simple raw imaging and allows storage of supporting case information in a similar way as more advanced forensic formats. The technique uses SquashFS as a forensic evidence container together with a small shell script, sfsimage, which manages various aspects of the container. This method creates a compressed image combined with imaging logs, information about the disk device, and any other information (photographs, chain of custody forms, and so on) into a single package. The files are contained in a read-only SquashFS filesystem, which you can access without any special forensic tools.

SquashFS Background

SquashFS is a highly compressed, read-only filesystem written for Linux. It was created by Phillip Lougher in 2002 and was merged into the Linux kernel tree in 2009, starting with kernel version 2.6.29.

SquashFS was designed more for use with bootable CDs and embedded systems, but it has a number of features that make it attractive as a forensic evidence container:

- SquashFS is a highly compressed filesystem.
- It is read-only; items can be added but not removed or modified.
- It stores investigator's uid/gid and creation timestamps.
- It supports very large file sizes (theoretically up to 16EiB).
- It is included in the Linux kernel and trivial to mount as a read-only filesystem.
- The filesystem is an open standard (tools exist for Windows, OS X).
- The mksquashfs tool uses all available CPUs to create a container.

The use of SquashFS as a forensic evidence container is a practical alternative to using other forensic formats, because it facilitates the management of compressed raw images acquired with dd. The sfsimage tool, described next, provides the functionality you need to manage SquashFS forensic evidence containers.

---

2. M.I. Cohen, Simson Garfinkel, and Bradley Schatz, "Extending the Advanced Forensic File Format to Accommodate Multiple Data Sources, Logical Evidence, Arbitrary Information and Forensic Workflow," *Digital Investigation* 6 (2009): S57–S68.

SquashFS Forensic Evidence Containers

Modern Linux kernels include support for SquashFS filesystems by default. No additional kernel modules or recompiling are necessary to mount and access a SquashFS filesystem. However, to create a file, append a file, or list the contents of a SquashFS file, the squashfs-tools package is required.[3] Additional forensic software packages for imaging (dcfldd, dc3dd, ewfacquire) may be required, depending on your preferred imaging tool.

My sfsimage shell script is available at *http://digitalforensics.ch/sfsimage/*. Running sfsimage without any options provides you with some help text that describes its usage:

```
$ sfsimage
Sfsimage: a script to manage forensic evidence containers with squashfs
Version: Sfsimage Version 0.8
Usage:
        sfsimage -i diskimage container.sfs
        sfsimage -a file ... container.sfs
        sfsimage -l container.sfs ...
        sfsimage -m container.sfs ...
        sfsimage -m
        sfsimage -u container.sfs ...
Where:
diskimage is a disk device, regular file, or "-" for stdin
container.sfs is a squashfs forensic evidence container
file is a regular file to be added to a container
and the arguments are as follows:
  -i images a disk into a newly created *.sfs container
  -a adds a file to an existing *.sfs container
  -l lists the contents of an existing *.sfs container
  -m mounts an *.sfs container in the current directory
  -m without options shows all mounted sfs containers
  -u umounts an *.sfs container
```

To configure sfsimage, you can edit the script or create separate *sfsimage.conf* files for the script to use. The *config* file is documented with comments and examples, and it allows you to define the following parameters:

- Preferred imaging/acquisition command (dd, dcfldd, dc3dd, and so on)

- Preferred command to query a device (hdparm, tableu-parm, and so on)

- Default directory to mount the evidence container (the current working directory is the default)

- How to manage privileged commands (sudo, su, and so on)

- Permissions and uid/gid of created files

---

3. With Debian-based systems, the package is installed using apt-get install squashfs-tools.

The sfsimage script uses *.sfs* as the naming convention for SquashFS forensic evidence containers. The sfsimage(1) manual page is included with the script and provides more details.

To image a disk into a SquashFS forensic evidence container, run sfsimage using the -i flag, the disk device, and the name of the evidence container. An evidence container will be created with the image and initial metadata about the device just imaged. In this example, sfsimage is configured to use dc3dd as the imaging tool:

```
$ sfsimage -i /dev/sde kingston.sfs
Started: 2016-05-14T20:44:12
Sfsimage version: Sfsimage Version 0.8
Sfsimage command: /usr/bin/sfsimage -i /dev/sde
Current working directory: /home/holmes
Forensic evidence source: if=/dev/sde
Destination squashfs container: kingston.sfs
Image filename inside container: image.raw
Acquisition command: sudo dc3dd if=/dev/sde log=errorlog.txt hlog=hashlog.txt
    hash=md5 2>/dev/null | pv -s 7918845952
7.38GiB 0:01:19 [95.4MiB/s] [========================================>] 100%
Completed: 2016-05-14T20:45:31
```

Here, a SquashFS container is created, and a regular raw image is produced within it. Additional logs and information are also created or can be added separately.

You can add additional evidence to a container using sfsimage with the -a flag. For example, if you need to add a photograph of the physical disk to the forensic evidence container previously made, the following command will perform the task:

```
$ sfsimage -a photo.jpg kingston.sfs
Appending to existing 4.0 filesystem on kingston.sfs, block size 131072
```

To list the contents of a SquashFS forensic evidence container, run the sfsimage script with the -l flag as follows:

```
$ sfsimage -l kingston.sfs
Contents of kingston.sfs:
drwxrwxrwx holmes/holmes            135 2016-05-14 20:46 squashfs-root
-r--r--r-- holmes/holmes            548 2016-05-14 20:45 squashfs-root/errorlog.txt
-r--r--r-- holmes/holmes            307 2016-05-14 20:45 squashfs-root/hashlog.txt
-r--r--r-- holmes/holmes     7918845952 2016-05-14 20:44 squashfs-root/image.raw
-rw-r----- holmes/holmes         366592 2016-05-14 20:45 squashfs-root/photo.jpg
-r--r--r-- holmes/holmes            431 2016-05-14 20:45 squashfs-root/sfsimagelog.txt
```

This command output shows the contents of the *.sfs container (without mounting it). Also shown are the correct times when the files were created or added. The error log, hash log, and sfsimage log contain documentation about activity and errors. The *photo.jpg* is the photograph that was subsequently added to the container.

By mounting the *.sfs file, you can access an acquired image and added metadata files in the SquashFS container. The contents become accessible as a regular part of the filesystem. Because the SquashFS filesystem is read-only, there is no danger of the contents being modified.

In the following example, the *.sfs file is mounted with the -m flag, and regular forensic tools (sleuthkit mmls in this example) are used on the acquired image:

```
$ sfsimage -m kingston.sfs
kingston.sfs.d mount created
$ mmls kingston.sfs.d/image.raw
DOS Partition Table
Offset Sector: 0
Units are in 512-byte sectors

      Slot       Start       End          Length        Description
000:  Meta       0000000000  0000000000   0000000001    Primary Table (#0)
001:  -------    0000000000  0000002047   0000002048    Unallocated
002:  000:000    0000002048  0015466495   0015464448    Linux (0x83)
```

Note that the mounted *.sfs container (by default) appears as a *.sfs.d directory. Once mounted, you can access the files inside the directory by using regular OS tools or forensic tools or even by exporting the files as a shared drive over a network.

When the *.sfs.d mount is no longer needed, unmount it with the -u flag as follows:

```
$ sfsimage -u kingston.sfs.d
kingston.sfs.d unmounted
```

Running sfsimage -m without a mount point will list all mounted SquashFS containers. You can also mount multiple containers on a single system.

Disk image file sizes have always been difficult to work with in a forensic setting. Large disk sizes create space issues and logistical hurdles. Practical compression methods such as SquashFS help manage this problem. To illustrate the practicality of having a compressed filesystem, sfsimage was used to image an 8TB subject disk (*bonkers*) on an investigator system containing only 2TB of disk space. The entire acquisition took more than 16 hours, and the resulting compressed SquashFS file was only 1TB. The mounted

SquashFS file provides access to the full 8TB as a raw image file. The image is compressed on the fly without needing any temporary files. The file sizes of the *.sfs file and the image file are shown here:

```
$ ls -l bonkers.sfs bonkers.sfs.d/bonkers.raw
-rw-r----- 1 holmes  root 1042820382720 Jun 28 13:06 bonkers.sfs
-r--r--r-- 1 root root 8001562156544 Jun 27 20:19 bonkers.sfs.d/bonkers.raw
```

The use of SquashFS is a practical and effective solution for using raw files in a compressed way and offers an alternative forensic evidence container.

Closing Thoughts

This chapter introduced you to various forensic image formats. I provided a short overview and history of different tools that can be used to forensically acquire a drive. You also learned about the SquashFS filesystem and the sfsimage script used to create and manage SquashFS forensic evidence containers. The tools and formats presented in this chapter will be used in examples throughout the rest of the book.

4

PLANNING AND PREPARATION

This chapter describes the preparatory steps performed prior to imaging a disk or storage medium. These include setting up an audit trail of investigator activity, saving output for reports, and deciding on naming conventions. In addition, I describe various logistical challenges involved in the forensic acquisition of storage media and how to establish a protected write-blocking environment.

The subject of forensic readiness overlaps somewhat with the sections in this chapter. However, forensic readiness is a broader topic that includes general planning, budgeting, lab infrastructure, staff training, hardware and software purchasing, and so on. If you consider the preceding requirements needed as "macro" forensic readiness, you can consider the information in this chapter as "micro" forensic readiness. The focus is narrower and includes setting up a forensic examiner's workstation environment and the tools and individual tasks needed to analyze a disk or storage media.

It is worth noting that forensic readiness in a private sector organization (in a corporate forensic lab, for example) is different from forensic readiness in some public sector organizations, such as law enforcement agencies. Private sector organizations, especially large corporate IT environments, can dictate how their IT infrastructure is built and operated. Forensic readiness in this controlled environment can be built into the IT infrastructure, providing advantages for a forensic examiner in the event of an investigation or incident. This chapter focuses on preparatory forensic tasks, which the private sector and public sector have in common.

Maintain an Audit Trail

An audit trail or log maintains a historical record of actions, events, and tasks. It can have various levels of detail and can be either manual or automated. This section covers several command line methods for manually tracking tasks as well as automated logging of command line activity.

Task Management

During a forensic examination, it's beneficial to keep a high-level log of pending and completed activity. Pending tasks turn into completed tasks, and completed tasks make up the examination's historical record. Often while working, you'll think of a task that you need to address sometime in the future or a task you've completed and should note. Making quick notes and more comprehensive task lists becomes increasingly valuable as the length of the examination grows (possibly to many hours, days, or longer) or when more than one examiner is involved.

Maintaining a list of pending and completed tasks during an examination is important for a number of reasons:

- Helps ensure nothing was forgotten
- Avoids duplicating work already done
- Improves collaboration and coordination when working in teams
- Shows compliance with policies and procedures
- Facilitates accounting, including billing
- Helps produce documentation and reports (formal incident reports or forensic reports)
- Allows for post-incident review to identify lessons learned and support process optimization
- Helps to maintain a longer-term historical record of completed activity
- Supports learning and education for new team members
- Serves as a guide to remember complex procedures
- Provides information for troubleshooting problems and getting support
- Maintains a record of work done by external and third-party examiners

Many commercial task managers and investigation management tools are available, but the focus in this section is on simple task management that you can do from the command line. Using the command line permits you to quickly track tasks and activity without leaving the terminal to access some other graphical or web-based application.

Many open source command line task managers are available and can be used to manage a forensic examiner's activity. The most important criteria include reliable task recording and a detailed timestamp (not just dates).

Taskwarrior

Taskwarrior is a popular task manager with many features for managing large task lists in a quick and efficient manner. You'll find more information about Taskwarrior at *http://taskwarrior.org/*. The following examples show Taskwarrior commands in practical use in a forensic lab context.

To add several pending tasks:

```
$ task add acquire PC disk and transfer to evidence safe due:friday
Created task 1.
$ task add have a meeting with investigation team to plan analysis
Created task 2.
```

To list the current task list (task info will show times and more detailed information):

```
$ task list

ID Due       Age Description
 1 2015-06-05 1m  acquire PC disk and transfer to evidence safe
 2             3s  have a meeting with investigation team to plan analysis

2 tasks
```

To complete a task on the task list:

```
$ task 2 done
Completed task 2 'have a meeting with investigation team to plan analysis'.
Completed 1 task.
```

To log a completed task without placing it on the task list:

```
$ task log requested history of PC use at the firm
Logged task.
```

Taskwarrior is useful for managing large numbers of tasks. It provides reports, searching, sorting, and various levels of customizable detail. Taskwarrior maintains timestamps and unique identifiers (UUID) for each task, manages prioritization of pending tasks, and keeps a history of completed tasks. The ability to create user-defined attributes makes it customizable for specific settings, such as a forensics lab or examination process.

Todo.txt

You can also maintain a list of completed tasks and pending work by editing a simple text file. An example is the *todo.txt* file format by Gina Trapani (see *http://todotxt.com/* for more information). The *todo.txt* system defines a file format for task creation and completion dates, priorities, projects, and contexts. It also provides a shell script to manage the *todo.txt* file. Although the todo.sh script performs all the necessary operations on the *todo.txt* task list, the file format can be managed using a regular text editor. The notation indicates priority with parentheses ((A), (B), and so on), context keywords with @, and project keywords with +. Completed tasks are prefixed with an x. Here is an example *todo.txt* file:

```
(A) Sign chain of custody forms @reception
(B) Start forensic acquisition +Disk_A @imagingstation
Discuss analysis approach with investigation team @meetingroom
x 2015-05-30 08:45 upgrade ram in imaging PC @imagingstation
```

The *todo.txt* apps don't use timestamps, only dates. If you use this system, you must manually include the time with the completed task.

Shell Alias

You can also maintain an examiner activity log of completed tasks without the use of task management software. For example, here is a simple shell alias that redirects a short description into a file with a timestamp:

```
$ alias log="echo $2 \`date +%FT%R\` >> ~/examiner.log"
```

You can customize the log filename and date format as desired. Making a quick note of activity or viewing past activity takes a simple one-line command, which you can enter anytime during the examination process. When something significant or notable occurs, enter **log** followed by the short description of the action taken. For example:

```
$ log removed hdd from PC and attached to examiner machine
...
$ log started forensic acquisition of the disk
...
$ log acquisition completed, disk sealed in evidence bag
...
$ cat ~/examiner.log
2015-05-30T09:14 informed that seized PC was enroute to forensic lab
2015-05-30T10:25 PC arrived, chain of custody forms signed
2015-05-30T10:47 removed hdd from PC and attached to examiner machine
2015-05-30T10:55 started forensic acquisition of the disk
```

```
2015-05-30T15:17 acquisition completed, disk sealed in evidence bag
2015-05-30T16:09 disk transferred to evidence safe for storage
```

Simple systems for managing tasks are useful for staff who spend much of their time working on the command line. They are also advantageous for remotely working on systems with secure shell (ssh).

Shell History

This section discusses how to set up automated logging of shell commands entered by the examiner on the command line. Ideally, this command logging should not increase complexity or interfere with the forensic work in progress. Using various tools, you can log the examiner's command line activity with automated background processes. This approach is completely transparent to the examiner during the course of a forensic investigation.

The Unix/Linux shell was not originally designed with logging or audit trails in mind. In the past, patches have been created to augment the history mechanism, hacks have attempted to capture commands as the shell is used, and commercial products have performed various enterprise logging. Developing a robust auditing and compliance system to log all commands with timestamps, including shell builtins as well as executed programs and pipelines, is beyond the scope of this book.

The Bash shell history can be configured to satisfy the following basic requirements:

- Record the command entered by the examiner

- Record a timestamp for each command entered

- Record all commands, including duplicates, comments, and space-prefixed commands

- Avoid truncating or overwriting history files

- Avoid conflicts when using multiple terminal windows on the same system

- Include root and non-root command history

Using basic Bash shell history as an audit trail is rudimentary. Important information, such as the command completion time, the working directory where the command was executed, and the return code, are not logged. The Bash history is also not a tamper-resistant system: the examiner can easily modify or delete the history. Creating a secure and tamper-resistant audit environment with restricted access is beyond the scope of this book.

Some shells, such as zsh, have additional history features that allow for the logging of elapsed time. Other proposed solutions to improve shell logging include the use of PS1, PROMPT_COMMAND, trap and DEBUG, and key bindings to modify a command before executing. Using sudo logging; auditd logging; or special scripts, such as preexec.sh, can also increase command line logging. A useful tutorial at *http://www.pointsoftware.ch/ en/howto-bash-audit-command-logger/* discusses this problem at length and proposes a solution. The command line audit trail should be tailored to particular lab policies or expectations.

For basic shell command logging, the built-in shell history functionality can be configured to record command line activity. Bash provides some useful functionality, including the ability to enable the time stamping of the commands entered. You can add the following commands to the Linux startup scripts (.bashrc and so on) to enable the basic requirements outlined in the previous list:

```
set -o history
shopt -s histappend
export HISTCONTROL=
export HISTIGNORE=
export HISTFILE=~/.bash_history
export HISTFILESIZE=-1
export HISTSIZE=-1
export HISTTIMEFORMAT="%F-%R "
```

These commands ensure that history is enabled and in append mode (as opposed to overwriting with each new login). The two variables HISTCONTROL and HISTIGNORE control which commands are saved to the history file. A common default setting is to ignore duplicates and commands beginning with a space. To ensure complete logging of all commands, the HISTCONTROL and HISTIGNORE variables are explicitly set to null. The HISTFILE variable is explicitly set to ensure command history held in memory is saved when a shell exits. HISTFILESIZE and HISTSIZE are set to -1 to ensure history is not truncated or overwritten. The HISTTIMEFORMAT variable enables timestamps to be written to the history file and allows you to set a time format. The format can include regional settings and should include a timestamp, not just the date.

At the end of the examination, the history can be saved to a text file and included in the examination's supporting data files. The history can then be reset and made ready for the next examination by using the following commands:

```
$ history > examiner_bash_history.txt
$ history -c; history -w
```

Synchronizing the history across multiple shell instances can be tricky because each shell keeps its history in memory and writes it to the history file only on exit. Setting the variable PROMPT_COMMAND='history -a; history -r' will write (append) and read new commands from the Bash history file every time the command prompt is displayed.

A command logger that is actively developed is Snoopy: it provides a number of features, including logging the commands to syslog. Snoopy is a preloaded library that functions as a wrapper around the execv() and execve() system calls. It is transparent to users, and you can enable and configure it by adding the Snoopy library to */etc/ld.so.preload* and editing the */etc/snoopy.ini* file. For example, suppose the following series of commands are entered on the Bash command prompt:

```
# fls -p -r  /dev/sda1 | grep -i "\.doc$" |wc -l
10
```

These commands are individually logged to syslog with various details:

```
Jun  5 10:47:05 lab-pc snoopy[1521]: [uid:0 sid:1256 tty:(none) cwd:/ filename:
    /bin/grep]: grep -i \.doc$
Jun  5 10:47:05 lab-pc snoopy[1522]: [uid:0 sid:1256 tty:(none) cwd:/ filename:
    /usr/bin/wc]: wc -l
Jun  5 10:47:05 lab-pc snoopy[1520]: [uid:0 sid:1256 tty:/dev/pts/0 cwd:/ filename:
    /usr/bin/fls]: fls -p -r /dev/sda1
```

You'll find more information and the latest release of Snoopy at *https://github.com/a2o/snoopy/*.

Terminal Recorders

In some cases, it might be useful to show the work done in the terminal, complete with command output (stdout), error messages (stderr), and other messages or activity visible in a terminal session. Several tools exist to capture session activity and even provide playback of the session.

The most well-known tool is script. In this example, script is started and the output appended to a file together with timing data for replay. After running script, you can execute any normal shell commands, and they'll be saved for later viewing.

```
$ script -a -tscript.timing script.output
Script started, file is script.output
```

When the recorded session is finished, enter exit or press CTRL-D. You can view the recording using the scriptreplay command as follows:

```
$ scriptreplay -m1 -tscript.timing script.output
...[session plays back here]...
```

Common issues that make this method challenging are the handling of control characters and events such as terminal resizing. Other TTY recorders and sniffers, such as ttyrec and termrec, are available with similar functionality and features.

Terminal multiplexers, such as tmux and GNU screen, also provide some level of logging that can be useful in certain situations. With screen, you can set up logging for a detached session from within a session

(CTRL-A followed by H). The tmux terminal multiplexer now supports logging by using the `pipe-pane` option, as shown here:

```
$ tmux pipe-pane -o -t session_index:window_index.pane_index 'cat >> ~/output
   .window_index-pane_index.txt'
```

Linux Auditing

Professional labs might want to implement more robust logging or an audit trail to satisfy stricter organizational policies or regulatory requirements. One possibility to achieve this is through auditd, a Linux audit package. Typically, this involves running the `auditd` daemon with *pam_tty_audit.so* configured as a pam module. You can review audit trail activity using the `aureport` command.

Using auditd provides several security advantages, especially when used with granular access control, such as `sudo`. Audit trails, in particular those logging to a central log host, can be made relatively tamper resistant, ensuring an increased level of integrity when recording examination work.

Comprehensive audit trails can record all TTY activity (including keystrokes), as well as monitor file access and many other events on a system. Setting up auditing and audit reporting can be a complex process, one beyond the scope of this book.

You'll find discussions of other solutions and hacks in various places, including *http://www.pointsoftware.ch/en/howto-bash-audit-command-logger/* and *http://whmcr.com/2011/10/14/auditd-logging-all-commands/*.

As of Bash version 4.1, a new feature allowing command history logging to syslog has been added (it may require recompilation to enable).

Organize Collected Evidence and Command Output

When conducting a forensic examination on the command line, it's common to save command output from various tools and utilities to files for future reference and reporting. You can do this by redirecting the output of commands to text files. Those files can be saved with the rest of the examination data collected. During the process of collecting and saving large amounts of evidence data, it is important to keep your file and directory structure organized and understandable. This section talks about various strategies to achieve this goal.

Naming Conventions for Files and Directories

To reduce confusion among all the files, directories, mount points, images, and other saved data collected during an examination, it's best to follow a naming convention. Make it descriptive enough to be intuitive, but avoid redundancy in the wording and file extensions. Most important, make naming conventions consistent throughout an investigation or incident and across multiple incidents.

Certain unique identifiers are associated with systems, storage media devices, and removable media. Such identifiers can be useful when deciding on a naming convention:

- Company asset tag or inventory number for PCs
- Manufacturer serial number for disk drives
- 64-bit World Wide Name (WWN) for disk drives
- Block device UUID for filesystems and RAIDs
- Forensic hash value for disk drive images
- 48-bit MAC address for network interface cards (NICs)
- Forensic lab evidence number (possibly a sticker or tag on the drive)
- Forensic lab evidence bag number (evidence bag containing the disc)

Wherever sensible, start all numbering with 1, not 0. Programmers and engineers have a tendency to start at 0, but people who read and review the examination reports may not have a technical background (lawyers, judges, managers, and so on) and expect numbering to start with 1.

Raw image files use the extension *.raw throughout this book. The commonly used *.dd extension implies that a dd tool was used, which might not be the case. The *.raw extension describes the file accurately without associating it with the particular tool used to acquire the image.

Ideally, a raw image's filename should link a forensic image to a unique attribute of the physical object. If a forensic format is used, this unique information can be embedded as metadata in the forensic image file. This allows you to associate a lone physical disk with an image and associate a lone image with a physical disk. The disk and the image then remain linked without any dependencies on surrounding context (directory names, evidence shelves, and so on). This establishes a chain of custody link between the physical and digital worlds.

If large numbers of disks are under analysis, possibly include a serial number in the image filename. You can include varying levels of detail in a filename. Although the filename *server12-slot3-seagate-3.5in-disk-500gb -SN12345ACBDEE.raw* is very descriptive, it might be too detailed and cumbersome to work with. A practical naming convention for many basic incidents could simply be the storage media type with a number, for example, *disk1, tape1, ssd1, stick1, card1, cdrom1, dvd1, bluray1, floppy1,* and so on. In some cases, using a short description of the disk and the serial number might be the most suitable approach, for example, *crucial-ssd -15030E69A241.raw.* Often, it's helpful to create image names that examiners can easily discuss in conversation, such as, "We found the file on disk1." Terms used in conversations, raw examination output, and final reports should have a consistent nomenclature.

When you're extracting files from disk images, archive files, or other compound images, add an underscore to the filename to indicate it has been extracted. This will prevent you and others from accidentally opening malware, HTML pages with tracking bugs, macros in Office documents, or other executables and scripts that might execute on opening. Some examples are shown here:

```
$ icat image.raw 68 > photo.jpg_
$ icat image.raw 34 > customerlist.xls_
$ icat image.raw 267 > super-updater57.exe_
```

If an extracted file already ends with an underscore, add another one. An appended underscore make it obvious that a file has been extracted as evidence from a suspect drive.

When you're analyzing an extracted file, saving tool output, or making manual notes, create a text file with the original name and append _.*txt* to it. For example:

```
$ exif photo.jpg_ > photo.jpg_.txt
$ vi customerlist.xls_.txt
$ objdump -x super-updater57.exe_ > super-updater57.exe_.txt
```

The _.*txt* extension signifies that the text file contains notes, tool output, and results of forensic analysis work about the extracted file. The filename is associated with the file originally extracted from the image. The text file may contain bookmarks and examiner annotations that can be searched. Unless it's otherwise clear where an extracted file came from (which disk, partition, and so on), it's good practice to have such corresponding text files; they can also indicate why it was chosen for extraction.

A file extension should always indicate the format of the content. For example:

- **.txt* can be opened and read using a text editor.
- **.raw* is a raw data dump (disk, memory, and so on).
- **.pcap* is captured network traffic.
- **.db* is a database (possibly a Sleuth Kit file list).
- **.sfs* is a SquashFS evidence container.
- **.e01* and **.aff* are forensic formats.

Each case, incident, or investigation will have an associated physical storage media. Storage media will have a corresponding forensic image and associated output from various programs (hdparm, smartctl, and so on). Each forensic image will have associated output from various programs (mmls, fls, and so on), and each extracted file may have associated output from various programs (exif, objdump, and so on). A naming convention will help keep everything organized and allow the organizing system to scale as the investigation data grows.

How much information should be embedded into filenames and directory names? When is it more sensible to have a corresponding description text file with additional information? How should the corresponding file be associated with an image? Consider the following examples of two representations of the same incident.

An example of information embedded into filenames looks like this:

```
case42.txt
image6.case42.raw
image6.case42.raw.txt
mmls.image6.case42.txt
fls.part1.image6.case42.txt
```

An example of that same information embedded into a directory structure looks like this:

```
./case42/case.txt
./case42/image6/image.raw
./case42/image6/image.raw.txt
./case42/image6/mmls.txt
./case42/image6/part1/fls.txt
```

For manually written notes, further descriptions, caveats, issues, and other random comments within a certain context, storing the information in simple *notes.txt* or *readme.txt* files within working directories can be useful. They can provide reminders, hints, or warnings for you or other examiners to read at a later date.

When you're noting web URLs that might pose a risk if opened, replace *http* with *hxxp* to prevent others from accidentally clicking them. Such links might take the user to malware, personal sites monitored by a suspect, sites with tracking bugs, or other content that should not be accessed without understanding the consequences.

Scalable Examination Directory Structure

Each incident, case, or investigation should have a single unique directory (for example, *case42*). All collected evidence, images, and analysis work should be contained within a hierarchy under that one root directory. As investigations scale, a well-planned directory structure can scale with it. Having a single directory is also practical when multiple forensic examiners are working on the same incident and sharing the directory structure. Be prepared to reorganize the directory structure if an incident grows in complexity. If a large number of files are being extracted for individual analysis, consider having an *export* directory (similar to EnCase).

Examinations often scale unexpectedly, and a forensic examination that starts with a single disk under suspicion might expand into a larger examination involving multiple PCs with many disks. For example, suppose someone reports strange or suspicious behavior of a PC or employee. A single disk is seized for examination. Preliminary examination results find a USB stick is also involved. It is found and examined, and a second PC is linked to the incident. That PC has two internal hard disks and DVD burner. Further search reveals a box of DVDs full of data hidden in a closet. Then it turns out that an external USB hard disk and a spare notebook in another building are also involved in the incident. The collected evidence has grown from a single hard disk to 16 storage media items. This hypothetical incident is not uncommon in large organizations. When preparing for an examination, expanded coverage should be anticipated. The naming convention should be designed to scale as the size of an investigation grows.

Some PCs are used by multiple people, and some people use multiple PCs. Notebooks are not necessarily bound to a physical location. Removable media can be shared and attached to multiple PCs and notebooks. Over long periods of time, PC hardware will change, offices may change, departments will experience staff turnover, and organizational restructuring may occur. Be sure to design file and directory names to accommodate these changes.

As an examination progresses, the number of output files will grow as more collected data is analyzed and output is produced. A good practice is to create a directory structure to separate the files and organize the output of the examination. As with filenames, the directory name should indicate the contents without revealing confidential information. Creating a separate directory for each disk or image analyzed segregates files and allows an investigation to scale up.

The smallest examination usually consists of a single disk. A slightly larger examination might consist of a PC containing multiple disks; consider the following example directory structure:

```
├── HDD1
├── HDD2
└── HDD3
```

As another example, consider the examination of an entire workplace that consists of a desktop PC (possibly with multiple disks), a notebook, several USB drives, multiple CD-ROMs and DVDs, and an external disk pack. A convenient directory structure would organize each piece of storage media where the command output files are stored, allowing an examination to easily scale further. Consider a larger investigation consisting of multiple workplaces, across multiple office buildings, spread out across multiple countries. In large global organizations, such investigations can occur; therefore, having a well-thought-out naming convention will maintain the organization of the examination process.

It's advantageous to rely on a directory structure to separate command output from different disks, PCs, users, and locations. As a result, you won't need to embed this information into the output filenames. For example:

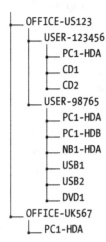

```
└─ OFFICE-US123
    └─ USER-123456
        └─ PC1-HDA
        └─ CD1
        └─ CD2
    └─ USER-98765
        └─ PC1-HDA
        └─ PC1-HDB
        └─ NB1-HDA
        └─ USB1
        └─ USB2
        └─ DVD1
└─ OFFICE-UK567
    └─ PC1-HDA
```

In this example, two office locations are US123 and UK567, in the United States and the United Kingdom, respectively. The US office is divided by user workplaces, and a directory is used for each piece of storage media under examination. The UK office PC is not associated with any particular user (possibly located in a meeting room), and this is reflected in the directory structure.

Instead of using an employee identifier for the storage media, an organization's IT inventory number can be used for the storage media in the directory structure. This unique identifier will likely have additional information associated with it (date of purchase, department, office location, user details, software installed, history of use, and so on). Confidentiality reasons might require you to omit information from the filenames and directory structure. For example, names of suspected or targeted individuals should not be embedded into filenames. Rather, you should use an identifier, initials, or an employee number. Code names for investigations might also be used. They provide a minimal level of protection if the information is lost, stolen, or otherwise accessed at a later date.

Save Command Output with Redirection

After creating the directory structure to store the analysis results from various items under examination, typical shell command output is redirected into files from stdout as shown here:

```
# fls /dev/sda1 > fls-part1.txt
# fls /dev/sda2 > fls-part2.txt
```

To include regular output and error messages, you need to redirect stdout and stderr file descriptors to the file. Newer versions of Bash provide an easy-to-remember method by adding an ampersand to the redirection (this also applies when piping to another program):

```
# fls /dev/sda &> fls-part1.txt
```

Other shells and earlier Bash versions might require 2>&1 notation for combining stderr and stdin. For example:

```
# fls /dev/sda > fls-part1.txt 2>&1
```

When a text file already exists and you need to add additional information to it, you can use the >> notation to specify an append operation. For example:

```
# grep clientnames.xls fls-part1.txt >> notes.txt
```

Here, all instances of a known filename are added to the end of the *notes.txt* file.[1] If *notes.txt* doesn't exist, it will be created.

Many forensic tasks performed on the command line are time-consuming and may take many hours to complete (disk imaging, performing operations on very large files, and so on). Having a timestamp indicating the duration of the command can be useful. The time command provides this functionality. There are two common implementations of the time command: one is a shell builtin with rudimentary features, and the other is a GNU utility with additional features. The primary advantage of the shell builtin time version is that it will time an entire pipeline of commands, whereas GNU time will only time the first command in a pipeline.

Here is an example of using the time command to run a disk-imaging program:

```
# time dcfldd if=/dev/sdc of=./ssd-image.raw
3907328 blocks (122104Mb) written.
3907338+1 records in
3907338+1 records out

real    28m5.176s
user    0m11.652s
sys     2m23.652s
```

The zsh shell can log the elapsed time of a command as part of the history file. This functionality is currently not available in Bash.

---

1. The dot in this example may be interpreted as a regular expression. This is ignored here for simplicity.

Another useful command for some situations is the timestamp output command `ts`. Any output piped into `ts` will have a timestamp appended to each line of output.

```
# (ls -l image.raw; cp -v image.raw /exam/image.raw; md5sum /exam/image.raw) |ts
May 15 07:45:28 -rw-r----- 1 root root 7918845952 May 15 07:40 image.raw
May 15 07:45:40 'image.raw' -> '/exam/image.raw'
May 15 07:45:53 4f12fa07601d02e7ae78c2d687403c7c  /exam/image.raw
```

In this example, three commands were executed (grouped together with parentheses) and the command outputs were sent to `ts`, creating a timeline.

Assess Acquisition Infrastructure Logistics

Various logistical issues are important when performing forensic acquisition of storage media. Managing large acquired forensic images is not a trivial task and so requires planning and forethought. Factors such as disk capacity, time duration, performance, and environmental issues need to be considered.

Image Sizes and Disk Space Requirements

Forensic images of storage media are orders of magnitude larger than the small file sizes a PC typically handles. Managing disk image files of this size takes additional thought and planning. You also need to consider certain logistical factors when you're preparing an examination system. Careful preparation and planning for an examination will save you time and effort, as well as help you avoid problems that might disrupt the process.

When creating a forensic image of a disk (hundreds of gigabytes or terabytes), it is not files that are copied, but the individual disk sectors. If a 1TB disk has only a single 20K Microsoft Word document on it, an uncompressed forensic image will still be 1TB. As of this writing, 10TB disks are now on the market, increasing the challenge for performing forensic acquisition.

When managing disk images, the examiner's time and the examiner host's disk capacity are the main logistical factors that need to be considered. Before beginning a forensic acquisition of a subject disk or storage media, you need to ask a number of questions:

- Can the attached storage be analyzed *in place* without taking a forensic image?
- What is the size of the subject disk?
- What is the available space on the examiner's machine?

- What is the potential for image compression?

- How much space do forensic tools need for processing and temporary files?

- What is the estimated number of files to be extracted for further analysis?

- How much memory and swap space is available on the examiner's machine?

- Is there a possibility of more subject disks being added to the same case or incident?

- Is there an expectation to separately extract all slack or unallocated disk space?

- Are there plans to extract individual partitions (possibly including swap)?

- Is there a potential need to convert from one forensic format to another?

- Do disk images need to be prepared for transport to another location?

- Do subject disks contain virtual machine images to separately extract and analyze?

- Do subject disks contain large numbers of compressed and archive files?

- Are subject disks using full-disk encryption?

- Is there a need to burn images to another disk or DVDs for storage or transport?

- Is there a need to carve files from a damaged or partially overwritten filesystem?

- How are backups of the examiner host performed?

In some situations, it may not be necessary to image a disk. When certain triage or cursory searching is conducted, it may be enough to attach the disk to an examiner host and operate on the live subject disk. Depending on the triage or search findings, you can decide whether or not to take a forensic image. In a corporate environment, this approach could translate into downtime for an employee, because they must wait for a seized disk to be reviewed or analyzed. Corporate environments typically have a standard end-user PC build, which is designed without local user data (all data is saved to servers or clouds). It could be more economical simply to swap the original disk with a new disk. End-user PC disks are cheap, and replacing a subject disk with a new one could be a cost-saving alternative when factoring in the cost of employee downtime and the time needed to image a disk in the field.

File Compression

Using compression solves a number of the capacity challenges faced by a forensic examiner. You can use a compressed forensic format to store the resulting acquired image, but the effectiveness depends on a number of factors.

The compression algorithms you choose will have some effect on the size and time needed to compress a subject disk. A better compression ratio will take more time to compress (and subsequently uncompress).

A relatively new PC disk that contains a large number of untouched disk sectors (original manufacturer's zeroed contents) will compress better than an older disk containing significant amounts of residual data in the unallocated sectors.

Disks that contain large amounts of compressed files (*.mp3*, *.avi*, and so on) will not compress much further, and as a result, forensic imaging tools will benefit less from added compression.

Encrypted subject disks or disks with large numbers of encrypted files will not compress as well as unencrypted content due to the data's higher entropy level.

Sparse Files

Sparse files are worth mentioning because they have some advantages; however, they can also be problematic when calculating disk capacity. Some filesystems use metadata to represent a sequence of zeros in a file instead of actually writing all the zeros to the disk. Sparse files contain "holes" where a sequence of zeros is known to exist. To illustrate, a new drive containing mostly zeroed sectors is acquired with GNU dd,[2] first as a regular raw file and then as a sparse file.

```
# dd if=/dev/sde of=image.raw
15466496+0 records in
15466496+0 records out
7918845952 bytes (7.9 GB, 7.4 GiB) copied, 112.315 s, 70.5 MB/s

# dd if=/dev/sde of=sparse-image.raw conv=sparse
15466496+0 records in
15466496+0 records out
7918845952 bytes (7.9 GB, 7.4 GiB) copied, 106.622 s, 74.3 MB/s
```

The GNU dd command provides a conv=sparse flag that creates a sparse destination file. In these dd examples, you can see the number of blocks transferred is the same for both the normal and sparse files. In the following

---

2. The GNU cp command also allows for the creation of sparse files during copy.

output, the file size and the MD5 hash are also identical. However, notice how the block size used on the filesystem is very different (7733252 blocks versus 2600 blocks):

```
# ls -ls image.raw sparse-image.raw
7733252 -rw-r----- 1 root root 7918845952 May 15 08:28 image.raw
   2600 -rw-r----- 1 root root 7918845952 May 15 08:30 sparse-image.raw

# md5sum image.raw sparse-image.raw
325383b1b51754def26c2c29bcd049ae  image.raw
325383b1b51754def26c2c29bcd049ae  sparse-image.raw
```

Although the sparse file requires much less space, the full byte size is still reported as the file size. This can cause confusion when calculating the real available disk capacity. Sparse files are often used by VM images and can become an issue when extracted for analysis.

You can also use sparse files as a method of compacting image files, but using compressed forensic formats or SquashFS containers is preferred and recommended. Not all programs and utilities can handle sparse files correctly, and the files can become problematic when moved between filesystems and platforms. Some programs may even expand sparse files when reading them.

Reported File and Image Sizes

Reporting data sizes is an important concept to grasp. When you're working with forensic tools, size can refer to bytes, disk sectors, filesystem blocks, or other units of measurement. The notation for bytes can be prefixed with a multiplier (such as kilobytes, megabytes, gigabytes, terabytes, and so on), and the multiplier can refer to multiples of either 1000 or 1024. Disk sectors could represent sector sizes of either 512 bytes or 4096 bytes. The filesystem block size depends on the type of filesystem and the parameters used during creation. When you're documenting sizes in a forensic context, it's important to always include descriptive units.

Many Linux tools support the -h flag to report file sizes in a human readable form. For example, you can use ls -lh, df -h, and du -h to more easily view the size of files and partitions. An example ls output with several file sizes is shown here:

```
# ls -l
total 4
-rw-r----- 1 root root 2621440000 Jan 29 14:44 big.file
-rw-r----- 1 root root  104857600 Jan 29 14:41 medium.file
-rw-r----- 1 root root      51200 Jan 29 14:42 small.file
-rw-r----- 1 root root         56 Jan 29 14:44 tiny.file
# ls -lh
total 4.0K
-rw-r----- 1 root root 2.5G Jan 29 14:44 big.file
```

```
-rw-r----- 1 root root 100M Jan 29 14:41 medium.file
-rw-r----- 1 root root  50K Jan 29 14:42 small.file
-rw-r----- 1 root root   56 Jan 29 14:44 tiny.file
```

The sizes in the second command's output are much easier to read and understand.

Moving and Copying Forensic Images

Moving and copying forensic disk images from one place to another requires planning and foresight. Don't think of image files in the same way as typical end-user files (even though technically they're the same).

Acquiring, copying, and moving large disk images may take many hours or even days depending on the size and speed of the source disk and other performance factors. Consider the following list of typical file and disk image sizes and the average amount of time needed to copy the file from one disk to another disk:[3]

- 5KB simple ASCII text email: less than 1 second

- 5MB typical MP3 music file: less than 1 second

- 650MB CD ISO image: about 5 seconds

- 5–6GB typical DVD or iTunes movie download: about 1 minute

- 64GB common mobile phone image: about 10 minutes

- 250GB common notebook disk image: 30-40 minutes

- 1TB typical desktop PC image: more than 2 hours

- 2TB typical external USB disk image: more than 4 hours

- 8TB internal disk image: more than 16 hours

Once a copy or move process has been started, disrupting it could leave the data in an incomplete state or require additional time to revert to the original state. A copy or move operation could create temporary files or result in two copies of the images existing temporarily.

In general, think carefully beforehand about the copying and moving of large data sets, and don't interrupt the process once it has started.

Estimate Task Completion Times

The forensic acquisition process takes time to complete. During this time, people and other processes may be waiting. Therefore, it's important to calculate and estimate the completion time needed for various processes. Also, determine whether you need to report estimated completion times to other parties, such as management, legal teams, law enforcement, or other investigators. It is important to manage expectations with regard to the time needed for completion.

---

3. Tested on a typical i7 PC with two SATA3 disks using dd.

Some important questions to consider include:

- Can the acquisition be safely left running overnight while nobody is around?
- Is the examiner machine unusable during the acquisition process (for performance reasons or other reasons)?
- Can other examination work be done while the forensic image is being acquired?
- When can several tasks be completed in parallel?
- Are there certain tasks or processes that can only be done sequentially?
- Are there tasks that will block other tasks until they're completed?
- Can the workload be shared, delegated, or distributed across multiple examiners?

You can calculate an estimated completion time for an acquisition. From previous work and processes, you should know the approximate initial setup time. This includes factors such as completing paperwork, creating necessary directory structure, documenting the hardware, attaching suspect drives to the examiner host, deciding on the approach for acquisition, and so on. This will give you a time estimate for the preacquisition phase.

You can calculate the expected storage media acquisition time based on the amount of data (known) passing through the slowest component in the system (the bottleneck).

Performance and Bottlenecks

To improve the efficiency of a forensic acquisition, you can optimally tune the examiner host and assess the bottlenecks.

A performance bottleneck always occurs; this is simply the slowest component in the system, which all other components must wait for. In a forensic setting, the bottleneck should ideally be the subject disk. This is the evidence source and is the only performance variable that you can't (or shouldn't) modify.

You can assess the performance of various system components by reading the vendor specifications, querying the system with various tools, or running various benchmarking and measurement tests.

Useful tools to check the speed of various components include dmidecode, lshw, hdparm, and lsusb. Several command line examples are shown here.

To check the CPU family and model, current and maximum speed, number of cores and threads, and other flags and characteristics, use this command:

```
# dmidecode -t processor
```

Here is a command to view the CPU's cache (L1, L2, and L3):

```
# dmidecode -t cache
```

To view the memory, including slots used, size, data width, speed, and other details, use this command:

```
# dmidecode -t memory
```

Here is a command to view the number of PCI slots, usage, designation, and type:

```
# dmidecode -t slot
```

A command to view the storage interfaces, type (SATA, NVME, SCSI, and so on), and speed:

```
# lshw -class storage
```

To view the speed, interface, cache, rotation, and other information about the attached disks (using device */dev/sda* in this example), use this:

```
# hdparm -I /dev/sda
```

To view the speed of the external USB interfaces (and possibly an attached write blocker), use this command:

```
# lsusb -v
```

NOTE   *There are many different methods and commands to get this information. The commands shown here each present one example of getting the desired performance information. Providing an exhaustive list of all possible tools and techniques is beyond the scope of this book.*

Reading the vendor documentation and querying a system will identify the speeds of various components. To get an accurate measurement, it's best to use tools for hardware benchmarking and software profiling. Some tools for benchmarking include mbw for memory and bonnie++ for disk I/O.

The health and tuning of the OS is also a performance factor. Monitoring the logs (syslog, dmesg) of the examiner hardware can reveal error messages, misconfiguration, and other inefficiency indicators. Tools to monitor the performance and load of the live state of an examiner machine include htop, iostat, vmstat, free, or nmon.

You can also optimize the OS by ensuring minimal processes are running in the background (including scheduled processes via cron), tuning the kernel (`sysctl -a`), tuning the examiner host's filesystems (`tunefs`), and managing disk swap and caching. In addition, ensure that the examiner OS is running on native hardware, not as a virtual machine.

When you're looking for bottlenecks or optimizing, it's helpful to imagine the flow of data from the subject disk to the examiner host's disk. During an acquisition, the data flows through the following hardware interfaces and components:

- Subject disk platters/media (rotation speed? latency?)
- Subject disk interface (SATA-X?)
- Write blocker logic (added latency?)
- Write blocker examiner host interface (USB3 with UASP?)
- Examiner host interface (USB3 sharing a bus with other devices? bridged?)
- PCI bus (PCI Express? speed?)
- CPU/memory and OS kernel (speed? DMA? data width?)

These components will be traversed twice, once between the subject disk and the examiner host, and again between the host and the examiner disk where the acquired image is being saved.

Ensure that the data flow between the subject disk and the CPU/memory is not using the same path as for the data flow between the CPU/memory and the destination disk on the examiner host. For example, if a field imaging system has a write blocker and an external disk for the acquired image, and both are connected to local USB ports, it is possible they're sharing a single bus. As a result, the available bandwidth will be split between the two disks, causing suboptimal performance.

For network performance tuning, the speed of the underlying network becomes a primary factor, and performance enhancements include the use of jumbo Ethernet frames and TCP checksum offloading with a high-performance network interface card. It is also beneficial to assess when various programs are accessing the network and for what reason (automatic updates, network backups, and so on).

To summarize, have an overall plan or strategy for the acquisition actions you intend to take. Have well-tested processes and infrastructure in place. Ensure that the right capacity planning and optimizing has been done. Be able to monitor the activity while it's in progress.

The most common bus speeds relevant for a forensic examination host (in bytes/second) are listed in Table 4-1 for comparison. You'll find a good reference of the bit rates for various interfaces and buses at *https://en.wikipedia.org/wiki/List_of_device_bit_rates*.

Table 4-1: Common Bus/Interface Speeds

Bus/interface	Speed
Internal buses	
PCI Express 3.0 x16	15750 MB/s
PCI Express 3.0 x8	7880 MB/s
PCI Express 3.0 x4	3934 MB/s
PCI 64-bit/133MHz	1067 MB/s
Storage drives	
SAS4	2400 MB/s
SAS3	1200 MB/s
SATA3	600 MB/s
SATA2	300 MB/s
SATA1	150 MB/s
External interfaces	
Thunderbolt3	5000 MB/s
Thunderbolt2	2500 MB/s
USB3.1	1250 MB/s
USB3.0	625 MB/s
GB Ethernet	125 MB/s
FW800	98 MB/s
USB2	60 MB/s

Heat and Environmental Factors

During a forensic disk acquisition, every accessible sector on the disk is being read, and the reading of the disk is sustained and uninterrupted, often for many hours. As a result, disk operating temperatures can increase and cause issues. When disks become too hot, the risk of failure increases, especially with older disks. Researchers at Google have produced an informative paper on hard disk failure at *http://research.google.com/archive/disk_failures.pdf*.

To reduce the risk of read errors, bad blocks, or total disk failure, it's worthwhile to monitor the disk temperature while a disk is being acquired. Most disk vendors publish the normal operating temperatures for their drives, including the maximum acceptable operating temperature.

You can also use several tools to manually query the temperature of a drive. A simple tool that queries the SMART interface for a drive's temperature is hddtemp, as shown here:

```
# hddtemp /dev/sdb
/dev/sdb: SAMSUNG HD160JJ: 46C
```

The hddtemp tool can be run as a daemon and periodically log to syslog, where you can monitor it for certain thresholds.

For more detailed output on a disk's temperature, and in some cases a temperature history, use the smartctl tool. Here is an example:

```
# smartctl -x /dev/sdb
...
```

```
Vendor Specific SMART Attributes with Thresholds:
ID# ATTRIBUTE_NAME          FLAGS     VALUE WORST THRESH FAIL RAW_VALUE
...
190 Airflow_Temperature_Cel -O---K    100   055   000    -    46
194 Temperature_Celsius     -O---K    100   055   000    -    46
...
Current Temperature:                  46 Celsius
Power Cycle Max Temperature:          46 Celsius
Lifetime    Max Temperature:          55 Celsius

SCT Temperature History Version:      2
Temperature Sampling Period:          1 minute
Temperature Logging Interval:         1 minute
Min/Max recommended Temperature:      10/55 Celsius
Min/Max Temperature Limit:             5/60 Celsius
Temperature History Size (Index):     128 (55)

Index    Estimated Time   Temperature Celsius
  56     2015-06-07 19:56    50  *****************************
...
  62     2015-06-07 20:02    55  **********************************
  63     2015-06-07 20:03    55  **********************************
  64     2015-06-07 20:04    51  ******************************
...
  55     2015-06-07 22:03    46  *************************
```

   If a disk begins to overheat during a disk acquisition, take action to
reduce the temperature. As an immediate step, temporarily suspend the
acquisition process and continue it when the disk has cooled. Depending
on the acquisition method you use, this could be a simple matter of sending
a signal to the Linux process by pressing CTRL-Z or entering kill -SIGTSTP
followed by a process id. When the temperature decreases to an acceptable
level, the acquisition process can be resumed from the same place it was
suspended.

   Suspending and resuming a process in this way should not affect the
forensic soundness of the acquisition. The process is suspended with its
operational state intact (current sector, destination file, environment variables, and so on). An example of suspending and resuming an imaging
process on the shell by pressing CTRL-Z looks like this:

```
# dcfldd if=/dev/sdb of=./image.raw
39424 blocks (1232Mb) written.^Z
[1]+ Stopped                 dcfldd if=/dev/sdb of=./image.raw
# fg
dcfldd if=/dev/sdb of=./image.raw
53760 blocks (1680Mb) written.
...
```

Here an executing `dcfldd` command is suspended by pressing CTRL-Z on the keyboard. Resume the process by using the `fg` command (foreground). The process can also be resumed with a `kill -SIGCONT` command. See the Bash documentation and the SIGNAL(7) manual page for more about job control and signals.

Using tools such as Nagios, Icinga, or other infrastructure-monitoring systems, you can automate temperature monitoring and alerting. Such systems monitor various environmental variables and provide alerts when critical thresholds are approached or exceeded.

Many forensic labs use heat sinks or disk coolers when imaging to reduce the problem of overheating subject disks. This is recommended during long acquisition sessions, especially when you're working with older drives.

If you attempt to use certain power management techniques to reduce heat, they will be of little use. These methods work by spinning down the drive after a period of idle time; however, during a sustained imaging operation, there is little or no idle time.

Establish Forensic Write-Blocking Protection

A fundamental component of digital evidence collection is performing a forensically sound acquisition of storage media. You can achieve part of this goal[4] by ensuring that a write-blocking mechanism is in place before you attach the disk to the forensic acquisition host.

When you attach a disk to a PC running a modern OS, automated processes significantly increase the risk of data modification (and therefore evidence destruction). Attempts to automatically mount partitions, generate thumbnail images for display in graphical file managers, index for local search databases, scan with antivirus software, and more all put an attached drive at risk of modification. Timestamps might be updated, destroying potential evidence. Deleted files in unallocated parts of the disk might be overwritten, also destroying evidence. Discovered malware or viruses (the very evidence an investigator might be looking for) could be purged. Journaling filesystems could have queued changes in the journal log written to disk. There may be attempts to repair a broken filesystem or assemble/synchronize RAID components.

In addition to automated potential destruction of evidence, human error poses another significant risk. People might accidentally copy or delete files; browse around the filesystem (and update last-accessed timestamps); or mistakenly choose the wrong device, resulting in a destructive action.

Write blockers were designed to protect against unwanted data modification on storage media. Requiring the use of write blockers in a forensic lab's standard processes and procedures demonstrates due diligence. It satisfies industry best practice for handling storage media as evidence in a digital

---

4. Forensically sound acquisition also deals with data completeness and preserving integrity.

forensic setting. Write blockers guarantee a read-only method of attaching storage media to an examiner's workstation.

NIST Computer Forensic Tool Testing (CFTT) provides formal requirements for write blockers. The Hardware Write Block (HWB) Device Specification, Version 2.0 is available at *http://www.cftt.nist.gov/hardware_write_block. htm*. This specification identifies the following top-level tool requirements:

- An HWB device shall not transmit a command to a protected storage device that modifies the data on the storage device.
- An HWB device shall return the data requested by a read operation.
- An HWB device shall return without modification any access-significant information requested from the drive.
- Any error condition reported by the storage device to the HWB device shall be reported to the host.

Both hardware and software write blockers are available, as stand-alone hardware, installable software packages, or bootable forensic CDs. In some cases, media might have built-in read-only functionality.

Hardware Write Blockers

The preferred method of write blocking uses hardware devices situated between a subject disk and an examiner's workstation. A hardware write blocker intercepts drive commands sent to the disk that might modify the data. A photograph of a portable write-blocking device protecting a SATA drive (Tableau by Guidance Software) is shown in Figure 4-1.

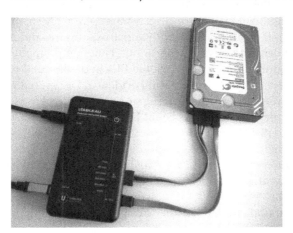

Figure 4-1: Portable SATA write blocker

Hardware write blockers usually have a switch or LED to indicate whether write blocking functionality is in operation. A photograph of a multifunctional write-blocking device designed to be built directly into the examiner workstation (Tableau by Guidance Software) is shown in Figure 4-2. It can protect SATA, SAS, IDE, FireWire, and USB drives.

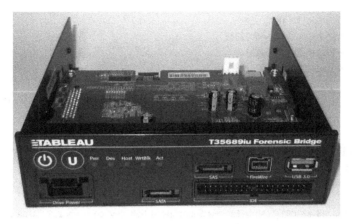

Figure 4-2: Multifunction drive bay write blocker

Write blockers can provide status information to the acquisition host
system. An example is the tableau-parm tool (*https://github.com/ecbftw/
tableau-parm/*), which can query the Tableau hardware write blocker for
information. You can use this open source tool to verify the write-blocking
status of a disk attached with a Tableau write blocker. For example:

```
$ sudo tableau-parm  /dev/sdg
WARN: Requested 255 bytes but got 152 bytes)
## Bridge Information ##
chan_index: 0x00
chan_type: SATA
writes_permitted: FALSE
declare_write_blocked: TRUE
declare_write_errors: TRUE
bridge_serial: 000ECC550035F055
bridge_vendor: Tableau
bridge_model: T35u-R2
firmware_date: May 23 2014
firmware_time: 09:43:37

## Drive Information ##
drive_vendor: %00%00%00%00%00%00%00%00
drive_model: INTEL SSDSA2CW300G3
drive_serial: CVPR124600ET300EGN
drive_revision: 4PC10302

## Drive HPA/DCO/Security Information ##
security_in_use: FALSE
security_support: TRUE
hpa_in_use: FALSE
hpa_support: TRUE
dco_in_use: FALSE
```

```
dco_support: TRUE
drive_capacity: 586072368
hpa_capacity: 586072368
dco_capacity: 586072368
```

According to Tableau's documentation, the drive_vendor field may not contain any information for some drives.[5]

During the final stages of editing this book, the first PCI Express write blockers appeared on the market. An example is shown here from Tableau. Attaching an NVME drive using a PCI Express write blocker produces the following dmesg output:

```
[194238.882053] usb 2-6: new SuperSpeed USB device number 5 using xhci_hcd
[194238.898642] usb 2-6: New USB device found, idVendor=13d7, idProduct=001e
[194238.898650] usb 2-6: New USB device strings: Mfr=1, Product=2, SerialNumber=3
[194238.898654] usb 2-6: Product: T356789u
[194238.898658] usb 2-6: Manufacturer: Tableau
[194238.898662] usb 2-6: SerialNumber: 0xecc3500671076
[194238.899830] usb-storage 2-6:1.0: USB Mass Storage device detected
[194238.901608] scsi host7: usb-storage 2-6:1.0
[194239.902816] scsi 7:0:0:0: Direct-Access     NVMe     INTEL SSDPEDMW40 0174
    PQ: 0 ANSI: 6
[194239.903611] sd 7:0:0:0: Attached scsi generic sg2 type 0
[194240.013810] sd 7:0:0:0: [sdc] 781422768 512-byte logical blocks: (400 GB/
    373 GiB)
[194240.123456] sd 7:0:0:0: [sdc] Write Protect is on
[194240.123466] sd 7:0:0:0: [sdc] Mode Sense: 17 00 80 00
[194240.233497] sd 7:0:0:0: [sdc] Write cache: disabled, read cache: enabled,
    doesn't support DPO or FUA
[194240.454298]  sdc: sdc1
[194240.673411] sd 7:0:0:0: [sdc] Attached SCSI disk
```

The write blocker operates as a USB3 bridge and makes the NVME drive available as a SCSI device. This particular write blocker supports PCI Express drives using both AHCI and NVME standards. The hardware interfaces supported are regular PCI Express slots (Figure 4-3) and M.2 (Figure 4-4). Standard adapters from mini-SAS to PCI Express or M.2 can be used to attach U.2 (SFF-8639) NVME drives. PCI write blockers with NVME support are also available from Wiebetech.

The primary advantage of hardware-based write blockers is their OS independence. They operate transparently and separately from the acquisition host, eliminating the need to maintain drivers or OS compatibility. This makes them ideal for use in a Linux acquisition environment.

---

5. "Tableau Bridge Query—Technical Documentation," accessed 8 December 2005, previously available for download. Contact Guidance Software for more information.

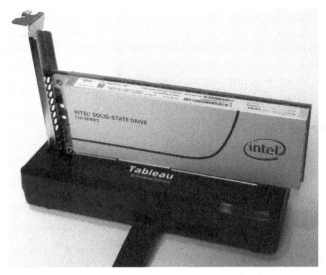

Figure 4-3: Write blocker dock for PCI Express slot drives

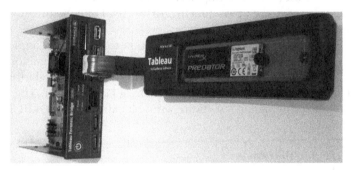

Figure 4-4: Multifunction write blocker and dock for PCI Express M.2 drives

Special thanks to Arina AG in Switzerland for providing the write blocker equipment used for test purposes in this book.

Software Write Blockers

Software write blockers have a somewhat controversial history. They've become increasingly difficult to develop and maintain with modern OSes. System updates by the OS vendor, configuration tweaks by the examiner, and additionally installed software all create a risk of disabling, overwriting, bypassing, or causing the failure of write-blocking functionality implemented in software.

Software write blockers are difficult to implement. Simply mounting a disk as read-only (`mount -o ro`) will *not* guarantee that the disk won't be modified. The *read-only* property in this context refers to the filesystem, not the disk device. The kernel may still write to the disk for various reasons. Software write blocking must be implemented in the kernel, below the virtual filesystem layer and even below the other device drivers that implement a particular drive interface (AHCI for example). Several low-level software write-blocking methods have been used under Linux but with limited success.

Tools such as hdparm and blockdev can set a disk to read-only by setting a kernel flag. For example:

```
# hdparm -r1 /dev/sdk

/dev/sdk:
 setting readonly to 1 (on)
 readonly     =  1 (on)
```

The same flag can be set with blockdev, like this:

```
# blockdev --setro /dev/sdk
```

The method of setting kernel flags is dependent on properly configuring udev to make newly attached drives read-only before any other process has a chance to modify them.

A kernel patch has also been written to specifically implement forensic write-blocking functionality. You'll find more information about it at *https://github.com/msuhanov/Linux-write-blocker/*. Several forensic boot CDs use Maxim Suhanov's write-blocking kernel patch. The following helper script manages software write blocking on the DEFT Linux forensic boot CD:

```
% cat /usr/sbin/wrtblk
#!/bin/sh

# Mark a specified block device as read-only
[ $# -eq 1 ] || exit
[ ! -z "$1" ] || exit
bdev="$1"
[ -b "/dev/$bdev" ] || exit
[ ! -z $bdev##loop*$ ] || exit
blockdev --setro "/dev/$bdev" || logger "wrtblk: blockdev --setro /dev/$bdev
    failed!"

# Mark a parent block device as read-only
syspath=$(echo /sys/block/*/"$bdev")
[ "$syspath" = "/sys/block/*/$bdev" ] && exit
dir=$syspath%/*$
parent=$dir##*/$
[ -b "/dev/$parent" ] || exit
blockdev --setro "/dev/$parent" || logger "wrtblk: blockdev --setro /dev/$parent
    failed!"
```

The patch is implemented in the kernel and is turned on (and off) using helper scripts. The helper scripts simply use the blockdev command to mark the device as read-only.

NIST CFTT has performed software write blocker tool tests, which you'll find at *http://www.cftt.nist.gov/software_write_block.htm*.

Hardware write blockers are still the safest and recommended method of protecting storage media during forensic acquisition.

Linux Forensic Boot CDs

The need to perform incident response and triage in the field has led to the development of bootable Linux CDs that contain the required software to perform such tasks. These CDs can boot a subject PC and access the locally attached storage using various forensic tools. Forensic boot CDs are designed to write protect discovered storage in the event it needs to be forensically imaged. You can make an attached disk writable by using a command (like wrtblk shown in the previous example), which is useful in acquiring an image when you attach an external destination disk. Forensic boot CDs also have network functionality and enable remote analysis and acquisition.

Forensic boot CDs are useful when:

- A PC is examined without opening it to remove a disk.

- A write blocker is not available.

- PCs need to be quickly checked during triage for a certain piece of evidence before deciding to image.

- Linux-based tools (Sleuth Kit, Foremost, and so on) are needed but not otherwise available.

- A forensic technician needs to remotely perform work via ssh.

Several popular forensic boot CDs that are currently maintained include:

- Kali Linux (formerly BackTrack), which is based on Debian: *https://www.kali.org/*

- Digital Evidence & Forensics Toolkit (DEFT), which is based on Ubuntu Linux: *http://www.deftlinux.net/*

- Pentoo, a forensic CD based on Gentoo Linux: *http://pentoo.ch/*

- C.A.I.N.E, Computer Forensics Linux Live Distro, which is based on Ubuntu Linux: *http://www.caine-live.net/*

Forensic boot CDs require a lot of work to maintain and test. Many other forensic boot CDs have been available in the past. Because of the changing landscape of forensic boot CDs, be sure to research and use the latest functional and maintained versions.

Media with Physical Read-Only Modes

Some storage media have a write-protect mechanism that can be useful in a forensic context. For example, most tapes have a sliding switch or tab that instructs the tape drive to treat them as read-only, as shown on the left of Figure 4-5. On the LTO-5 tape (bottom left), a closed tab indicates it is write protected; on the DAT160 tape (top left), an open tab indicates it is write protected.

SD memory cards have a *lock* switch that write protects the memory card, as shown on the right of Figure 4-5.

Figure 4-5: Write-protect tabs on tapes and SD cards

Older USB thumb drives may have a write-protect switch. Some very old IDE hard disks have a jumper that you can set to make the drive electronics treat the drive as read-only.

CD-ROMs, DVDs, and Blu-ray discs do not need a write blocker, because they are read-only by default. The simple act of accessing a rewritable disc will not make modifications to timestamps or other data on the disc; changes to these optical media must be explicitly burned to the disc.

Closing Thoughts

In this chapter, you learned how to set up basic auditing, activity logging, and task management. I covered topics such as naming conventions and scalable directory structures, as well as various challenges with image sizes, drive capacity planning, and performance and environmental issues. Finally, this chapter discussed the crucial component of forensic write blocking. You are now ready to attach a subject drive to the acquisition host in preparation for executing the forensic acquisition process.

5

ATTACHING SUBJECT MEDIA TO AN ACQUISITION HOST

This chapter discusses the physical attachment of subject storage media to an examination host, identification of the subject device on the system, and querying the device firmware for information. You'll also learn about methods for removing HPA and DCO, unlocking ATA passwords, and decrypting self-encrypting drives. The chapter ends with several special storage topics. Let's start by examining the subject PC hardware.

Examine Subject PC Hardware

When a PC or notebook is seized in the field or delivered to a forensic lab for examination, more than just the internal disks can be examined. Included in the examination should be a complete review of the PC hardware configuration, BIOS settings, hardware clock, and so on.

NOTE   *The scope of this book covers "dead" disk acquisition, that is, drives and PCs that are already powered off. Depending on the organization, a triage process will exist for arriving at a crime or incident scene with live, running machines. This triage process may include taking photographs of screens, using mouse jigglers to prevent password-protected screensavers from activating, or running memory-dumping tools. First responder triage of live PCs is outside the scope of this book.*

Physical PC Examination and Disk Removal

Before you unplug any drive cables or unscrew any drives from the drive bays, take photographs of the subject PC to document the hardware configuration, the number of disks it contains, and how the disks are cabled to the mainboard.

Remove disks with care, especially if they're in old PCs that may not have been opened for many years. The top of each drive can be photographed to capture the serial number and other information on the label. For each disk, note the cable location on the mainboard. If a mainboard has multiple SATA ports, note which port each disk was using.

Open optical drive trays to confirm they don't contain any discs. Most optical drives have a pinhole that can manually release the drive door without powering on the drive.

Examine the PCI slots for PCI SATA Express drives or PCI NVME drives. If a mainboard has an M.2 or mSATA slot, check for SSD circuit boards.

Subject PC Hardware Review

After removing all the drives from the subject PC enclosure, power on the subject mainboard and note the BIOS configuration, clock, boot order, potential BIOS logs, version, and so forth.

If you require further information about the subject PC, examine it using a forensic boot CD that contains various hardware analysis tools, such as lshw, dmidecode, biosdecode, lspic, and more.

You might be able to retrieve some vendor-specific information by using vendor-specific tools—for example, vpddecode for IBM and Lenovo hardware or ownership for Compaq hardware ownership tags.

Examine and document any additional hardware components as well, such as memory modules or PCI cards.

Attach Subject Disk to an Acquisition Host

After physically attaching the subject drive to the examiner workstation (using a write-blocking mechanism), you need to identify the correct block device associated with the subject drive. To reliably identify the subject drive on the acquisition host, list the storage media devices, confirm any unique identifiers associated with the physical drive, and determine the corresponding device file in */dev*. This section examines these steps in more detail.

View Acquisition Host Hardware

Understanding the examination host's hardware configuration is useful for performance tuning, capacity planning, maintaining a stable platform, troubleshooting, isolating faults, and reducing the risk of human error. In this section, you'll see examples of tools you can use for listing and viewing PC hardware.

Using the lshw tool, you can generate a quick overview of the examiner workstation hardware:

```
# lshw -businfo
```

The bus information describes the device specific addresses, such as pci@domain:bus:slot.function, scsi@host.channel.target.lun, and usb@bus:device.

You can also use lshw to specifically look for an attached device type. For example:

```
# lshw -businfo -class storage
Bus info        Device    Class      Description
=========================================================
...
usb@2:5.2       scsi22    storage    Forensic SATA/IDE Bridge
...
# lshw -businfo -class disk
Bus info        Device    Class      Description
=========================================================
...
scsi@22:0.0.0   /dev/sdp  disk       120GB SSD 850
...
```

Note that scsi22 links to scsi@22:.0.0.0, which links to */dev/sdp*. Identifying the Linux device file for an attached physical drive is discussed further in the following sections.

If the subject drive has been externally attached, it's likely connected via USB, Thunderbolt, FireWire, or eSATA (and in rare cases, possibly Fibre Channel).

If the drive has been internally attached, it's likely connected via SATA cable, a PCI Express slot, an M.2 interface, or SAS cable (or possibly legacy interfaces, such as parallel SCSI or IDE).

You can list the devices attached to the PCI bus (including parallel PCI and PCI Express) using the lspci tool:

```
# lspci
```

The PCI bus categorizes devices by class (see *http://pci-ids.ucw.cz/* for more information about PCI IDs and device classes). Devices matching the *Mass storage controller* class (class ID 01) are of interest because they manage attached storage media.

Newer versions of lspci (as of pciutils version 3.30) can list the PCI bus by device class, which can be useful to isolate specific hardware of interest. The following command lists all SATA mass storage controller (class ID 01, subclass ID 06) devices:

```
# lspci -d ::0106
```

This command enumerates all the SCSI, IDE, RAID, ATA, SATA, SAS, and NVME mass storage controller devices on a system:

```
# for i in 00 01 04 05 06 07 08; do lspci -d ::01$i; done
```

Another PCI class that can manage connected storage media is the *serial bus controller* class (class ID 0C). The following command lists all devices with the USB serial bus controller class (class ID 0C, subclass ID 03):

```
# lspci -d ::0C03
```

This command enumerates all FireWire, USB, and Fibre Channel serial bus controllers on the examiner host:

```
# for i in 00 03 04; do lspci -d ::0C$i; done
```

If the subject drive is attached via USB, it won't appear on the PCI bus. You can list USB devices separately using lsusb. Without options, the command generates a list of all attached USB devices:

```
# lsusb
...
Bus 001 Device 005: ID 0951:1665 Kingston Technology
Bus 001 Device 002: ID 8087:0024 Intel Corp. Integrated Rate Matching Hub
Bus 001 Device 001: ID 1d6b:0002 Linux Foundation 2.0 root hub
```

Here a USB thumb drive is attached to USB bus 1 and assigned a USB device ID of 5. Running lsusb -v will provide more detailed output about the USB device.[1]

The preceding tools and examples provide an overview of the storage media controllers and the hardware attached to an examiner workstation. The lshw(1), lspci(8), and lsusb(8) manual pages explain additional parameters and features, which you can use to view more detail about the hardware.

---

1. From the lsusb -v output, the iSerial device descriptor in Linux Foundation...root hub devices will point to the USB controller's PCI device address.

Identify the Subject Drive

Having an understanding of the examiner workstation hardware, especially the available bus systems and controllers, will help you locate where a subject disk is attached. The next step is to positively confirm the identity of the subject drive using some distinct information, such as a serial number, unique model number, or other unique property.

You can use multiple approaches to identify the subject device. If the subject disk is attached via the USB bus and listed with the lsusb tool, you can retrieve more information by specifying the subject disk's *vendor:productID*, as shown here:

```
# lsusb -vd 0781:5583

Bus 004 Device 002: ID 0781:5583 SanDisk Corp.
...
    idVendor          0x0781 SanDisk Corp.
    idProduct         0x5583
    bcdDevice           1.00
    iManufacturer          1 SanDisk
    iProduct               2 Ultra Fit
    iSerial                3 4C530001200627113025
...
    wSpeedsSupported   0x000e
      Device can operate at Full Speed (12Mbps)
      Device can operate at High Speed (480Mbps)
      Device can operate at SuperSpeed (5Gbps)
...
```

From this output, you can use the unique information (serial number and so on) about the device to confirm the identity of the attached device as the subject drive. If the serial number or other unique properties match the physically attached drive, you've identified the correct device.

Nearly all drives are accessible via SCSI commands (directly attached NVME drives are a notable exception) . To query for an attached storage device, you can use the lsscsi tool. It supports a number of transport layer protocols, including SATA, USB, SAS, FireWire, ATA, SCSI, Fibre Channel, and more. lsscsi is also useful for linking kernel device paths with device files in */dev*:

```
# lsscsi -v
...
[6:0:0:0]   disk    ATA      INTEL SSDSA2CW30 0302  /dev/sda
  dir: /sys/bus/scsi/devices/6:0:0:0  [/sys/devices/pci0000:00/0000:00:1f.2/ata7/
    host6/target6:0:0/6:0:0:0]
...
```

The kernel outputs an informational message when devices are attached or detached from a host system. This is the kernel *ring buffer* and is viewed with the dmesg tool. Running dmesg with the -T flag prints human-readable timestamps, which are useful when you're determining which device was added at a known time:

```
# dmesg -T
...
[Sun May 15 13:44:45 2016] usb 2-1: new SuperSpeed USB device number 9 using
    xhci_hcd
[Sun May 15 13:44:45 2016] usb 2-1: New USB device found, idVendor=0781,
    idProduct=5583
[Sun May 15 13:44:45 2016] usb 2-1: New USB device strings: Mfr=1, Product=2,
    SerialNumber=3
[Sun May 15 13:44:45 2016] usb 2-1: Product: Ultra Fit
[Sun May 15 13:44:45 2016] usb 2-1: Manufacturer: SanDisk
[Sun May 15 13:44:45 2016] usb 2-1: SerialNumber: 4C530001141203113173
[Sun May 15 13:44:45 2016] usb-storage 2-1:1.0: USB Mass Storage device detected
[Sun May 15 13:44:45 2016] scsi host24: usb-storage 2-1:1.0
[Sun May 15 13:44:46 2016] scsi 24:0:0:0: Direct-Access     SanDisk  Ultra Fit
    1.00 PQ: 0 ANSI: 6
[Sun May 15 13:44:46 2016] sd 24:0:0:0: Attached scsi generic sg5 type 0
[Sun May 15 13:44:46 2016] sd 24:0:0:0: [sdf] 30375936 512-byte logical blocks:
    (15.6 GB/14.5 GiB)
[Sun May 15 13:44:46 2016] sd 24:0:0:0: [sdf] Write Protect is off
[Sun May 15 13:44:46 2016] sd 24:0:0:0: [sdf] Mode Sense: 43 00 00 00
[Sun May 15 13:44:46 2016] sd 24:0:0:0: [sdf] Write cache: disabled, read cache:
    enabled, doesn't support DPO or FUA
[Sun May 15 13:44:46 2016]  sdf: sdf1
[Sun May 15 13:44:46 2016] sd 24:0:0:0: [sdf] Attached SCSI removable disk
```

You can use this output to identify an attached physical device, linking the USB device to a SCSI host ID and a block device name. In this example, usb 2-1: refers to bus 2 and physical port 1 (the plug). The USB drive is assigned device number 9 and uses the *xhci_hcd driver* (which has USB3 support). The vendor and product ID strings, idVendor=0781, idProduct=5583, are displayed, followed by informational strings for the manufacturer, product, and serial number (these can be different from idVendor and idProduct). The Bulk-Only Transport usb-storage driver detects the device (not needed for UASP devices), and scsi host24: indicates a SCSI host number has been assigned to the device and corresponds to the SCSI address 24:0:0:0:. Two devices are created, sg5 (generic SCSI) and sdf (block device), which correspond to */dev/sg5* and */dev/sdf*. Some information about the (now established) SCSI device is queried, and partition tables are detected (sdf1).

A simpler command to list all attached storage devices, including descriptive information and device paths, is the lsblk command. Newer versions of lsblk provide output options for vendor, model, revision, serial number, and

WWN (*World Wide Name*; *https://en.wikipedia.org/wiki/World_Wide_Name*) number. In addition, lsblk provides useful technical details, such as the device name, size, physical and logical sector size, transport (USB, SATA, SAS, and so on), SCSI address, and more:

```
# lsblk -pd -o TRAN,NAME,SERIAL,VENDOR,MODEL,REV,WWN,SIZE,HCTL,SUBSYSTEMS,HCTL
```

Most of the tools demonstrated here are simply reading different files and directories from the Linux */proc* directory. You'll find more information about attached drives and other kernel structures in the */proc* tree. Consult the proc(5) manual page for more information about the proc filesystem.

Query the Subject Disk for Information

After attaching the subject drive to the examiner workstation and positively identifying the correct Linux device to work with, you can gather additional meta information about the device. You can query the device directly for information about the drive, the firmware, SMART data, and other configuration details.

A number of tools are available to query information stored in the hard drive. Typically, you access this firmware information using lower-level ATA or SCSI interface commands, which interact directly with the drive electronics.

Document Device Identification Details

At this point, you should have a number of details and technical identifiers about the drive attached to the examiner host, including the following:

- Vendor, make, and model
- Serial number or WWN
- Linux device name
- PCI *domain:bus:slot.function*
- PCI *vendorID:deviceID*
- USB *bus:device*
- USB *vendorID:productID*
- SCSI *host:channel:target:lun*

You can save this information for reporting purposes by redirecting the various tool command outputs to text files.

Document evidence for the use of a write blocker. If you're using a hardware write blocker, such as Tableau, query it and save the results:

```
# tableau-parm  /dev/sdc > write-blocked.txt
```

Here */dev/sdc* should be replaced with the relevant device of the subject drive.

If you're using a software write blocker, such as wrtblk, query `blockdev` for a report on the current status of the device (including the read-only flag):

```
# blockdev --report /dev/sda > wrtblk.txt
```

Here */dev/sda* should be replaced with the relevant device of the subject drive.

If the subject drive is attached via USB, you can specify it either by the *bus:device* (using -s) or by *vendor:product* (using -d). The following two commands will produce and save the same verbose output:

```
# lsusb -v -s 2:2 > lsusb.txt
# lsusb -v -d 13fe:5200 > lsusb.txt
```

Here 2:2 and 13fe:5200 should be replaced with the relevant values for the subject drive on your acquisition host.

The `lsblk` command can specify a Linux device, and the -O flag will output all available columns in the output:

```
# lsblk -O /dev/sda  > lsblk.txt
```

Here */dev/sda* should be replaced with the relevant device of the subject drive on your acquisition host.

The `lsscsi` command can also save a certain perspective of the attached drive, specifying the SCSI address to use:

```
# lsscsi -vtg -L 16:0:0:0 > lsscsi.txt
```

Here 16:0:0:0 should be replaced with the relevant SCSI address of the subject drive on your acquisition host.

Relevant dmesg output could also be copied into a text file if desired.

The examples shown in this section illustrated how to save command output for a specific subject drive. For brevity, subsequent chapters sometimes will not include examples of saving data to files, focusing instead on the construction of commands.

Query Disk Capabilities and Features with hdparm

Many of the tools discussed previously (lsusb, lspci, lsblk, and so on) have queried the Linux system and kernel structures for information. However, it's possible to query a drive directly for additional information. The hdparm tool is useful for sending commands to most drives attached to a Linux system.

The hdparm tool operates by sending requests to the OS disk drivers (using ioctls) to retrieve information about the disk. From a forensics perspective, a number of items may be of interest or useful to document:

- Details about the drive geometry (physical and logical)
- The disk's supported standards, features, and capabilities
- States and flags related to the drive configuration
- DCO and HPA information
- Security information
- Vendor information, such as make, model, and serial number
- The WWN device identifier (if it exists)
- Time needed for secure erase (for most disks, this is roughly the acquisition time)

For more detailed information about hdparm's features, see the hdparm(8) manual page.

The following example shows how to use hdparm to get an overview of the disk using the -I flag together with the raw disk device. The listing is annotated with comments relevant to forensic investigators.

The output begins with documenting information about the drive, including manufacturer, model, serial number, and the standards with which it is compliant. Also in the output are various drive parameters, such as physical and logical sector size, number of sectors, form factor, and other physical properties.

```
# hdparm -I /dev/sda

/dev/sda:

ATA device, with non-removable media
        Model Number:       WDC WD20EZRX-00D8PB0
        Serial Number:      WD-WCC4NDA2N98P
        Firmware Revision:  80.00A80
        Transport:          Serial, SATA 1.0a, SATA II Extensions, SATA Rev 2.5,
    SATA Rev 2.6, SATA Rev 3.0
Standards:
        Supported: 9 8 7 6 5
        Likely used: 9
Configuration:
        Logical         max     current
        cylinders       16383   16383
        heads           16      16
        sectors/track   63      63
        --
        CHS current addressable sectors:   16514064
        LBA     user addressable sectors:  268435455
```

```
        LBA48  user addressable sectors: 3907029168
        Logical  Sector size:                 512 bytes
        Physical Sector size:                4096 bytes
        device size with M = 1024*1024:   1907729 MBytes
        device size with M = 1000*1000:   2000398 MBytes (2000 GB)
        cache/buffer size  = unknown
        Nominal Media Rotation Rate: 5400
Capabilities:
        LBA, IORDY(can be disabled)
        Queue depth: 32
        Standby timer values: spec'd by Standard, with device specific minimum
        R/W multiple sector transfer: Max = 16  Current = 16
        DMA: mdma0 mdma1 mdma2 udma0 udma1 udma2 udma3 udma4 udma5 *udma6
            Cycle time: min=120ns recommended=120ns
        PIO: pio0 pio1 pio2 pio3 pio4
            Cycle time: no flow control=120ns  IORDY flow control=120ns

...
```

The next section of the output describes the features available on a
drive, and the star (*) indicates if a feature is currently enabled. (To understand vendor-specific features, you might need additional proprietary documentation.) This is useful when you're preparing for a forensic acquisition,
because it indicates the status of security feature sets and other things like
the DCO (Device Configuration Overlay feature set).

```
...
Commands/features:
        Enabled Supported:
            *    SMART feature set
                 Security Mode feature set
            *    Power Management feature set
            *    Write cache
            *    Look-ahead
            *    Host Protected Area feature set
            *    WRITE_BUFFER command
            *    READ_BUFFER command
            *    NOP cmd
            *    DOWNLOAD_MICROCODE
                 Power-Up In Standby feature set
            *    SET_FEATURES required to spinup after power up
                 SET_MAX security extension
            *    48-bit Address feature set
            *    Device Configuration Overlay feature set
            *    Mandatory FLUSH_CACHE
            *    FLUSH_CACHE_EXT
            *    SMART error logging
            *    SMART self-test
            *    General Purpose Logging feature set
```

```
    *    64-bit World wide name
    *    WRITE_UNCORRECTABLE_EXT command
    *    {READ,WRITE}_DMA_EXT_GPL commands
    *    Segmented DOWNLOAD_MICROCODE
    *    Gen1 signaling speed (1.5Gb/s)
    *    Gen2 signaling speed (3.0Gb/s)
    *    Gen3 signaling speed (6.0Gb/s)
    *    Native Command Queueing (NCQ)
    *    Host-initiated interface power management
    *    Phy event counters
    *    NCQ priority information
    *    READ_LOG_DMA_EXT equivalent to READ_LOG_EXT
    *    DMA Setup Auto-Activate optimization
         Device-initiated interface power management
    *    Software settings preservation
    *    SMART Command Transport (SCT) feature set
    *    SCT Write Same (AC2)
    *    SCT Features Control (AC4)
    *    SCT Data Tables (AC5)
         unknown 206[12] (vendor specific)
         unknown 206[13] (vendor specific)
         unknown 206[14] (vendor specific)
...
```

The next section of the hdparm output provides more detail about the
currently active security features, which are important when you're determining if a drive is locked or encrypted. The time needed for a secure erase
is also a rough estimate of how long an acquisition might take (if the subject
drive is the performance bottleneck).

```
...
Security:
        Master password revision code = 65534
                supported
        not     enabled
        not     locked
        not     frozen
        not     expired: security count
                supported: enhanced erase
        324min for SECURITY ERASE UNIT. 324min for ENHANCED SECURITY ERASE UNIT.
...
```

The final section of the hdparm output displays the WWN again, but
this time it's broken down into the NAA (which describes the rest of the
WWN), the IEEE OUI assigned vendor ID, and the rest of the WWN (which
is unique to the drive).

```
...
Logical Unit WWN Device Identifier: 50014ee25fcfe40c
        NAA            : 5
        IEEE OUI       : 0014ee
        Unique ID      : 25fcfe40c
Checksum: correct
```

The hdparm output contains a number of items of interest to forensic investigators, either for documentation or as information for further analysis. To include the entire output of hdparm -I in a forensic report, you can redirect it to a text file.

A similar tool for querying SCSI drives is sdparm, which you can use to access SCSI mode pages. Running sdparm with the flags -a -1 retrieves a verbose list of disk parameters. A more concise query using sdparm -i can extract the Vital Product Data (VPD), which provides unique identifying information about the make, model, and serial number of SCSI and SAS drives.

Extract SMART Data with smartctl

SMART was developed in the early 1990s to help monitor hard disks and predict failures. It was added to the SCSI-3 standard in 1995(SCSI-3 standard: X3T10/94-190 Rev 4) and the ATA-3 standard in 1997 (ATA-3 standard: X3.298-1997). Because certain details about the disk hardware may be of value in forensic investigations, in this section, you'll learn several techniques to extract SMART information about the disk hardware.

The smartctl command is part of the smartmontools package and provides access to the SMART interface built into nearly all modern hard drives. The smartctl command queries attached ATA, SATA, SAS, and SCSI hardware.

SMART provides a number of variables and statistics about a disk, some of which could be of interest to a forensic investigator. For example:

- Statistics about errors on the disk and the overall health of the disk

- Number of times the disk was powered on

- Number of hours the disk was in operation

- Number of bytes read and written (often expressed in gigabytes)

- Various SMART logs (temperature history, and so on)[2]

The following example shows SMART data requested from a drive. The listing is annotated with comments relevant to forensic investigators.

The -x flag instructs smartctl to print all available information. The first block of output is the information section, which provides unique

---

2. SMART statistics and logs available vary among hard disk vendors.

identifying information about the drive. You can also retrieve most of this information using other tools, such as hdparm, as shown in previous examples.

```
# smartctl -x /dev/sda
smartctl 6.4 2014-10-07 r4002 [x86_64-linux-4.2.0-22-generic] (local build)
Copyright (C) 2002-14, Bruce Allen, Christian Franke, www.smartmontools.org

=== START OF INFORMATION SECTION ===
Model Family:     Western Digital Green
Device Model:     WDC WD20EZRX-00D8PB0
Serial Number:    WD-WCC4NDA2N98P
LU WWN Device Id: 5 0014ee 25fcfe40c
Firmware Version: 80.00A80
User Capacity:    2,000,398,934,016 bytes [2.00 TB]
Sector Sizes:     512 bytes logical, 4096 bytes physical
Rotation Rate:    5400 rpm
Device is:        In smartctl database [for details use: -P show]
ATA Version is:   ACS-2 (minor revision not indicated)
SATA Version is:  SATA 3.0, 6.0 Gb/s (current: 6.0 Gb/s)
Local Time is:    Thu Jan  7 12:33:43 2016 CET
SMART support is: Available - device has SMART capability.
SMART support is: Enabled
AAM feature is:   Unavailable
APM feature is:   Unavailable
Rd look-ahead is: Enabled
Write cache is:   Enabled
ATA Security is:  Disabled, NOT FROZEN [SEC1]
Wt Cache Reorder: Enabled
...
```

The following SMART data section shows the health of the drive and the results of self-tests. An unhealthy drive is an early warning of possible acquisition issues. Additional SMART capabilities are then listed.

```
...
=== START OF READ SMART DATA SECTION ===
SMART overall-health self-assessment test result: PASSED

General SMART Values:
Offline data collection status:  (0x82) Offline data collection activity
                                        was completed without error.
                                        Auto Offline Data Collection: Enabled.
Self-test execution status:      (   0) The previous self-test routine completed
                                        without error or no self-test has ever
                                        been run.
Total time to complete Offline
data collection:                 (30480) seconds.
```

```
Offline data collection
capabilities:                    (0x7b) SMART execute Offline immediate.
                                        Auto Offline data collection on/off support.
                                        Suspend Offline collection upon new
                                        command.
                                        Offline surface scan supported.
                                        Self-test supported.
                                        Conveyance Self-test supported.
                                        Selective Self-test supported.
SMART capabilities:            (0x0003) Saves SMART data before entering
                                        power-saving mode.
                                        Supports SMART auto save timer.
Error logging capability:        (0x01) Error logging supported.
                                        General Purpose Logging supported.
Short self-test routine
recommended polling time:        (   2) minutes.
Extended self-test routine
recommended polling time:        ( 307) minutes.
Conveyance self-test routine
recommended polling time:        (   5) minutes.
SCT capabilities:              (0x7035) SCT Status supported.
                                        SCT Feature Control supported.
                                        SCT Data Table supported.

...
```

The next section provides more statistics about the drive. Of possible forensic interest here are statistics on the history of the drive usage; for example, the cumulative number of hours the drive has been powered on (Power_On_Hours) and how many times the drive has been powered up (Power_Cycle_Count). Both attributes may correlate with the PC from where they were taken. The total logical block addresses (LBAs) read and written indicates the drive volume usage in the past.

```
...
SMART Attributes Data Structure revision number: 16
Vendor Specific SMART Attributes with Thresholds:
ID# ATTRIBUTE_NAME          FLAGS    VALUE WORST THRESH FAIL RAW_VALUE
  1 Raw_Read_Error_Rate     POSR-K   200   200   051    -    0
  3 Spin_Up_Time            POS--K   181   180   021    -    5908
  4 Start_Stop_Count        -0--CK   100   100   000    -    61
  5 Reallocated_Sector_Ct   PO--CK   200   200   140    -    0
  7 Seek_Error_Rate         -OSR-K   200   200   000    -    0
  9 Power_On_Hours          -0--CK   099   099   000    -    989
 10 Spin_Retry_Count        -0--CK   100   253   000    -    0
 11 Calibration_Retry_Count -0--CK   100   253   000    -    0
 12 Power_Cycle_Count       -0--CK   100   100   000    -    59
```

```
192 Power-Off_Retract_Count -O--CK   200   200   000   -   33
193 Load_Cycle_Count         -O--CK   199   199   000   -   3721
194 Temperature_Celsius      -O---K   119   110   000   -   31
196 Reallocated_Event_Count  -O--CK   200   200   000   -   0
197 Current_Pending_Sector   -O--CK   200   200   000   -   4
198 Offline_Uncorrectable    ----CK   200   200   000   -   4
199 UDMA_CRC_Error_Count      -O--CK   200   200   000   -   0
200 Multi_Zone_Error_Rate    ---R--   200   200   000   -   4
                             ||||||_  K auto-keep
                             |||||__  C event count
                             ||||___  R error rate
                             |||____  S speed/performance
                             ||_____  O updated online
                             |_____  P prefailure warning
...
```

The next section is the log directory, which describes the SMART logs available on the drive. The logs are included in the smartctl -x output with repeating entries removed ("skipped"). Some of these logs may be of interest in a forensic investigation.

```
...
General Purpose Log Directory Version 1
SMART          Log Directory Version 1 [multi-sector log support]
Address   Access  R/W  Size  Description
0x00      GPL,SL  R/O    1   Log Directory
0x01          SL  R/O    1   Summary SMART error log
0x02          SL  R/O    5   Comprehensive SMART error log
0x03      GPL     R/O    6   Ext. Comprehensive SMART error log
0x06          SL  R/O    1   SMART self-test log
0x07      GPL     R/O    1   Extended self-test log
0x09          SL  R/W    1   Selective self-test log
0x10      GPL     R/O    1   SATA NCQ Queued Error log
0x11      GPL     R/O    1   SATA Phy Event Counters log
0x80-0x9f GPL,SL  R/W   16   Host vendor specific log
0xa0-0xa7 GPL,SL  VS    16   Device vendor specific log
0xa8-0xb7 GPL,SL  VS     1   Device vendor specific log
0xbd      GPL,SL  VS     1   Device vendor specific log
0xc0      GPL,SL  VS     1   Device vendor specific log
0xc1      GPL     VS    93   Device vendor specific log
0xe0      GPL,SL  R/W    1   SCT Command/Status
0xe1      GPL,SL  R/W    1   SCT Data Transfer
...
```

The next section of log information displays the results of self-tests. Failed self-tests are an early warning that the acquisition could have issues.

```
...
SMART Extended Comprehensive Error Log Version: 1 (6 sectors)
No Errors Logged

SMART Extended Self-test Log Version: 1 (1 sectors)
Num Test_Description  Status                Remaining  LifeTime(hours)  LBA_of...
# 1  Short offline    Completed without error    00%          0            -

SMART Selective self-test log data structure revision number 1
 SPAN  MIN_LBA  MAX_LBA  CURRENT_TEST_STATUS
    1        0        0  Not_testing
    2        0        0  Not_testing
    3        0        0  Not_testing
    4        0        0  Not_testing
    5        0        0  Not_testing
Selective self-test flags (0x0):
  After scanning selected spans, do NOT read-scan remainder of disk.
If Selective self-test is pending on power-up, resume after 0 minute delay.

SCT Status Version:              3
SCT Version (vendor specific):   258 (0x0102)
SCT Support Level:               1
Device State:                    Active (0)
...
```

The next output block describes a drive's temperature statistics. This information could be useful to monitor during the acquisition process. For investigation purposes, the minimum and maximum temperatures reached during the drive's lifetime might be of interest if correlated with environmental factors linked to a suspect's PC. Vendor-specific SMART data is not part of the generic SMART standard, and you may need additional proprietary documentation to understand it.

```
...
Current Temperature:                   31 Celsius
Power Cycle Min/Max Temperature:    22/31 Celsius
Lifetime   Min/Max Temperature:    20/41 Celsius
Under/Over Temperature Limit Count:  0/0
Vendor specific:
01 00 00 00 00 00 00 00 00 00 00 00 00 00 00 00
00 00 00 00 00 00 00 00 00 00 00 00 00 00 00 00
...
```

Some SMART-capable drives maintain a log of temperature history. You can calculate the history from the interval multiplied by the history size. In this example, 478 minutes are roughly 8 hours of temperature data. Some disks have a temperature-logging interval set much higher (one hour or more). The temperature-logging interval is potentially useful for investigations: if a disk were seized immediately after a crime, known temperature variations might be correlated with the disk temperature record.

```
...
SCT Temperature History Version:      2
Temperature Sampling Period:          1 minute
Temperature Logging Interval:         1 minute
Min/Max recommended Temperature:       0/60 Celsius
Min/Max Temperature Limit:           -41/85 Celsius
Temperature History Size (Index):     478 (175)

Index   Estimated Time    Temperature Celsius
 176   2016-01-07 05:00       ?  -
 ...   ..(300 skipped).      ..  -
 477   2016-01-07 10:01       ?  -
   0   2016-01-07 10:02      29  **********
   1   2016-01-07 10:03      30  ***********
 ...   ..( 68 skipped).      ..  ***********
  70   2016-01-07 11:12      30  ***********
  71   2016-01-07 11:13      31  ************
 ...   ..(103 skipped).      ..  ************
 175   2016-01-07 12:57      31  ************
...
```

The final section of output in this example shows statistics of physical errors. It can be useful to compare these statistics with values during or at the end of an acquisition to ensure no physical errors arose during the process.

```
...
SCT Error Recovery Control command not supported

Device Statistics (GP/SMART Log 0x04) not supported

SATA Phy Event Counters (GP Log 0x11)
ID       Size    Value   Description
0x0001   2          0    Command failed due to ICRC error
0x0002   2          0    R_ERR response for data FIS
0x0003   2          0    R_ERR response for device-to-host data FIS
0x0004   2          0    R_ERR response for host-to-device data FIS
0x0005   2          0    R_ERR response for non-data FIS
0x0006   2          0    R_ERR response for device-to-host non-data FIS
0x0007   2          0    R_ERR response for host-to-device non-data FIS
0x0008   2          0    Device-to-host non-data FIS retries
0x0009   2          6    Transition from drive PhyRdy to drive PhyNRdy
0x000a   2          6    Device-to-host register FISes sent due to a COMRESET
0x000b   2          0    CRC errors within host-to-device FIS
```

```
0x000f  2           0  R_ERR response for host-to-device data FIS, CRC
0x0012  2           0  R_ERR response for host-to-device non-data FIS, CRC
0x8000  4       14532  Vendor specific
```

Other SMART logs might exist depending on the drive vendor. Consult the smartctl(8) manual page for more information about additional flags and queries that you can send to attached subject drives.

Enable Access to Hidden Sectors

Forensic literature often includes handling the HPA and DCO as part of the imaging process. Indeed, some imaging software has the capability to detect and remove these hidden areas at acquisition time. This book positions the detection and removal of the HPA/DCO as part of the preparation process, not the actual imaging. There is no special technique to image these hidden areas once they've been made accessible. They're simply disk sectors protected by drive configuration parameters. It is a simple preparatory step to make them available for a subsequent imaging process. Removing the HPA or DCO modifies the drive's configuration, but it does not modify its contents.[3]

This section also covers drive maintenance sectors and service areas on a disk, but this topic is mentioned only briefly, because these areas are not easily accessible using common open source tools.

Remove a DCO

The DCO was developed to allow PC system manufacturers to make different drive models appear to have the same features. Using a DCO, certain features can be disabled, and the capacity of a drive (number of usable sectors) can be reduced to fit a vendor's requirements. Identifying and removing the DCO is standard forensic practice when you're analyzing a suspect drive.

The DCO is a general configuration overlay, and multiple features can be overridden. It does not only refer to the number of sectors on a drive.

Two hdparm commands can determine if a DCO exists and provide the number of real sectors available. The first command determines if the drive has the DCO feature set enabled. In this example, the current size of the disk is reported to be 474GB or 926773168 sectors (512-byte sector size) and the asterisk (*) next to Device Configuration Overlay feature set indicates it is active:

```
# hdparm -I /dev/sdl

/dev/sdl:
```

---

3. For a paper on the forensics of HPA and DCO areas, see Mayank R. Gupta, Michael D. Hoeschele, and Marcus K. Rogers, "Hidden Disk Areas: HPA and DCO," *International Journal of Digital Evidence* 5, no. 1 (2006).

```
ATA device, with non-removable media
        Model Number:        WDC WD5003AZEX-00MK2A0
...
        LBA48  user addressable sectors:  926773168
        Logical  Sector size:                    512 bytes
        Physical Sector size:                    4096 bytes
        device size with M = 1024*1024:      452525 MBytes
        device size with M = 1000*1000:      474507 MBytes (474 GB)
...
        *    Device Configuration Overlay feature set
...
```

The second command specifically queries for the features modified by a DCO:

```
# hdparm --dco-identify /dev/sdl

/dev/sdl:
DCO Revision: 0x0002
The following features can be selectively disabled via DCO:
        Transfer modes:
                udma0 udma1 udma2 udma3 udma4 udma5 udma6
        Real max sectors: 976773168
        ATA command/feature sets:
                security HPA
        SATA command/feature sets:
                NCQ interface_power_management SSP
```

In this example, "Real max sectors" is 976773168, which is 25GB less than the reported size, indicating the existence of a DCO. The reported size of 474GB is also a mismatch to the 500GB label on the physical drive. You can confirm the expected number of sectors by checking the drive model number with the vendor's product documentation.

Having confirmed the existence of a DCO using hdparm, you can use the same command to remove it. First, run **hdparm** to ensure the drive configuration is not locked or frozen:

```
# hdparm -I /dev/sdl

/dev/sdl:

ATA device, with non-removable media
        Model Number:        WDC WD5003AZEX-00MK2A0
...
Security:
...
        not      locked
```

```
not     frozen
```
...

Some BIOSes or OSes will issue an ATA command to freeze the DCO configuration during boot to prevent malicious changes. In this case, hot plugging the drive power cable after booting should cause the drive to spin up in an unfrozen state.[4] Many USB bridges automatically spin up an attached disk in an unfrozen state. If the drive is locked, refer to "Identify and Unlock ATA Password-Protected Disks" on page 126.

Once the drive is ready, you can send the appropriate ATA command to reset the DCO, making the additional hidden sectors available.

Simply running the hdparm command with the --dco-restore option will do nothing but generate a warning message:

```
# hdparm --dco-restore /dev/sdl

/dev/sdl:
Use of --dco-restore is VERY DANGEROUS.
You are trying to deliberately reset your drive configuration back to the factory
    defaults.
This may change the apparent capacity and feature set of the drive, making all data
    on it inaccessible.
You could lose *everything*.
Please supply the --yes-i-know-what-i-am-doing flag if you really want this.
Program aborted.
```

Following the instructions, and including the --yes-i-know-what-i-am-doing flag, you can remove the DCO as follows:

```
# hdparm --yes-i-know-what-i-am-doing --dco-restore /dev/sdl

/dev/sdl:
 issuing DCO restore command
```

Now when you run the hdparm -I command again, the full sectors will be revealed.

```
# hdparm -I /dev/sdl

/dev/sdl:

ATA device, with non-removable media
        Model Number:       WDC WD5003AZEX-00MK2A0
...
        LBA48  user addressable sectors:  976773168
```

---

4. Some mainboards require SATA ports to be configured for hot plugging in the BIOS.

```
Logical  Sector size:                  512 bytes
Physical Sector size:                  4096 bytes
device size with M = 1024*1024:     476940 MBytes
device size with M = 1000*1000:     500107 MBytes (500 GB)
...
```

Now you can acquire the drive or analyze it with forensic tools. It's important to note the DCO hidden area's exact sector offset, which will be useful when you want to extract only the DCO sectors for separate analysis.

Removing the DCO using hdparm can be tricky. Read the hdparm(8) manual page if a particular drive is causing problems with the removal commands.

The tableau-parm tool has an -r flag that should remove the DCO (and possibly the HPA) from the drive.

Remove an HPA

The HPA was developed to allow PC system manufacturers to store data in a way that is normally inaccessible to a customer. Examples of HPA uses include diagnostic tools, recovery partitions, and so on. These special areas are often activated with BIOS hotkeys during startup.

You can detect the existence of an HPA using a single hdparm command:

```
# hdparm -N /dev/sdl

/dev/sdl:
 max sectors   = 879095852/976773168, HPA is enabled
```

Here HPA is enabled indicates that an HPA exists. The max sectors provides the visible sector count followed by the real sector count. In this example, subtracting the two sector counts reveals a 50GB difference, which is the host protected area.

You can temporarily remove the HPA using the same command (as with the DCO removal, a warning message appears, and you need to use the --yes-i-know-what-i-am-doing flag):

```
# hdparm --yes-i-know-what-i-am-doing -N 976773168 /dev/sdl

/dev/sdl:
 setting max visible sectors to 976773168 (temporary)
 max sectors   = 976773168/976773168, HPA is disabled
```

The result of this command is only temporary; the original HPA will be in place next time you cycle the drive's power. To make the change permanent, add p to the sector count number as follows:

```
# hdparm --yes-i-know-what-i-am-doing -N p976773168 /dev/sdl

/dev/sdl:
```

```
setting max visible sectors to 976773168 (permanent)
max sectors    = 976773168/976773168, HPA is disabled
```

The HPA is now removed, and you can acquire the drive or analyze it with forensic tools. It's important to note the HPA hidden area's exact sector offset, which will be useful when you want to extract only the HPA sectors for separate analysis.

Removing the HPA with hdparm can be tricky. Read the hdparm(8) manual page if a particular drive is causing problems with the removal commands.

Previously, the Sleuth Kit forensic suite had two utilities to detect and temporarily remove the HPA: disk_stat and disk_sreset. These were removed in 2009 because other tools, such as hdparm, included the same features.

Drive Service Area Access

Hard disk drives need to store information such as SMART logs, ATA passwords, bad sector lists, firmware, and other persistent information. This information is typically stored on the disk platters in reserved, user-inaccessible sectors called the *system area* (also known as the *service area*, *negative sectors*, or *maintenance sectors*). Access to this area is done through proprietary vendor commands, which are usually not public.

There is no common systematic approach to access a disk's system areas. Each disk manufacturer implements system areas differently, there are no industry standards, and there are few publicly available tools. Some specialized commercial tools exist, such as Ace Laboratory's PC-3000 (*http://www.acelaboratory.com/catalog/*) or Atola Insight Forensic (*http://www.atola.com/products/insight/supported-drives.html*), which can access service areas of many disks.[5, 6]

In some cases, it's possible to bypass the standard SATA, USB, or SAS interfaces and access storage media using debug or diagnostic ports built into the drive electronics. These interfaces may use serial RS-232/TTL, JTAG for chip access,[7] or undocumented vendor proprietary commands over the regular drive interface. Media access in this manner is not standard across manufacturers or even across drives from the same manufacturer.

For illustration purposes, the following example shows reading information over a serial interface on a Seagate Barracuda ST500DM002 drive. The drive has a serial port next to the SATA data plug and can be accessed with a USB 3V TTL cable. Standard serial terminal emulation software such as the Linux cu (connect UNIX) command is used in this example.

---

5. For research into the possibility of hiding data in the service sectors, see Ariel Berkman, "Hiding Data in Hard-Drive's Service Areas," Recover Information Technologies LTD, February 14, 2013, *http://www.recover.co.il/SA-cover/SA-cover.pdf*.

6. Todd G. Shipley and Bryan Door, "Forensic Imaging of Hard Disk Drives: What We Thought We Knew," *Forensic Focus*, January 27, 2012, *http://articles.forensicfocus.com/2012/01/27/forensic-imaging-of-hard-disk-drives-what-we-thought-we-knew-2/*.

7. The Joint Test Action Group (JTAG) defines a standardized debug interface for accessing electronic components.

Figure 5-1 shows a photo of the USB cable connected to the pin block at the back of the drive.

Figure 5-1: Serial port access to disk firmware

NOTE **Warning:** *This method should not be used without specialized training or tools. There is a risk of physically damaging the disk beyond repair.*

After connecting a terminal and powering on the drive, a boot message is displayed. Entering CTRL-Z puts the drive in diagnostic mode with a command prompt from the drive firmware (similar to UNIX terminals or analog modems).

```
$ cu -s 38400 -l /dev/ttyUSB0
Connected.

Boot 0x10M
 Spin Up[0x00000000][0x0000B67C][0x0000BA10]
 Trans.

Rst 0x10M
 MC Internal LPC Process
 Spin Up
(P) SATA Reset

ASCII Diag mode

F3 T>
```

From this diagnostic interface, detailed underlying information about the disk can be retrieved. In the following example, a Level 2 x command reveals the internal physical drive geometry and partitioning for User and System areas:

```
F3 2>x

User Partition


 LBAs 000000000000-0000075D672E
 PBAs 000000000000-0000076F8EDD
 HdSkew 006E, CylSkew 002D
 ZonesPerHd 11


 Head 0, PhyCyls 000000-040001, LogCyls 000000-03F19C

     Physical      Logical      Sec   Sym   Sym    Data
  Zn Cylinders     Cylinders    Track Wedge Track  Rate
  00 000000-0003FB 000000-0003FB 010F  0D77  000F4D40 1263.750
  01 0003FC-005A41 0003FC-005A41 0130  0F1A  00112A40 1417.500
 ...


 Head 1, PhyCyls 000000-039877, LogCyls 000000-038B61

     Physical      Logical      Sec   Sym   Sym    Data
  Zn Cylinders     Cylinders    Track Wedge Track  Rate
  00 000000-00035B 000000-00035B 0130  0F16  001124A0 1415.625
  01 00035C-004E72 00035C-004E72 0145  1025  00125E80 1516.875
 ...
System Partition


 LBAs 000000000000-0000000972CF
 PBAs 000000000000-00000009811F
 HdSkew 006E, CylSkew 0018
 ZonesPerHd 02


 Head 0, PhyCyls 040002-040155, LogCyls 000000-000152

     Physical      Logical      Sec   Sym   Sym    Data
  Zn Cylinders     Cylinders    Track Wedge Track  Rate
  00 040002-0400AB 000000-0000A9 0394  063D  00072AE0 592.500
  01 0400AC-040155 0000AA-000152 0394  063D  00072AE0 592.500


 Head 1, PhyCyls 039878-0399CB, LogCyls 000000-000152

     Physical      Logical      Sec   Sym   Sym    Data
  Zn Cylinders     Cylinders    Track Wedge Track  Rate
```

```
00  039878-039921  000000-0000A9  0394   063D   00072AE0   592.500
01  039922-0399CB  0000AA-000152  0394   063D   00072AE0   592.500
```

Diagnostic interfaces, such as this one, can provide access to disk sectors in the system areas and other information that is not otherwise accessible.

Online forums exist that discuss low-level disk access and recovery, for example, HDDGURU (*http://forum.hddguru.com/index.php*) and The HDD Oracle (*http://www.hddoracle.com/index.php*).

Methods of accessing the underlying areas of SSD or flash storage media include the physical removal (desoldering) of memory chips, sometimes called *chip-off*. The memory contents from these chips can then be extracted and reconstructed into readable blocks of data.

Some devices (Internet-of-Things, mobile devices, and so on) may have a JTAG interface providing access to memory contents. JTAG is a well-documented standard and can be applied in a forensic context to extract data (see *http://www.evidencemagazine.com/index.php?option=com_content&task=view&id=922*).

Covering these techniques in more depth is beyond the scope of this book. I've mentioned JTAG interfaces and Serial access to disks for illustration purposes to make you aware that such techniques exist in the forensics industry.

ATA Password Security and Self-Encrypting Drives

This section covers the standard security features implemented by the disk vendors. These features include drive locking, password protection, self-encrypting drives, and other security mechanisms. Although some of the features discussed here are not widely used, they are still important to understand in a professional forensic lab setting.

Password recovery techniques are not described in detail here. The examples demonstrate how to attach password-protected media to an acquisition host in preparation for imaging. It is assumed that passwords are already known.

Methods of acquiring passwords are beyond the scope of this book, but recovery techniques may include the following:

- Brute force, exhaustively attempting multiple passwords until the correct one is found.

- Finding passwords hidden or stored in an accessible location.

- Knowledge of password reuse across different accounts or devices. Recovery from one location provides access to all.

- Depending on the jurisdiction, a person may be legally compelled to provide passwords.

- The password may be volunteered by a friendly or cooperative owner (the victim perhaps) or a cooperating accomplice.

- Enterprise IT environments may have key escrow or backups in place.

Identify and Unlock ATA Password-Protected Disks

The ATA/ATAPI commands (*http://www.t13.org/*) specify a security feature set that restricts access to a disk using passwords. When this feature is enabled, the firmware prevents the execution of certain ATA commands, including access to content, until the required password is provided. This is only an access control feature and doesn't use encryption to protect data on the disk.

The hdparm tool can determine if a disk has the security feature set enabled. For example:

```
# hdparm -I /dev/sda
...
Commands/features:
        Enabled Supported:
...
        *       Security Mode feature set
...
Security:
        Master password revision code = 1
                supported
                enabled
                locked
        not     frozen
        not     expired: security count
                supported: enhanced erase
        Security level high
        60min for SECURITY ERASE UNIT. 60min for ENHANCED SECURITY ERASE UNIT.
...
```

The Commands/features: information indicates the Security Mode feature set exists and is enabled, and the Security: information also confirms the feature is supported and enabled.

If Security: has enabled listed, a user password has been set, and the drive will be locked on boot. If the drive is locked, as in the preceding example, access to the drive is prevented until a correct password is provided. The OS may generate a device error or failed command error as it tries to access the disk. The T13 standard outlines which commands are allowed when a disk is locked. Access to a number of commands, including to query SMART information, is still possible when a disk is locked.

Two passwords can be set, user and master. If the user password is set, security is enabled (as shown in the preceding example). Setting the master password alone does not enable security.

If a master password has never been set (it may still have a factory default password set), the Master password revision code will be set to 65534. The first time the master password is set, this value is set to 1 and incremented each time the master password is set again.

Two security levels control how correct passwords behave. The Security level refers to the MASTER PASSWORD CAPABILITY bit in the T13 standard and can be "high" or "maximum." If the security level is set to high, either user or master passwords can unlock the drive. If the security level is set to maximum, the master password will allow security erase commands but only the user password can unlock the drive.

Some PCs might issue a security freeze command after booting to prevent further security commands from being sent, even with correct passwords (to prevent malicious password-setting attacks). The Security output from hdparm will indicate if a drive is frozen. Many USB bridges automatically spin up an attached disk in an unfrozen state, but if you still have difficulty, here are several possibilities to try:

- Checking the BIOS for settings to enable/disable the freeze command
- Using a forensic boot CD that prevents freeze commands from being issued
- Attaching the disk to a separate controller card (not built into the mainboard)
- Hot plugging the disk into the system (if supported)
- Using a mainboard that does not issue freeze commands

If you know the user password and the drive security is not frozen, you can unlock the drive as follows:

```
# hdparm --security-unlock "mysecret99" /dev/sdb
security_password="mysecret99"

/dev/sdb:
 Issuing SECURITY_UNLOCK command, password="mysecret99", user=user
```

By default, the user password is provided using hdparm, and the master password needs to be explicitly specified with an additional command line parameter. If you know the master password and the security level is set to high, you can use the master password to unlock the drive as follows:

```
# hdparm --user-master m --security-unlock "companysecret22" /dev/sdb
security_password="companysecret22"

/dev/sdb:
 Issuing SECURITY_UNLOCK command, password="companysecret22", user=master
```

If no passwords are known, access to the disk is not possible with regular tools. The password information is stored on the service/system areas of a disk and is generally not accessible without special hardware or tools. However, several further options are available and are discussed here.

The master password might be set to a factory default and can be used to gain access to the drive (if the security level is set to high and not maximum). You can easily find lists of factory default master passwords on the internet.

Using brute force to identify either the master or user password is inefficient, because the drive must be reset after five failed attempts. However, if you have a small set of likely passwords, multiple attempts become feasible and may lead to lucky success.

Specialized data recovery companies provide services and hardware tools that can recover or reset ATA Security Feature Set passwords from the service areas of a disk. Success is not guaranteed for all disks, but data recovery firms often list the disks they do support. In some cases, you might have to ship the disk to the firm's laboratory, which may have chain-of-custody implications. See "Drive Service Area Access" on page 122 for more information.

The hard disk vendor may be able to provide assistance to disable or reset the ATA password. This will depend on the cooperation of the drive vendor, the ability to prove ownership of the disk and its contents, the authority of the requesting party, and the motivation for recovering the data.

Hardware and firmware hacks and published methods by researchers may exist that provide access for certain hard drive models. The security research community is regularly finding innovative ways to access and modify data in hard-to-reach places.

Identify and Unlock Opal Self-Encrypting Drives

Self-encrypting drives (SEDs) are a form of full-disk encryption (FDE). Unlike software-based FDE (TrueCrypt, FileVault, LUKS, and so on) where the OS manages the encryption, SEDs have encryption capabilities built directly into the drive electronics and firmware. SEDs are OS agnostic and are based on vendor-independent standards. The international body responsible for defining the standard is the Trusted Computing Group (TCG; *http://www.trustedcomputinggroup.org/*). The standard is the TCG Storage Security Subsystem Class: Opal, Specification Version 2.00.

This section identifies drives with Opal encryption and describes how appropriate keys can be used to unlock the drive. The recovery of encryption keys is outside the scope of this book. The examples shown here assume the key is known.

A physical examination of the drive can already indicate if it is an Opal SED. The existence of a *Physical Secure ID (PSID)* string printed on the label of the drive is shown in Figure 5-2. This string is used for the Opal RevertSP feature, which generates a new key securely, destroying all data and resetting the drive to its original factory state. The PSID cannot be queried from the drive and must be physically read or scanned if a QR code exists. The existence of a PSID string does not mean the drive is locked and passwords are set; it just indicates the drive supports Opal full-disk encryption.

```
'SHZ41
6Gb/s SED    5V  1.7A
'510E69A241                 PSID: 54BADE82-5B0B-6578-E100-000089C981B5
'007   HALOGEN FREE
NA
```

Figure 5-2: Opal SED PSID

Full-disk encryption has a chicken-and-egg problem. If an entire drive is encrypted, including the boot sector, how can the system execute the master boot record (MBR) and ask for a password or other security credentials? The solution was to implement a *shadow MBR* and store it in the system area of a disk (the same place where SMART data, bad block lists, and so on are stored). When an Opal disk is in a locked state, only the shadow MBR is visible to the host. It is a group of unencrypted sectors (can be large—150MB in size, for example) that is executed as a normal MBR (the host is completely unaware that it is using a shadow MBR). This alternate boot area can execute code to request a password, access a Trusted Platform Module (TPM) chip or smartcard, or get other credentials. Once the disk has been unlocked, the proper MBR becomes visible, and a normal boot process can begin.

An open source command line tool was created to manage Opal SED encryption under Linux. Originally called msed, it was available at *https://github.com/r0m30/msed/*, but the tool was recently renamed sedutil-cli and moved to *https://github.com/Drive-Trust-Alliance/sedutil/*. This tool is still under development and may not work on all drives. Follow the instructions carefully and ensure that libata.allow_tpm is enabled in the kernel.

The following command scans the local system for all Opal-compliant SED drives. Out of four attached drives, one disk is detected as Opal version 2:

```
# sedutil-cli --scan

Scanning for Opal compliant disks
/dev/sda  2   Crucial_CT250MX200SSD1              MU01
/dev/sdb No   WDC WD20EZRX-00D8PB0                80.00A80
/dev/sdc No   INTEL SSDSA2CW300G3                 4PC10302
/dev/sdd No   Kingston SHPM2280P2H/240G           0C34L5TA
No more disks present ending scan
```

You can query the drive to find information about the Opal status, including if a disk is encrypted, locked, or has a shadow MBR (all three are shown in this example):

```
# sedutil-cli --query /dev/sda

/dev/sda ATA Crucial_CT250MX200SSD1              MU01         15030E69A241
...
Locking function (0x0002)
```

```
Locked = Y, LockingEnabled = Y, LockingSupported = Y, MBRDone = N,
MBREnabled = Y, MediaEncrypt = Y
```
...

Two commands can be issued: one to disable locking and the second to inform the disk that the shadow MBR is not needed (MBR is "Done"). In this example, *xxmonkey* is the password:

```
# sedutil-cli --disableLockingRange 0 xxmonkey /dev/sda
- 16:33:34.480 INFO: LockingRange0 disabled
# sedutil-cli  --setMBRDone on xxmonkey /dev/sda
- 16:33:54.341 INFO: MBRDone set on
```

At this point, a kernel message (dmesg) might show a change in available devices. The status in this example now shows the following:

```
# sedutil-cli --query /dev/sda

/dev/sda ATA Crucial_CT250MX200SSD1                    MU01        15030E69A241
...
Locking function (0x0002)
   Locked = N, LockingEnabled = Y, LockingSupported = Y, MBRDone = Y,
   MBREnabled = Y, MediaEncrypt = Y
...
```

The drive is no longer locked, and the shadow MBR is no longer visible. The proper MBR and the rest of the decrypted disk are available, and they can be accessed with regular forensic tools. Now the partition table of a Linux installation becomes visible, as shown in this example:

```
# mmls /dev/sda
DOS Partition Table
Offset Sector: 0
Units are in 512-byte sectors

     Slot    Start        End          Length       Description
00:  Meta    0000000000   0000000000   0000000001   Primary Table (#0)
01:  -----   0000000000   0000002047   0000002048   Unallocated
02:  00:00   0000002048   0471887871   0471885824   Linux (0x83)
03:  -----   0471887872   0471889919   0000002048   Unallocated
04:  Meta    0471889918   0488396799   0016506882   DOS Extended (0x05)
05:  Meta    0471889918   0471889918   0000000001   Extended Table (#1)
06:  01:00   0471889920   0488396799   0016506880   Linux Swap / Solaris x86 (0x82)
07:  -----   0488396800   0488397167   0000000368   Unallocated
```

A locked drive that has no shadow MBR enabled will produce multiple error messages in the kernel dmesg output.

The simple example described in this section was provided for illustration purposes only. Some Opal disks may behave differently with this tool. In real scenarios, the key might not be a simple password but instead be tied to the TPM or some other enterprise security mechanism. If the wrong commands are given in this situation, the data on the disk can be irrevocably destroyed (in an instant if the key is destroyed).

From a forensics perspective, it may be useful to image the shadow MBR for analysis as well. It could contain interesting artifacts from the time the disk encryption was set up. It is also conceivable that data could be hidden in the shadow MBR region of Opal-capable drives.

Encrypted Flash Thumb Drives

USB thumb drives sold as "secure" devices often come with a proprietary software encryption solution provided by the vendor. Some drives offer OS-independent encryption with authentication using keypads, fingerprint readers, or smartcards (see Figure 5-3).

Figure 5-3: Encrypted USB sticks

Proprietary solutions might not have a compatible tool to manage access, making it difficult to acquire decrypted data with Linux. Devices with an onboard authentication mechanism should appear as a normal USB storage device after authentication.

Secure thumb drives that are locked may behave differently when attached to a host. Some don't provide any indication that they've been plugged into the host. Some appear as a removable media device without media (like a memory card reader). Some will appear as a CD-ROM and have software available to run or install, which manages the drive.

Larger hardware-encrypted external drives also exist and may require a pin to unlock. An exmple of such a drive is described in Chapter 7 (see Figure 7-1 on page 216).

Attach Removable Media

This section covers the attachment of devices that use removable storage media. The most common examples of removable media are optical discs, memory cards, and magnetic tapes. In a way, attaching removable storage media to an acquisition host occurs twice. First the device electronics are attached, and then in an additional step, the removable media is inserted. Let's begin with a discussion on optical media drives.

Optical Media Drives

Optical drives are typically attached internally via SATA or externally via USB. The drives appear in the Linux device tree but without media. Running forensic commands on an empty drive produces obvious results, as shown here:

```
# mmls /dev/cdrom
Error opening image file (raw_open: file "/dev/cdrom" - No medium found)
```

Two useful commands provide information about the attached drive and inserted discs. The cd-drive command provides details about an attached optical drive (internal or external), including various features, supported media, and so on:

```
# cd-drive
cd-drive version 0.83 x86_64-pc-linux-gnu
...
CD-ROM drive supports MMC 3

                          Drive: /dev/cdrom
Vendor                    : ASUS
Model                     : BW-16D1HT
Revision                  : 1.01
Profile List Feature
        Blu Ray BD-RE
        Blu Ray BD-R random recording
        Blu Ray BD-R sequential recording
        Blu Ray BD-ROM
        DVD+R Double Layer - DVD Recordable Double Layer
        DVD+R - DVD Recordable
        DVD+RW - DVD Rewritable
        DVD-R - Double-layer Jump Recording
        DVD-R - Double-Layer Sequential Recording
        Re-recordable DVD using Sequential Recording
        Re-recordable DVD using Restricted Overwrite
        Re-writable DVD
        Re-recordable DVD using Sequential recording
        Read only DVD
```

```
        CD-RW Re-writable Compact Disc capable
        Write once Compact Disc capable
        Read only Compact Disc capable
...
Removable Medium Feature
        Tray type loading mechanism
        can eject the medium or magazine via the normal START/STOP command
        can be locked into the Logical Unit
...
```

When you insert a disc into the drive, you can retrieve information about the media using the cd-info command. The result includes the mode, format, and information about the publisher:

```
# cd-info
cd-info version 0.83 x86_64-pc-linux-gnu
Disc mode is listed as: CD-DA
CD-ROM Track List (1 - 1)
  #: MSF       LSN     Type    Green? Copy? Channels Premphasis?
  1: 00:02:00  000000 data    false  no
170: 39:42:20  178520 leadout (400 MB raw, 400 MB formatted)
Media Catalog Number (MCN): 0000000000000
TRACK  1 ISRC: 000000000000
Last CD Session LSN: 0
audio status: invalid


CD Analysis Report
CD-ROM with ISO 9660 filesystem
ISO 9660: 154301 blocks, label `SOLARIS_2_5_1_SPARC       '
Application: NOT SPECIFIED
Preparer   : SOLARIS_PRODUCT_ENGINEERING
Publisher  : SUNSOFT_INC
System     : SUNSOFT_INC
Volume     : SOLARIS_2_5_1_SPARC
Volume Set : SOLARIS_2_5_1_SERIES
```

You can eject the optical media using the eject shell command.

Using write blockers on optical drives is unnecessary. No timestamps are updated simply by accessing files on a disc. Modifying an optical disc requires explicit burn instructions, reducing the risk of accidental modification.

Magnetic Tape Drives

You can determine a list of attached tape drives using the lshw tool and the tape class. The output provides information about the drive vendor, serial number, and device information.

In this example, two tape drives are found (LTO and DAT):

```
# lshw -class tape
  *-tape
       description: SCSI Tape
       product: LTO-5 HH
       vendor: TANDBERG
       physical id: 0.0.0
       bus info: scsi@13:0.0.0
       logical name: /dev/nst0
       version: Y629
       serial: HU1246T99F
       capabilities: removable
       configuration: ansiversion=6
  *-tape
       description: SCSI Tape
       product: DAT160
       vendor: HP
       physical id: 0.0.0
       bus info: scsi@15:0.0.0
       logical name: /dev/nst1
       version: WU8A
       serial: HU10123NFH
       capabilities: removable
       configuration: ansiversion=3
```

Magnetic tape drives are typically SCSI devices, which you can query using standard SCSI commands. The standard tool for controlling tapes is mt, which provides information about the drive status, controls the position of the tape, and ejects the media. The mt tool can provide basic information about the tape, but the tapeinfo tool is more comprehensive. In this example, the mt and tapeinfo tools query the status of an LTO tape drive with a loaded tape:

```
# mt -f /dev/nst0 status
SCSI 2 tape drive:
File number=1, block number=0, partition=0.
Tape block size 0 bytes. Density code 0x58 (no translation).
Soft error count since last status=0
General status bits on (81010000):
 EOF ONLINE IM_REP_EN

# tapeinfo -f /dev/nst0
Product Type: Tape Drive
Vendor ID: 'TANDBERG'
Product ID: 'LTO-5 HH      '
Revision: 'Y629'
Attached Changer API: No
```

```
SerialNumber: 'HU1246T99F'
MinBlock: 1
MaxBlock: 16777215
SCSI ID: 0
SCSI LUN: 0
Ready: yes
BufferedMode: yes
Medium Type: Not Loaded
Density Code: 0x58
BlockSize: 0
DataCompEnabled: yes
DataCompCapable: yes
DataDeCompEnabled: yes
CompType: 0x1
DeCompType: 0x1
Block Position: 166723430
Partition 0 Remaining Kbytes: 1459056
Partition 0 Size in Kbytes: 1459056
ActivePartition: 0
EarlyWarningSize: 0
NumPartitions: 0
MaxPartitions: 1
```

The tape head is positioned at the second file on the tape (file 1 is after file 0). The block offset and file offset are useful when you're forensically acquiring individual files from a tape.

Using mt, you can rewind tapes and take them offline (eject them):

```
# mt -f /dev/nst0 status
```

When a tape device is attached to a Linux system, a number of corresponding devices are created.

```
# ls -1 /dev/*st0*
/dev/nst0
/dev/nst0a
/dev/nst0l
/dev/nst0m
/dev/st0
/dev/st0a
/dev/st0l
/dev/st0m
```

The st* devices auto-rewind the tape after each command (which is not always desired), and the nst* devices are the nonrewinding devices. The a, l, and m characters represent the same device but with different characteristics (block size, compression). When you're performing a forensic acquisition, you should use the nst* devices (without an additional a, l, or m character).

Memory Cards

Memory cards typically attach to a host using a USB adapter with multiple slots for different types of memory cards. When attached, the adapter creates a removable SCSI device for each slot (even when the slots are empty). This behavior can be observed in the following dmesg output.

```
[ 2175.331711] usb 1-7: new high-speed USB device number 10 using xhci_hcd
[ 2175.461244] usb 1-7: New USB device found, idVendor=058f, idProduct=6362
[ 2175.461249] usb 1-7: New USB device strings: Mfr=1, Product=2, SerialNumber=3
[ 2175.461252] usb 1-7: Manufacturer: Generic
[ 2175.461938] usb-storage 1-7:1.0: USB Mass Storage device detected
[ 2175.462143] scsi host15: usb-storage 1-7:1.0
[ 2176.458662] scsi 15:0:0:0: Direct-Access     Generic  USB SD Reader   1.00
    PQ: 0 ANSI: 0
[ 2176.459179] scsi 15:0:0:1: Direct-Access     Generic  USB CF Reader   1.01
    PQ: 0 ANSI: 0
[ 2176.459646] scsi 15:0:0:2: Direct-Access     Generic  USB SM Reader   1.02
    PQ: 0 ANSI: 0
[ 2176.460089] scsi 15:0:0:3: Direct-Access     Generic  USB MS Reader   1.03
    PQ: 0 ANSI: 0
[ 2176.460431] sd 15:0:0:0: Attached scsi generic sg11 type 0
[ 2176.460641] sd 15:0:0:1: Attached scsi generic sg12 type 0
[ 2176.460863] sd 15:0:0:2: Attached scsi generic sg13 type 0
[ 2176.461150] sd 15:0:0:3: Attached scsi generic sg14 type 0
[ 2176.463711] sd 15:0:0:0: [sdj] Attached SCSI removable disk
[ 2176.464510] sd 15:0:0:1: [sdk] Attached SCSI removable disk
[ 2176.464944] sd 15:0:0:2: [sdl] Attached SCSI removable disk
[ 2176.465339] sd 15:0:0:3: [sdm] Attached SCSI removable disk
```

As you insert media into the slots, the media is made available as a USB mass storage device with a linear sequence of "sectors," which you can forensically acquire. Continuing on from the previous example, a memory card has now been inserted into a slot of the card reader and appears as block device:

```
[ 2310.750147] sd 15:0:0:0: [sdj] 7959552 512-byte logical blocks: (4.07 GB/3.79 GiB)
[ 2310.753162]  sdj: sdj1
```

Hardware-querying tools, such as hdparm and smartctl, may produce unreliable results, because memory cards don't have the ATA features of more complex drives with dedicated drive circuitry.

Attach Other Storage

Sometimes storage media is attached to a forensic acquisition host and behaves in a unique way. In particular, it is useful to know about special behavior with portable devices, Apple computer systems, and NVME drives.

Apple Target Disk Mode

TDM allows Apple computers with OpenBoot firmware or newer firmware to boot into a state where the Mac system appears as an external disk enclosure and the internal disks are available as SCSI target devices. Earlier TDM implementations used the FireWire bus but have since moved to Thunderbolt. You activate this mode by holding down the T key while powering on the Apple computer.

A Linux machine without a Thunderbolt adapter can use FireWire to achieve the same result with an adapter. Figure 5-4 shows a photo of a Thunderbolt-to-FireWire adapter.

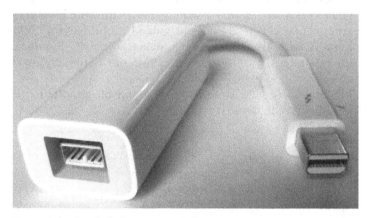

Figure 5-4: Thunderbolt to Firewire adapter

Be sure to boot the Apple device (while holding the T key) with the Thunderbolt-to-FireWire adapter already plugged in; otherwise, the Apple firmware will not use the FireWire adapter for the target device.

The following example shows dmesg output of an Apple notebook in TDM that is connected to a Linux machine using a Thunderbolt to FireWire adapter (Thunderbolt on the Apple; FireWire on the Linux machine):

```
[  542.964313] scsi host10: SBP-2 IEEE-1394
[  542.964404] firewire_core 0000:0e:00.0: created device fw1: GUID
   000a27020064d0ef, S800
[  543.163093] firewire_sbp2 fw1.0: logged in to LUN 0000 (0 retries)
[  543.163779] scsi 10:0:0:0: Direct-Access-RBC AAPL     FireWire Target  0000
   PQ: 0 ANSI: 3
[  543.164226] sd 10:0:0:0: Attached scsi generic sg10 type 14
[  543.165006] sd 10:0:0:0: [sdj] 236978176 512-byte logical blocks:
   (121 GB/113 GiB)
[  543.165267] sd 10:0:0:0: [sdj] Write Protect is off
[  543.165271] sd 10:0:0:0: [sdj] Mode Sense: 10 00 00 00
[  543.165759] sd 10:0:0:0: [sdj] Write cache: enabled, read cache: enabled,
   doesn't support DPO or FUA
```

```
[  543.171533] sdj: sdj1 sdj2 sdj3
[  543.173479] sd 10:0:0:0: [sdj] Attached SCSI disk
```

PC-based Linux systems with Thunderbolt ports are not common, and Linux kernel support is still under development. As an alternative, you can boot recent Apple computers with a forensic boot CD/USB device and acquire them to a locally attached evidence drive.

NVME SSDs

NVME drives compete with SATA Express in the way they attach directly to a PCI Express bus. As of this writing, hardware write blockers for NVME drives are very new. There are hot-pluggable USB bridges for NVME and SATA Express drives from Tableau (Guidance Software). For illustration purposes, the examples shown here use an NVME device directly attached to a Linux system.

You can use the nvme tool from the nvme-cli software package to list the attached NVME devices:

```
# nvme list
Node              Model                 Version  Namepace  Usage                        ...

----------------  --------------------  -------  --------  ---------------------------
/dev/nvme0n1      INTEL SSDPE2MW400G4   1.0      1         400.09  GB / 400.09  GB ...
/dev/nvme1n1      Samsung SSD 950 PRO   1.1      1           3.01  GB / 256.06  GB ...
...
```

You should also check each NVME drive for multiple namespaces by using the nvme tool. In this example, only a single namespace exists:

```
# nvme list-ns /dev/nvme1
[   0]:0x1
```

Multiple namespaces may need to be acquired individually. This is a fundamental difference from other drives where a single drive is viewed as a linear set of sectors, which you can acquire in a single pass. NVME drives with multiple namespaces will likely need special consideration.[8]

It's important to note that the NVME standard was created from scratch without backward compatibility with SCSI or ATA standards (AHCI, and so on). It has its own command set and operates independently from other disk systems. For this reason, some tools may not work as expected with NVME hardware. Any forensic tool operating directly on low-level device drivers, such as SATA or SAS, will not work with NVME. However, if forensic tools operate on the virtual block layer, they should continue to work normally. In addition, PCI forensic write blockers may act as a bridge and

---

8. At the time of this writing, I did not have testing access to any NVME drives with support for multiple namespaces. These conclusions are based on reading the standards and documentation.

make the device appear as a SCSI device. For example, here the Sleuth Kit mmls tool is used on an NVME drive attached to the examination host:

```
# mmls /dev/nvme1n1
DOS Partition Table
Offset Sector: 0
Units are in 512-byte sectors

     Slot    Start        End          Length       Description
00:  Meta    0000000000   0000000000   0000000001   Primary Table (#0)
01:  -----   0000000000   0000002047   0000002048   Unallocated
02:  00:00   0000002048   0167774207   0167772160   Linux (0x83)
03:  00:01   0167774208   0335546367   0167772160   Linux (0x83)
04:  00:02   0335546368   0500118191   0164571824   Linux (0x83)
```

Notice that the device is nvme1n1 and not simply nvme1. The namespace of the drive must be specified when you're using commands on NVME drives.

As with other drives, NVME drives have a SMART log, but you can't access it with current versions of smartctl (as of this writing). However, you can use the nvme tool to extract the SMART log as follows:

```
# nvme smart-log /dev/nvme1
Smart Log for NVME device:/dev/nvme1 namespace-id:ffffffff
critical_warning              : 0
temperature                   : 46 C
available_spare               : 100%
available_spare_threshold     : 10%
percentage_used               : 0%
data_units_read               : 2,616
data_units_written            : 5,874
host_read_commands            : 19,206
host_write_commands           : 56,145
controller_busy_time          : 0
power_cycles                  : 34
power_on_hours                : 52
unsafe_shutdowns              : 17
media_errors                  : 0
num_err_log_entries           : 7
```

The nvme tool has a number of features for querying attached NVME drives. See the nvme(1) manual page or visit *https://github.com/linux-nvme/* for more information.

As of this writing, NVME drives are an emerging technology. Because they have numerous benefits in terms of performance and efficiency, they may become more popular in the future.

Other Devices with Block or Character Access

You can image any device that is detected as a block device by the Linux kernel. Some devices will appear as a block device the moment they are attached to the host system. For example, many generic MP3/music players, cameras, and other mobile devices behave in this manner.

Some devices need to be switched into a different "disk" mode before they can become accessible as a block device. Often, you can select this mode from the device's user interface.

Some USB devices are multifunctional and may provide other USB modes in addition to storage. You might need to switch the mode on these devices to usb-storage before acquiring them. A Linux tool called usb_modeswitch is able to query some multifunction USB devices and switch modes.

Closing Thoughts

In this chapter, you learned to attach a subject drive to an acquisition machine and positively identify the device for imaging. You learned different aspects of PC hardware (USB, PCI, block devices, and so on), how to query your acquisition system, and how to query your drive for firmware and SMART information. I demonstrated the removal of the HPA and DCO as well as various types of security built into the hardware of some drives. You are now equipped with the knowledge necessary to perform a forensic acquisition, which will be the focus of Chapter 6.

6

FORENSIC IMAGE ACQUISITION

This chapter explains the forensic imaging of storage media, with an emphasis on performing forensically sound image acquisition. This means maximizing the amount of data extracted from a particular storage medium, minimizing the disturbance to the storage device and medium, preserving the collected evidence, and documenting the process (including errors).

You'll read about several tools and approaches here, as well as the strengths and weaknesses of each. As a result, you'll be able to make an informed decision about which tool is most appropriate in a particular situation. You'll learn how to use a variety of free or open source forensic imaging tools, such as dd, dcfldd, dc3dd, ewfacquire, and ftkimager-cli. In addition, I describe the sfsimage tool as a script that uses existing acquisition tools to create a SquashFS forensic evidence container.

How do you choose which tool to use when imaging a disk? To some extent, it's a matter of personal preference. You may know one tool better than another or trust one particular tool based on past experience (or distrust a tool based on past experience). Each tool has its strengths and unique features. Forensic labs that use EnCase or FTK extensively might choose ewfacquire or ftkimager-cli for compatibility and policy reasons.

Dcfldd and dc3dd are based on mature and well-tested software, and they were designed to forensically acquire raw images with extensive hashing and logging. For disks with many bad blocks, GNU ddrescue might be a good choice. For integrated hashing, encryption, and compression during acquisition, recent versions of dd_rescue might be an interesting alternative. Ultimately, the tool used will depend on the forensic lab's organizational policy, the type of examination, your personal preferences, and other circumstances. No particular tool is recommended in this book.

All the examples in this chapter make the following assumptions:

- The subject storage device is physically attached to the forensics examiner's acquisition workstation.

- The subject storage device has been positively identified.

- The appropriate write-blocking mitigation is in place to prevent modification of the subject drive.

- Disk capacity planning has been performed to ensure disk space is not an issue.

Acquire an Image with dd Tools

The resulting image file from dd-based tools is not a "format" in the same sense as other forensic formats, such as EnCase EWF or FTK SMART. Images created by dd-based tools don't have a header, a footer, internal markers, or descriptive metadata about a case or incident. They are simply a raw mirror image of a chunk of data, in this case, a mirror image of a subject disk or other mass storage.

NOTE *Warning: the dd tools are unforgiving if you make any mistakes and will irrevocably overwrite any unprotected disk if instructed.*

To reduce the risk of damaging evidence or an examiner workstation, always double-check the following:

- A write blocker is protecting the evidence/subject drive.

- The serial number of the input device (if=) matches the serial number on the physical subject disk label.

- Confirm the output file (of=) is a regular file located on the examiner system or a program that can handle the expected input to stdin.

Standard Unix dd and GNU dd

The command syntax for dd simply specifies an input file and an output file, and it may include other options that modify the command's behavior. The following example shows the use of dd to copy a disk block device to a file:

```
# dd if=/dev/sde of=image.raw
15466496+0 records in
```

```
15466496+0 records out
7918845952 bytes (7.9 GB) copied, 130.952 s, 60.5 MB/s
```

Here if= specifies the input file, which in this case is a raw disk device attached to the acquisition system. The of= parameter is the output file, which is a normal file that contains the raw data copied from the disk device. On completion, dd reports how many bytes were transferred. You can divide the number of bytes transferred by the sector size, and the result should exactly match the number of sectors identified when you attached the device.

There can be challenges when using dd to forensically image a disk. If read errors occur in the middle of an acquisition, dd will abort with an "Input/output error." Address this issue by adding conv=noerror, which will force dd to skip over the unreadable block and continue. The problem with skipping over unreadable blocks is that the sector offset on the destination file changes for filesystem blocks on the rest of the disk, causing the rest of the filesystem on the disk to appear corrupted. To illustrate, consider the pages of a book. Suppose page 99 is ripped out. If the table of contents points to a chapter starting at page 200, it's still possible to find it. The book's page numbers are intact, even with the missing page. But this is not the case when sector 99 is ripped out of a disk image (due to a read error). The rest of the sectors are renumbered, and the filesystem's "table of contents" will point to the wrong blocks after sector 99.

The sync parameter corrects this by padding the unreadable output block with zeros, essentially creating a "fake" sector or block (full of zeros) to represent the missing one. The rest of the disk image will then have the correct sector numbers (offsets) expected by the filesystem it contains.

Using the previous example, but this time with protection from unreadable blocks (skipping and padding them with zeros), gives this result:

```
# dd if=/dev/sde of=image.raw conv=noerror,sync
15466496+0 records in
15466496+0 records out
7918845952 bytes (7.9 GB) copied, 136.702 s, 57.9 MB/s
```

Padding the output impacts the forensic acquisition in that the image is modified and new data (the zeros) has been added. Cryptographic checksums of the disk will not match the original data on the disk (especially if there are new or changing unreadable areas of a disk). This problem can be managed by logging hash windows. This is discussed in "Hash Windows" on page 152.

Another issue with dd is that the transfer block size can be larger than the physical media sector size. This is problematic when a read error occurs, because the remaining sectors in the larger block are padded with zeros, not just the one unreadable sector. This means some normal readable sectors might be excluded from the forensic image. A block size larger than the sector size could also cause additional padding sectors to be added to the end of a forensic image (if the image size is not divisible by the block size). The potential performance gained from increasing the block size must be weighed against the risk of losing evidence from a large padded block.

Traditional dd has no capability for hashing, logging to a file, or other features you would expect of a forensic acquisition tool. Because the raw image contains no metadata about the original subject disk, you must separately document any information that describes the disk (or partially embed some information in the filename).

The dcfldd and dc3dd Tools

Two popular dd derivatives, dcfldd and dc3dd, were independently developed specifically for use in a forensic context.

Because dcfldd and dc3dd originate from GNU dd, they use a similar command syntax. Neither tool has built-in support for writing to forensic formats (FTK, EnCase, AFF), compression, or image encryption. But you can achieve these functions through the use of command piping, which I'll demonstrate in subsequent sections.

The following example uses dcfldd to image a disk, ensuring blocks containing unreadable sectors are padded and don't cause an abort:

```
# dcfldd if=/dev/sde of=image.raw conv=noerror,sync errlog=error.log
241664 blocks (7552Mb) written.
241664+0 records in
241664+0 records out
```

Errors are written to a separate error log file. The dcfldd tool does not use conv=noerror,sync by default; you must add it manually.

A similar imaging command for dc3dd is shown in the next example. By default, dc3dd does a good job of managing errors during acquisition. No conv=noerror,sync flag is needed because it's built in. The output is well documented, both to stdout and to the log file. Here is a simple example acquisition:

```
# dc3dd if=/dev/sde of=image.raw log=error.log

dc3dd 7.2.641 started at 2016-05-07 14:37:10 +0200
compiled options:
command line: dc3dd if=/dev/sde of=image.raw log=error.log
device size: 15466496 sectors (probed),    7,918,845,952 bytes
sector size: 512 bytes (probed)
  7918845952 bytes ( 7.4 G ) copied ( 100% ),   80 s, 95 M/s

input results for device `/dev/sde':
   15466496 sectors in
   0 bad sectors replaced by zeros
```

```
output results for file `image.raw`:
   15466496 sectors out

dc3dd completed at 2016-05-07 14:38:30 +0200
```

You can also configure the sfsimage script to use either dcfldd or dc3dd for imaging into a SquashFS forensic container. In the following example, a 4K native (4096-byte native sector size) drive is imaged using sfsimage:

```
# sfsimage -i /dev/sdd 4Knative.sfs
Started: 2016-05-07T17:16:54
Sfsimage version: Sfsimage Version 0.8
Sfsimage command: /usr/bin/sfsimage -i /dev/sdd
Current working directory: /exam
Forensic evidence source: if=/dev/sdd
Destination squashfs container: 4Knative.sfs
Image filename inside container: image.raw
Aquisition command: sudo dc3dd if=/dev/sdd log=errorlog.txt hlog=hashlog.txt
     hash=md5 2>/dev/null | pv -s 3000592982016
2.73TiB 5:29:31 [ 144MiB/s] [==========================================>] 100%
Completed: 2016-05-07T22:47:42
# cat /sys/block/sdd/queue/logical_block_size
4096
# cat /sys/block/sdd/queue/physical_block_size
4096
```

This example also illustrates that the physical and logical sector size of a drive does not impact the acquisition when using dd-style imaging tools.

Both dcfldd and dc3dd have additional features for cryptographic hashing, image splitting, and piping to external programs. I'll demonstrate these features in various situations throughout the rest of the book.

Acquire an Image with Forensic Formats

Several imaging formats were specifically designed with forensics in mind. Some of these, FTK and EnCase for example, are commercial proprietary formats and have been reverse engineered to allow development of open source–compatible tools. The next two sections describe tools for acquisition using these proprietary formats.

The ewfacquire Tool

An acquisition tool that specializes in Guidance EnCase Expert Witness formats is ewfacquire from libewf (*https://github.com/libyal/libewf/*). This tool accepts informational parameters on the command line or asks for them interactively. You can choose from a number of commercial formats, including the various EnCase formats as well as FTK. The ewfacquire tool creates acquisition files that enable interoperability with EnCase, FTK, and Sleuth Kit. The tool can also convert raw images into other formats.

This example shows ewfacquire acquiring an attached disk device (a MacBook Air connected to the examiner workstation in Target Disk Mode with a Thunderbolt-to-FireWire adapter):

```
# ewfacquire -c best -t /exam/macbookair /dev/sdf
ewfacquire 20160424


Device information:
Bus type:                        FireWire (IEEE1394)
Vendor:
Model:
Serial:


Storage media information:
Type:                            Device
Media type:                      Fixed
Media size:                      121 GB (121332826112 bytes)
Bytes per sector:                512


Acquiry parameters required, please provide the necessary input
Case number: 42
Description: The case of the missing vase
Evidence number: 1
Examiner name: holmes
Notes: The vase was blue.
Media type (fixed, removable, optical, memory) [fixed]:
Media characteristics (logical, physical) [physical]:
Use EWF file format (ewf, smart, ftk, encase1, encase2, encase3, encase4, encase5,
    encase6, encase7, encase7-v2, linen5, linen6, linen7, ewfx) [encase6]:
Start to acquire at offset (0 <= value <= 121332826112) [0]:
The number of bytes to acquire (0 <= value <= 121332826112) [121332826112]:
Evidence segment file size in bytes (1.0 MiB <= value <= 7.9 EiB) [1.4 GiB]:
The number of bytes per sector (1 <= value <= 4294967295) [512]:
The number of sectors to read at once (16, 32, 64, 128, 256, 512, 1024, 2048, 4096,
    8192, 16384, 32768) [64]:
The number of sectors to be used as error granularity (1 <= value <= 64) [64]:
The number of retries when a read error occurs (0 <= value <= 255) [2]:
Wipe sectors on read error (mimic EnCase like behavior) (yes, no) [no]:


The following acquiry parameters were provided:
Image path and filename:         /exam/macbookair.E01
Case number:                     42
Description:                     The case of the missing vase
Evidence number:                 1
Examiner name:                   holmes
Notes:                           The vase was blue.
```

```
Media type:                      fixed disk
Is physical:                     yes
EWF file format:                 EnCase 6 (.E01)
Compression method:              deflate
Compression level:               best
Acquiry start offset:            0
Number of bytes to acquire:      113 GiB (121332826112 bytes)
Evidence segment file size:      1.4 GiB (1572864000 bytes)
Bytes per sector:                512
Block size:                      64 sectors
Error granularity:               64 sectors
Retries on read error:           2
Zero sectors on read error:      no

Continue acquiry with these values (yes, no) [yes]:

Acquiry started at: May 07, 2016 14:54:52
This could take a while.

Status: at 0.0%
        acquired 60 MiB (62914560 bytes) of total 113 GiB (121332826112 bytes)
        completion in 2 hour(s), 8 minute(s) and 38 second(s) with 14 MiB/s
    (15712616 bytes/second)
...
Status: at 99.9%
        acquired 112 GiB (121329188864 bytes) of total 113 GiB (121332826112 bytes)
        completion in 0 second(s) with 51 MiB/s (54069886 bytes/second)

Acquiry completed at: May 07, 2016 15:32:16

Written: 113 GiB (121332826300 bytes) in 37 minute(s) and 24 second(s) with
    51 MiB/s (54069886 bytes/second)
MD5 hash calculated over data:      083e2131d0a59a9e3b59d48dbc451591
ewfacquire: SUCCESS
```

The ewfacquire acquisition completed successfully in 37 minutes, and
the 120GB file was split into 54 compressed *.E0 files totaling 79GB.

AccessData ftkimager

AccessData provides free, precompiled, command line versions of the
FTK Imager. The tool is called ftkimager and binaries (no source code)
are available for Debian Linux, Fedora Linux, OS X, and Windows, which
you can download from the AccessData website at *http://accessdata.com/
product-download/digital-forensics/*.

The ftkimager tool can take input from a raw device, a file, or stdin. It
outputs to an **FTK SMART** format, an EnCase EWF format, or stdout. The

stdin and stdout streams are especially useful for piping to and from other programs. A number of other features are supported, including the addition of case metadata into the saved formats, compression, output file splitting ("image fragments"), hashing, and encrypted images.

The following basic example shows the use of ftkimager to acquire an attached disk:

```
# ftkimager /dev/sdf --s01 --description "SN4C53000120 Ultra Fit" sandisk
AccessData FTK Imager v3.1.1 CLI (Aug 24 2012)
Copyright 2006-2012 AccessData Corp., 384 South 400 West, Lindon, UT 84042
All rights reserved.

Creating image...
Image creation complete.
```

In this example, the source device was a SanDisk thumb drive accessible via */dev/sdf*, and the destination filename was *sandisk*. Because the default format is raw, adding the --s01 flag saves it to FTK's SMART format. A serial number and model string was added to the metadata using the --description flag.

The ftkimager creates a log file with basic metadata and any additional information that was added using flags on the command line, as shown here:

```
# cat sandisk.s01.txt
Case Information:
Acquired using: ADI3
Case Number:
Evidence Number:
Unique description: SN4C53000120 Ultra Fit
Examiner:
Notes:


------------------------------------------------------------

Information for sandisk:

Physical Evidentiary Item (Source) Information:
[Device Info]
 Source Type: Physical
[Drive Geometry]
 Cylinders: 14832
 Heads: 64
 Sectors per Track: 32
 Bytes per Sector: 512
 Sector Count: 30375936
 Source data size: 14832 MB
 Sector count:    30375936
[Computed Hashes]
```

```
MD5 checksum:     a2a9a891eed92edbf47ffba9f4fad402
SHA1 checksum:    2e73cc2a2c21c9d4198e93db04303f9b38e0aefe

Image Information:
 Acquisition started:  Sat May  7 15:49:07 2016
 Acquisition finished: Sat May  7 15:53:07 2016
 Segment list:
  sandisk.s01
  sandisk.s02
```

You can extract this same information using the `--print-info` flag together with the filename.

SquashFS Forensic Evidence Container

The sfsimage tool is simply a shell wrapper script that you can configure to use any imaging tool that supports writing an image cleanly to stdout. The script takes this stream of imaged bytes and places them inside a SquashFS compressed filesystem.

In this example, sfsimage was configured to use dc3dd as the imaging tool by editing the DD variable in the beginning of the shell script:

```
DD="dc3dd if=$DDIN log=errorlog.txt hlog=hashlog.txt hash=md5"
```

Then the block device is imaged using the `-i` flag:

```
$ sfsimage -i /dev/sde philips-usb-drive.sfs
Started: 2016-05-07T15:40:03
Sfsimage version: Sfsimage Version 0.8
Sfsimage command: /usr/bin/sfsimage -i /dev/sde
Current working directory: /exam
Forensic evidence source: if=/dev/sde
Destination squashfs container: philips-usb-drive.sfs
Image filename inside container: image.raw
Aquisition command: sudo dc3dd if=/dev/sde log=errorlog.txt hlog=hashlog.txt
    hash=md5 2>/dev/null | pv -s 7918845952
7.38GiB 0:01:18 [95.7MiB/s] [====================================>] 100%
Completed: 2016-05-07T15:41:22
```

The following output shows the size of the compressed *.sfs* file:

```
$ ls -lh *.sfs
-rw-r----- 1 holmes holmes 4.5G May  7 15:41 philips-usb-drive.sfs
```

You can list the contents of the SquashFS container file using `sfsimage -l` or mount it (read-only) using `sfsimage -m`. During the acquisition process, sfsimage saves the error log, hash log, and its own log together with the raw image file. You can add additional files to the sfsimage container using sfsimage -a.

Acquire an Image to Multiple Destinations

The flexibility of the Unix piping mechanism allows the completion of multiple complex tasks in a single unattended step. Both dc3dd and dcfldd can specify multiple destination filenames, allowing you to make simultaneous image copies. The following example shows imaging a disk and simultaneously writing to multiple destination drives: a local copy on the acquisition host and a second copy on a mounted, external third-party drive. These two output files are specified using multiple of= flags as follows:

```
# dc3dd if=/dev/sde of=/exam/local-lab.raw of=/ext/third-party.raw

dc3dd 7.2.641 started at 2016-05-07 15:56:10 +0200
compiled options:
command line: dc3dd if=/dev/sde of=/exam/local-lab.raw of=/ext/third-party.raw
device size: 15466496 sectors (probed),    7,918,845,952 bytes
sector size: 512 bytes (probed)
  7918845952 bytes ( 7.4 G ) copied ( 100% ),    79 s, 95 M/s

input results for device `/dev/sde':
   15466496 sectors in
   0 bad sectors replaced by zeros

output results for file `/exam/local-lab.raw':
   15466496 sectors out

output results for file `/ext/third-party.raw':
   15466496 sectors out

dc3dd completed at 2016-05-07 15:57:30 +0200
```

This technique is useful if you're creating one image for analysis and another for backup, when you're creating an additional image for a third party, or for any other situation where multiple copies of the image are needed. The two images should be identical, and you can verify them by comparing cryptographic checksums.

Preserve Digital Evidence with Cryptography

Preserving the integrity of evidence is fundamental to the digital forensics process. Integrity can be maintained by using cryptographic hashes and further enhanced with cryptographic signatures by the technicians who performed the acquisition. The purpose of hashing or signing images is to verify that the image has not changed since it was acquired. Because court proceedings and the presentation of evidence can take months or even years, it's useful to confirm that evidence has not been modified during that time. This can be viewed as somewhat of a digital chain of custody.

The next few sections demonstrate the use of hash windows, signing with PGP and S/MIME, and RFC-3161 timestamping to preserve digital evidence. Let's begin with some examples of basic cryptographic hashing.

Basic Cryptographic Hashing

The cryptographic hashing of forensic images is typically included as part of the imaging process. The entire media image (each sector in sequence) is passed through a one-way hash function. As of this writing, the four primary forensic imaging tools discussed in this book support the cryptographic hashing algorithms shown in Table 6-1.

Table 6-1: Supported Cryptographic Hashing Algorithms

Tool	Hashing algorithms supported
dcfldd	MD5, SHA1, SHA256, SHA384, SHA512
dc3dd	MD5, SHA1, SHA256, SHA512
ewfacquire	MD5, SHA1, SHA256
ftkimager	MD5, SHA1

The tools using forensic formats usually produce a hash by default. Both ftkimager and ewfacquire automatically generate hashes during the acquisition process, which you saw in previous examples.

To create a hash (or multiple hashes) with dcfldd, you specify the desired hash algorithms on the command line, as follows:

```
# dcfldd if=/dev/sde of=image.raw conv=noerror,sync hash=md5,sha256
241664 blocks (7552Mb) written.Total (md5): ebda11ffb776f183325cf1d8941109f8
Total (sha256): 792996cb7f54cbfd91b5ea9d817546f001f5f8ac05f2d9140fc0778fa60980a2

241664+0 records in
241664+0 records out
```

With dc3dd, you specify hash algorithms using hash= multiple times, as shown here:

```
# dc3dd if=/dev/sde of=image.raw hash=md5 hash=sha1 hash=sha512

dc3dd 7.2.641 started at 2016-05-07 16:02:56 +0200
compiled options:
command line: dc3dd if=/dev/sde of=image.raw hash=md5 hash=sha1 hash=sha512
device size: 15466496 sectors (probed),    7,918,845,952 bytes
sector size: 512 bytes (probed)
  7918845952 bytes ( 7.4 G ) copied ( 100% ),    80 s, 94 M/s
```

```
input results for device `/dev/sde':
   15466496 sectors in
   0 bad sectors replaced by zeros
   ebda11ffb776f183325cf1d8941109f8 (md5)
   62e5045fbf6a07fa77c48f82eddb59dfaf7d4d81 (sha1)
   f0d1132bf569b68d900433aa52bfc08da10a4c45f6b89847f244834ef20bb04f8c35dd625a31c2e3
    a29724e18d9abbf924b16d8f608f0ff0944dcb35e7387b8d (sha512)

output results for file `image.raw':
   15466496 sectors out

dc3dd completed at 2016-05-07 16:04:17 +0200
```

The traditional dd command doesn't support hashing. Instead, you must pipe the image into a separate program during the acquisition process, which you can do by using the Unix tee command:

```
# dd if=/dev/sde | tee image.raw | md5sum
15466496+0 records in
15466496+0 records out
7918845952 bytes (7.9 GB, 7.4 GiB) copied, 108.822 s, 72.8 MB/s
ebda11ffb776f183325cf1d8941109f8  -
```

When dd has no of= specified, the data is sent to stdout where it can be redirected or piped into another program. In this example, it's piped into the Unix tee command, which simultaneously saves the data to a file and sends it to stdout. Then it's piped into an independent hashing tool, md5sum, where it produces the hash. In addition to md5sum, the Linux coreutils software package includes other hashing programs: sha1sum, sha224sum, sha256sum, sha384sum, and sha512sum.

I explain the process of verifying the hashes produced in "Verify the Integrity of a Forensic Image" on page 197.

Hash Windows

When you image an older or damaged disk, block read errors can occur. These errors can happen in random places during the acquisition, and the frequency can increase over time. This creates a challenge when you're preserving the integrity of evidence, because the cryptographic hash might be different each time the disk is read (reacquired, duplicated, verified, and so on).

The solution to this problem is to use hash windows, or piecewise hashing. A hash window is a separate cryptographic hash taken over a smaller sequence of sectors on a disk. For example, a hash window size of 10MB during acquisition will generate a separate hash for every 10MB sequence of sectors and generate a list of hashes for a disk. If one sector becomes unreadable (or is modified for some reason), the hash of that window will be invalid. But all the other hash windows on the disk will maintain their integrity. So even if the hash of the full disk is invalid, if a hash window matches, the integrity of the data found within it will be preserved.

Among the commercial forensic formats, early versions of the Expert Witness Format (EWF) only use cyclic redundancy check (CRC) checksums for individual blocks of data. More recent versions are not open formats, and the ftkimager has no options for creating or viewing hash windows.

To create hash windows with dcfldd, you need to add the hashwindow= parameter to specify the window size. You can save the list of hash windows to a file during acquisition using the hashlog= parameter with a filename. The following example specifies a hash window size of 1MB, and the hashes for each sector range are logged to stdout:

```
# dcfldd if=/dev/sde of=image.raw conv=noerror,sync hashwindow=1M
0 - 1048576: e0796359399e85ecc03b9ca2fae7b9cf
1048576 - 2097152: 5f44a2407d244c24e261b00de65949d7
2097152 - 3145728: d6d8c4ae64b464dc77658730aec34a01
3145728 - 4194304: 0eae942f041ea38d560e26dc3cbfac48
4194304 - 5242880: 382897281f396b70e76b79dd042cfa7f
5242880 - 6291456: 17664a919d533a91df8d26dfb3d84fb9
6291456 - 7340032: ce29d3ca2c459c311eb8c9d08391a446
7340032 - 8388608: cd0ac7cbbd58f768cd949b082de18d55
256 blocks (8Mb) written.8388608 - 9437184: 31ca089fce536aea91d957e070b189d8
9437184 - 10485760: 48586d6dde4c630ebb168b0276bec0e3
10485760 - 11534336: 0969f7533736e7a2ee480d0ca8d9fad1
...
```

Groups of identical disk sectors will have the same hash value. This often occurs when large portions of a disk are zeroes or a repeating pattern.

With dc3dd, hash windows are referred to as *piecewise hashing*, and hashes can be created, not by sector range but per split file. In the following example, the hashes for the sector ranges in each split file are logged:

```
# dc3dd if=/dev/sda hof=image.raw ofs=image.000 ofsz=1G hlog=hash.log hash=md5

dc3dd 7.2.641 started at 2016-05-07 17:10:31 +0200
compiled options:
command line: dc3dd if=/dev/sda hof=image.raw ofs=image.000 ofsz=1G hlog=hash.log
    hash=md5
device size: 15466496 sectors (probed),    7,918,845,952 bytes
sector size: 512 bytes (probed)
  7918845952 bytes ( 7.4 G ) copied ( 100% ),   114 s, 66 M/s
  7918845952 bytes ( 7.4 G ) hashed ( 100% ),    24 s, 314 M/s

input results for device `/dev/sda':
  15466496 sectors in
  0 bad sectors replaced by zeros
  5dfe68597f8ad9f20600a453101f2c57 (md5)
```

```
c250163554581d94958018d8cca61db6, sectors 0 - 2097151
cd573cfaace07e7949bc0c46028904ff, sectors 2097152 - 4194303
83d63636749194bcc7152d9d1f4b9df1, sectors 4194304 - 6291455
da961f072998b8897c4fbed4c0f74e0e, sectors 6291456 - 8388607
4cd5560038faee09da94a0c829f07f7a, sectors 8388608 - 10485759
516ba0bdf8d969fd7e86cd005c992600, sectors 10485760 - 12582911
c19f8c710088b785c3f2ad2fb636cfcd, sectors 12582912 - 14680063
fb2eb5b178839878c1778453805b8bf6, sectors 14680064 - 15466495

output results for file `image.raw':
   15466496 sectors out
   [ok] 5dfe68597f8ad9f20600a453101f2c57 (md5)

output results for files `image.000':
   15466496 sectors out

dc3dd completed at 2016-05-07 17:12:25 +0200
```

If there is only one image file (that is, not split), there are no separate hash windows, just a single hash for the entire image. In the previous
example, eight image files were created, and the MD5 hashes of each file
match those reported during acquisition. This can be easily confirmed with
md5sum as follows:

```
# md5sum image.*
c250163554581d94958018d8cca61db6  image.000
cd573cfaace07e7949bc0c46028904ff  image.001
83d63636749194bcc7152d9d1f4b9df1  image.002
da961f072998b8897c4fbed4c0f74e0e  image.003
4cd5560038faee09da94a0c829f07f7a  image.004
516ba0bdf8d969fd7e86cd005c992600  image.005
c19f8c710088b785c3f2ad2fb636cfcd  image.006
fb2eb5b178839878c1778453805b8bf6  image.007
```

Sign an Image with PGP or S/MIME

The hash value is useful to preserve the integrity of an image over time, but
anyone can take a cryptographic hash of an image at any time. Consider
a disk modified by an unauthorized person who creates a new hash for the
disk image. Unless the original hash was properly secured at the original
time of acquisition, it's difficult to prove which hash (the old or the new) is
the correct one. Cryptographic signing of forensic images binds a person
(or that person's key) to the integrity of the image. The forensic examiner,
a superior, or an external neutral party can sign the image at the time of
acquisition.

This doesn't mean that you need to pass around multiterabyte images for people to sign. It's enough to sign the hash of the drive or the list of hash windows. The best option is to sign the entire output log containing the timestamps, bytes acquired, and all resulting cryptographic hashes.

In the same way an authorized individual signs paper forms with a pen, they can sign digital forms with a digital signature. Unlike pen and paper signatures, digital signatures are difficult to fake (unless the private key is stolen). Two popular standards for signing digital information are *Pretty Good Privacy (PGP)* and *Secure/Multipurpose Internet Mail Extensions (S/MIME)*.

The most common Linux implementation of the OpenPGP standard is GnuPG (GPG).[1] The three different signing methods include a regular binary signature, a clear text signature, and a detached signature. Using a clear text signature is the most beneficial, because it shows the text together with the signature and can be easily embedded into other documents and reports.

In the following example, S. Holmes has performed a forensic acquisition of a disk and signs the log output containing the MD5 hash and other details:

```
$ gpg --clearsign hash.log

You need a passphrase to unlock the secret key for
user: "Sherlock Holmes <holmes@digitalforensics.ch>"
2048-bit RSA key, ID CF87856B, created 2016-01-11

Enter passphrase:
```

The previous command created the *hash.log.asc* file, which contains the contents of the file together with the signature:

```
$ cat hash.log.asc
-----BEGIN PGP SIGNED MESSAGE-----
Hash: SHA1


dc3dd 7.2.641 started at 2016-05-07 17:23:49 +0200
compiled options:
command line: dc3dd if=/dev/sda hof=image.raw ofs=image.000 ofsz=1G hlog=hash.log
   hash=md5

input results for device `/dev/sda':
   5dfe68597f8ad9f20600a453101f2c57 (md5)
      c250163554581d94958018d8cca61db6, sectors 0 - 2097151
      cd573cfaace07e7949bc0c46028904ff, sectors 2097152 - 4194303
      83d63636749194bcc7152d9d1f4b9df1, sectors 4194304 - 6291455
```

---

1. It is assumed the authorized person has installed GnuPG and has securely generated a key pair.

```
        da961f072998b8897c4fbed4c0f74e0e, sectors 6291456 - 8388607
        4cd5560038faee09da94a0c829f07f7a, sectors 8388608 - 10485759
        516ba0bdf8d969fd7e86cd005c992600, sectors 10485760 - 12582911
        c19f8c710088b785c3f2ad2fb636cfcd, sectors 12582912 - 14680063
        fb2eb5b178839878c1778453805b8bf6, sectors 14680064 - 15466495

output results for file `image.raw':
  [ok] 5dfe68597f8ad9f20600a453101f2c57 (md5)

output results for files `image.000':

dc3dd completed at 2016-05-07 17:25:40 +0200

-----BEGIN PGP SIGNATURE-----
Version: GnuPG v1

iQEcBAEBAgAGBQJXLgnoAAoJEEg0vvzPh4VrdeAH/OEhCLFSWwTZDNUrIn++1rI3
XI6KuwES19EKR18PrK/Nhf5MsF3xyy3c/j7tjopkfnDGLYRA615ycWEvIJlevNh7
k7QHJoPTDnyJcF29uuTINPWk2MsBlkNdTTiyA6ab3U4Qm+DMC4wVKpOp/io52qq3
KP7Kh558aw8m+OFroc0/4sF7rer9xvBThA2cw+ZiyF5a8wTCBmavDchCfWm+NREr
RIncJV45nuHrQW8MObPOK6G34mruT9nSQFH1LR1FL830m/W69WHS2JX+shfk5g5X
I6I7jNEn6FgiRyhm+BizoSl5F6mv3ff6mRlVysGDJ+FXE3CiE6ZzK+jNB7Pw+Zg=
=6GrG
-----END PGP SIGNATURE-----
```

This signed text can be verified at a later date by any third party using a copy of Holmes's GPG public key.

Another encryption standard you can use to sign files is S/MIME. The use of S/MIME relies on X.509 certificates from a public key infrastructure (PKI), either privately within an organization or from a public certificate authority (CA). If an authorized person has a personal certificate (typically, the same one they use for signing and encrypting S/MIME email), they can use it to sign files containing acquisition details.

The gpgsm tool is part of GnuPG2 and supports managing X.509 keys, encryption, and signatures using the S/MIME standard. Once the necessary keys have been generated and certificates have been installed, you can use gpgsm to sign files in a similar manner to GPG. The following command produces a signature of a specified file:

```
$ gpgsm -a -r holmes@digitalforensics.ch -o hash.log.pem --sign hash.log
```

The -a flag specifies it should use ASCII armor, a method of encoding binary data in a plaintext format, instead of binary (because it's easier to copy into reports or emails). The -r flag specifies which recipient key to use for signing. In this command example, the email address is used, but the key can also be specified by key ID, fingerprint, or matching components of

X.509 strings. The -o specifies the output file for the signature, and --sign instructs gpgsm to create a signature over the specified *hash.log* file.

When used for signing, gpgsm will create a PEM[2] signature file that looks similar to the following:

```
-----BEGIN SIGNED MESSAGE-----
MIAGCSqGSIb3DQEHAqCAMIACAQExDzANBglghkgBZQMEAgEFADCABgkqhkiG9woB
BwGggCSABIICIApkYzNkZCA3LjIuNjQxIHN0YXJ0ZWQgYXQgMjAxNiOwMS0xMSAy
...
GR2YC4Mx5xQ63Kbxg/5BxT7rlC7DBjHOVMCMJzVPy40VUOXPnL2IdP2dhvkOtojk
UKIjSw40xIIAAAAAAA=
-----END SIGNED MESSAGE-----
```

Once a signature has been created by an authorized party, the hash values and details of the original forensic acquisition cannot be changed. Only the person who created the signature can make changes and sign it again.[3] With these signatures, it's possible to verify the integrity of the acquisition details without involving the person who signed it. I describe the signature verification process in Chapter 7.

You can purchase personal S/MIME certificates similar to SSL certificates for websites. You'll find an overview of CAs who offer personal S/MIME certificates at *https://www.sslshopper.com/email-certificates-smime -certificates.html.* Using a personal S/MIME certificate, you can also sign the acquisition details simply by sending a signed email message containing the contents of the output log.

The examples shown in this section are simple and use GNU Privacy Guard tools. There are other command line tools you can use to perform cryptographic signing. The OpenSSL command line tool provides a rich cryptographic toolkit that includes the ability to sign files using X.509 certificates and S/MIME. OpenSSL is used in the next section to demonstrate cryptographic timestamping.

RFC-3161 Timestamping

Signatures with PGP or S/MIME strongly bind an authorized individual (or multiple individuals) to the integrity of a file containing forensic acquisition results. In some cases, it's also useful to strongly bind the forensic acquisition results to a specific point in time. You can do this by using an independent timestamping service.

Timestamping is a formal standard defined in RFC-3161, which describes the format of a timestamp request and response. OpenSSL can create and send timestamp requests and verify responses. In the following

---

2. PEM was originally defined in the Privacy Enhanced Mail standard, and today it usually refers to the file format used to store X.509 certificates.

3. Multiple signatures from different people can also be used to reduce the risk of stolen keys or malicious changes by one person.

example, an RFC-3161 compliant timestamp request for the acquisition log is created, producing a request file with a *.tsq* extension:

```
$ openssl ts -query -data hash.log -out hash.log.tsq -cert
```

This timestamp request contains a hash of the *hash.log* file, not the actual file. The file is *not* sent to the timestamping server. This is important from an information security perspective. The timestamp service provider is only trusted with timestamp information, not the contents of the files being timestamped.

The generated request can then be sent to a timestamping service using the tsget command included with OpenSSL.[4] The following example uses the FreeTSA service:

```
$ tsget -h https://freetsa.org/tsr hash.log.tsq
```

On some Linux distributions, this script might be missing or broken. You can work around it by manually submitting the timestamp request with the curl command as follows:

```
$ curl -s -H "Content-Type: application/timestamp-query" --data-binary
    "@hash.log.tsq" https://freetsa.org/tsr > hash.log.tsr
```

If the timestamping server accepts the request, it returns an RFC-3161 compliant timestamp. In this example, the timestamp is saved with the *.tsr* file extension to hash.log.tsr. You can view the contents of the timestamp using the OpenSSL ts command:

```
$ openssl ts -reply -in hash.log.tsr -text
Status info:
Status: Granted.
Status description: unspecified
Failure info: unspecified

TST info:
Version: 1
Policy OID: 1.2.3.4.1
Hash Algorithm: sha1
Message data:
    0000 - 63 5a 86 52 01 24 72 43-8e 10 24 bc 24 97 d0 50   cZ.R.$rC..$.$..P
    0010 - 4a 69 ad a9                                       Ji..
Serial number: 0x0AF4
Time stamp: May  7 22:03:49 2016 GMT
Accuracy: 0x01 seconds, 0x01F4 millis, 0x64 micros
Ordering: yes
```

---

4. On some systems, this is a Perl script located in */usr/lib/ssl/misc*.

```
Nonce: 0xBC6F68553A3E5EF5
TSA: DirName:/O=Free TSA/OU=TSA/description=This certificate digitally signs
    documents and time stamp requests made using the freetsa.org online
    services/CN=www.freetsa.org/emailAddress=busilezas@gmail.com/L=Wuerzburg/
    C=DE/ST=Bayern
Extensions:
```

A copy of the *hash.log.tsr* file provides proof that the acquisition results existed at a specific point in time. An independent third party can also verify the validity of the timestamp. I'll demonstrate the validation of timestamps in Chapter 7.

A number of free and commercial timestamping services are available on the internet. Here are a few examples:

- Comodo RFC-3161 Timestamping Service: *http://timestamp.comodoca .com/?td=sha256*

- FreeTSA: *http://freetsa.org/index_en.php*

- Polish CERTUM PCC - General Certification Authority: *http://time .certum.pl/*

- Safe Creative Timestamping Authority (TSA) server: *http://tsa.safecreative .org/*

- StartCom Free RFC-3161 Timestamping Service: *http://tsa.startssl.com/ rfc3161*

- Zeitstempeldienst der DFN-PKI: *http://www.pki.dfn.de/zeitstempeldienst/*

The examples in the last two sections strongly bind an individual and a time to the integrity of an image. Cryptographic tokens such as smartcards or hardware security modules (HSMs) can be used to secure the private keys and guarantee physical possession of the token to sign the image. Cryptographic keys on hard tokens cannot be copied or stolen. Some examples of hard tokens that can be used to make cryptographic signatures include Nitrokey, Yubikey, and GnuPG OpenPGP smartcards.

Manage Drive Failure and Errors

Occasionally, a forensic lab receives a problematic hard disk to analyze. The disk might be old, damaged, or failing. It may have interface errors, platter read errors, head errors, motor resets, and other errors. In some cases, you can still acquire a partial forensic image of the drive. Depending on the disk size, the block size, and the number of unreadable sectors, imaging a bad disk could take several days.

It's important to understand that errors described here refer to the drive hardware. They don't refer to software errors such as corrupt file-systems, destroyed partition tables, and so on.

This section shows examples of different tools and how they handle error conditions. The dmsetup tool is useful for simulating disk errors and testing how forensic tools behave under various failing conditions, and was used in several of the following examples (the disk device is */dev/mapper/errdisk*). An overview of how dc3dd, dcfldd, ewfacquire, and ftkimager manage and report errors is shown in the following section.

Forensic Tool Error Handling

The following example shows the dcfldd tool encountering a disk with two errors. The locations (block offsets) of the errors on a disk are reported to stdout and logged to the specified file, as follows:

```
# dcfldd if=/dev/mapper/errdisk of=errdisk.raw conv=noerror,sync errlog=error.log
...
# cat error.log
dcfldd:/dev/mapper/errdisk: Input/output error
(null)+15 records in
(null)+16 records out
dcfldd:/dev/mapper/errdisk: Input/output error
(null)+29 records in
(null)+32 records out
(null)+62496 records in
(null)+62501 records out
```

Several bugs were encountered when testing dcfldd under Debian Linux. The block size used for padding remained at 4K, even when a 512-byte block size was specified (dd showed the same behavior). On some errors, dcfldd went into an endless loop and had to be manually terminated.

The dc3dd tool provides a very detailed overview of the errors encountered. Errors are sent to stout and saved in the specified log file, as follows:

```
# dc3dd if=/dev/mapper/errdisk of=errdisk.raw log=error.log
...
# cat error.log

dc3dd 7.2.641 started at 2016-01-12 19:42:26 +0100
compiled options:
command line: dc3dd if=/dev/mapper/errdisk of=errdisk.raw log=error.log
device size: 4000000 sectors (probed),    2,048,000,000 bytes
sector size: 512 bytes (probed)
[!!] reading `/dev/mapper/errdisk' at sector 1000 : Input/output error
[!!] 4 occurences while reading `/dev/mapper/errdisk' from sector 2001 to sector 2004
    : Input/output error
  2048000000 bytes ( 1.9 G ) copied ( 100% ), 5.74919 s, 340 M/s

input results for device `/dev/mapper/errdisk':
   4000000 sectors in
   5 bad sectors replaced by zeros
```

```
output results for file `errdisk.raw':
   4000000 sectors out

dc3dd completed at 2016-01-12 19:42:31 +0100
```

The ewfacquire tool offers a default error granularity of 64 sectors, and this can be changed to 1 to reduce the number of sectors padded to zero. In this example, ewfacquire only detected two read errors (similar to dcfldd; it skipped and padded a 4k block without checking the other sectors):

```
# ewfacquire -t errdisk /dev/mapper/errdisk
ewfacquire 20150126

...
The number of bytes per sector (1 <= value <= 4294967295) [512]:
The number of sectors to read at once (16, 32, 64, 128, 256, 512, 1024, 2048, 4096,
    8192, 16384, 32768) [64]:
The number of sectors to be used as error granularity (1 <= value <= 64) [64]: 1
The number of retries when a read error occurs (0 <= value <= 255) [2]: 1
Wipe sectors on read error (mimic EnCase like behavior) (yes, no) [no]: yes
...
Acquiry completed at: Jan 12, 2016 19:57:58

Written: 1.9 GiB (2048000804 bytes) in 14 second(s) with 139 MiB/s (146285771
    bytes/second).
Errors reading device:
        total number: 2
        at sector(s): 1000 - 1008 number: 8 (offset: 0x0007d000 of size: 4096)
        at sector(s): 2000 - 2008 number: 8 (offset: 0x000fa000 of size: 4096)

MD5 hash calculated over data:        4d319b12088b3990bded7834211308eb
ewfacquire: SUCCESS
```

The ftkimager reports errors and logs them. The following example uses an actual physically defective disk (an original first-generation iPod) because the ftkimager didn't work with simulated errors created with dmsetup:

```
# ftkimager /dev/sdg ipod
AccessData FTK Imager v3.1.1 CLI (Aug 24 2012)
Copyright 2006-2012 AccessData Corp., 384 South 400 West, Lindon, UT 84042
All rights reserved.

Creating image...
234.25 / 4775.76 MB (11.71 MB/sec) - 0:06:27 left
Image creation complete.
# cat ipod.001.txt
Case Information:
Acquired using: FTK
...
```

```
ATTENTION:
The following sector(s) on the source drive could not be read:
        491584 through 491591
        491928 through 491935
The contents of these sectors were replaced with zeros in the image.
...
```

Each of the forensic acquisition tools had some error detection, handling, and logging capabilities. However, for disks with a significant number of errors or hardware damage, using more specialized tools might be more appropriate. The next section describes the use of data recovery tools for this purpose.

Data Recovery Tools

Several disk block recovery tools are worth mentioning because of their robust error handling and aggressive recovery methods. Although these tools were not written with forensics in mind, they are useful in situations in which other forensic tools have failed.

The ddrescue tool (by Antonio Diaz Diaz) was designed to recover blocks from damaged disks. Unlike the dd family of tools, it has a multiphase recovery algorithm, and you can run it against a disk multiple times to fill gaps in the image. The algorithm includes reading problematic parts of the disk backward to increase the number of recovered sectors and performing various retry operations over multiple passes.

A completed ddrescue operation results in statistics that describe the recovery success rate:

```
# ddrescue /dev/sda image.raw image.log
rescued:    40968 MB,  errsize:   2895 kB,  current rate:       0 B/s
   ipos:    39026 MB,   errors:      38,  average rate:   563 kB/s
   opos:    39026 MB, run time:   20.18 h,  successful read:    8.04 h ago
Finished
```

The log file that ddrescue produces shows the start and end times and a detailed overview of the disk's problem areas:

```
# Rescue Logfile. Created by GNU ddrescue version 1.19
# Command line: ddrescue /dev/sda image.raw image.log
# Start time:   2015-06-13 22:57:39
# Current time: 2015-06-14 19:09:03
# Finished
# current_pos  current_status
0x9162CAC00     +
#      pos        size  status
0x00000000  0x4F29D000  +
0x4F29D000  0x00002000  -
```

```
0x4F29F000  0x00253000  +
...
```

The dd_rescue tool (note the underscore) was developed by Kurt Garloff in the late 1990s, and although the name contains *dd*, the command syntax is completely different and it doesn't perform data conversion (same with ddrescue). But it does transfer blocks of data similar to dd. Several features make this tool a possible option for use in a digital forensic laboratory. The block size is dynamically changed when disk errors occur, automatically decreasing to a physical block size. After a period without errors, the block size is changed again to improve performance. You can also image the disk backwards, from the end of the disk to the beginning. This technique is useful if the drive has difficulty reading past a certain point on the disk.

The myrescue tool is designed to initially avoid unreadable areas (no retries) and focuses on recovering as much of the readable areas as possible. After the readable sectors are copied, it works on the failed ranges. The tool documentation recommends letting difficult drives rest for a couple of hours between retries.

Another tool called recoverdm also performs data recovery. It is unique in that it can recover data from a damaged disk at the sector level or at an individual file level. The tool has additional features for floppies and optical media.

SMART and Kernel Errors

The SMART information on the disk can provide additional indicators about the health of the drive and the likelihood of a successful recovery. For example:

```
# smartctl -x /dev/sda
smartctl 6.4 2014-10-07 r4002 [x86_64-linux-3.19.0-18-generic] (local build)
Copyright (C) 2002-14, Bruce Allen, Christian Franke, www.smartmontools.org

=== START OF INFORMATION SECTION ===
Model Family:     Maxtor DiamondMax D540X-4K
Device Model:     MAXTOR 4K040H2
Serial Number:    672136472275
Firmware Version: A08.1500
User Capacity:    40,971,571,200 bytes [40.9 GB]
Sector Size:      512 bytes logical/physical
...
Vendor Specific SMART Attributes with Thresholds:
ID# ATTRIBUTE_NAME          FLAGS    VALUE WORST THRESH FAIL RAW_VALUE
  1 Raw_Read_Error_Rate     P--R-K   100   253   020    -    0
  3 Spin_Up_Time            POS--K   087   086   020    -    1678
  4 Start_Stop_Count        -O--CK   078   078   008    -    14628
  5 Reallocated_Sector_Ct   PO--CK   003   001   020    NOW  486
```

```
   7 Seek_Error_Rate           PO-R--  100  100  023   -    0
   9 Power_On_Hours            -O--C-  073  073  001   -    17814
  10 Spin_Retry_Count          -OS--K  100  100  000   -    0
  11 Calibration_Retry_Count   PO--C-  100  080  020   -    0
  12 Power_Cycle_Count         -O--CK  100  100  008   -    294
  13 Read_Soft_Error_Rate      PO-R--  100  100  023   -    0
 194 Temperature_Celsius       -O---K  094  083  042   -    17
 195 Hardware_ECC_Recovered    -O-RC-  100  031  000   -    7137262
 196 Reallocated_Event_Count   ----C-  100  253  020   -    0
 197 Current_Pending_Sector    -O--CK  003  001  020   NOW  486
 198 Offline_Uncorrectable     ----C-  100  253  000   -    0
 199 UDMA_CRC_Error_Count      -O-RC-  199  199  000   -    1
                               ||||||_ K auto-keep
                               |||||__ C event count
                               ||||___ R error rate
                               |||____ S speed/performance
                               ||_____ O updated online
                               |_____ P prefailure warning

Read SMART Log Directory failed: scsi error badly formed scsi parameters

ATA_READ_LOG_EXT (addr=0x00:0x00, page=0, n=1) failed: scsi error aborted command
Read GP Log Directory failed
...
ATA Error Count: 9883 (device log contains only the most recent five errors)
...
Error 9883 occurred at disk power-on lifetime: 17810 hours (742 days + 2 hours)
...
Error 9882 occurred at disk power-on lifetime: 17810 hours (742 days + 2 hours)
...
Error 9881 occurred at disk power-on lifetime: 17810 hours (742 days + 2 hours)
...
```

When performing forensic acquisition, you should note any error and failure messages appearing in dmesg or tool output. In cases where sectors could not be read and zeroed padding has been added, this needs to be recorded (depending on the forensic acquisition tool used, it will be logged).

Other Options for Failed Drives

In this section, I provide a few additional tips and comments to help you acquire problematic disks.

In some cases, a disk might only operate correctly for a few minutes when it's cold before it becomes inaccessible or unstable. If the disk functions properly for a few minutes before failing, you might still be able to make an image over time by repeatedly restarting the recovery. Some of the tools mentioned in "Data Recovery Tools" on page 162 maintain a file that contains the recovery state from the last attempt. A recovery operation can be interrupted and later restarted where it left off.

After attempting to image a drive for a while, let the drive cool down and try again. Sometimes as a drive overheats, the access problems can get worse. Again, the disk recovery tools' restart features are useful in this situation.

If you suspect the drive electronics are faulty and a second identical (meaning the same make, model, and firmware revision) functioning drive is available,[5] you might be able to swap the drive electronics temporarily to recover the data. You don't need to open the disk to perform this action, so the risk of damage (due to dust and so on) is minimal.

Professional data recovery firms have cleanrooms where trained staff can open drives, unstick drive heads, replace actuators, and perform other delicate operations on a drive. Do not attempt these procedures without the proper environment, equipment, and training. Just opening a drive outside of a cleanroom will expose it to dust particles, causing damage to the disk.

Damaged Optical Discs

Most of the tools mentioned earlier should also function on optical media. Some tools have added features or special behavior for optical media.

The ddrescue tool suggests specifying a 2048-byte sector size for optical media. Here's an example of ddrescue in the process of recovering a damaged CD-ROM disc:

```
# ddrescue -b 2048 /dev/cdrom cdrom.raw
GNU ddrescue 1.19
Press Ctrl-C to interrupt
rescued:    15671 kB,  errsize:   3878 kB,  current rate:       0 B/s
   ipos:   408485 kB,  errors:       126,  average rate:   12557 B/s
   opos:   408485 kB,  run time:  20.80 m,  successful read:    31 s ago
Copying non-tried blocks... Pass 2 (backwards)
```

Notice that ddrescue reads the CD-ROM backwards in an attempt to recover blocks.

For optical discs that are partially recoverable but have a corrupt filesystem, you can use carving tools to extract files. A data carver designed for optical discs is the dares carver (*ftp://ftp.heise.de/pub/ct/ctsi/dares.tgz*), which supports various optical disc filesystem formats.

This section has covered the management of drive failure and errors. Drive failure and errors do happen and can result in partial or total data loss. In cases where you experience problems with a drive, be sure you document the nature of the error and, wherever possible, the sector that was impacted.

---

5. In the data recover industry, this is called a *donor drive*.

Image Acquisition over a Network

Imaging a disk over a network can be useful for a number of reasons:

- A disk may be located in a remote location, and it might not be feasible to physically seize and ship the disk to a central forensic lab (possibly due to disruption of business, lack of resources, or other logistical issues).

- A time-critical incident might require a remote drive image as soon as possible without delays due to shipping (depending on network bandwidth, disk size, and shipping times, shipping a disk might still be faster).[6]

- A machine in a local forensic lab may have a disk in a PC that cannot be feasibly physically removed. This could be due to the design of the PC, the lack of tools needed, or the risk of causing damage or destroying evidence.

In general, seizing disks does not scale well in large organizations, and having a broadly deployed enterprise solution for remote disk triage and acquisition is common. EnCase Enterprise is a classic example, with many newer firms bringing similar products to the market.

As with disk imaging, many possibilities exist to perform forensic acquisition over a network. Most solutions involve booting a forensic CD on a remote machine, establishing a network connection, and piping the dd output over the network to a local file. You can do this simply by using a combination of dd and netcat. Secure connections can also be made using ssh or secure netcat alternatives, such as socat and cryptcat.

This section provides several examples that use ssh for a secure network connection. But first, let's start by looking at rdd, which was specifically designed with forensic acquisition in mind.

Remote Forensic Imaging with rdd

Designed for acquiring disk images over a network, the rdd tool was developed by the Netherlands Forensic Institute (NFI). The rdd tool has a number of useful features, including hashing, logging, compression, error handling, file splitting, progress indicators, and statistics. Support for EWF output can be included at compile time. The rdd tool uses a client-server model, where the subject PC (booted from a forensic boot CD) is the client and the examiner PC is the server. You perform an acquisition by starting a listening process on the server (examiner PC) and running the acquisition command on the client.

The rdd tool does not have built-in security; it must be added using a VPN, a secure shell, or the equivalent. When you are using rdd over untrusted or hostile networks, the network traffic needs to be encrypted,

---

6. The quote from Andrew S. Tanenbaum is appropriate here: "Never underestimate the bandwidth of a station wagon full of tapes hurtling down the highway."

and listening TCP ports should not be exposed. You can do this by using a two-step process of establishing a secure network channel and using it for the acquisition.

Without security, the rdd tool is still useful on a trusted network segment in a protected lab setting, when using crossed Ethernet cables, or when connecting two PCs with a FireWire cable. (FireWire interfaces can be used as network interfaces.)

On the examiner's workstation, run the server mode of rdd-copy by specifying -S, as shown in the following example. This needs to be started before the client starts. Make sure no firewalls or iptables packet filtering is blocking TCP port 4832 (the default port).

```
# rdd-copy -S --md5 -l server.log
# cat server.log
2016-01-13 01:34:21 +0100:
2016-01-13 01:34:21 +0100: 2016-01-13 01:34:21 CET
2016-01-13 01:34:21 +0100: rdd version 3.0.4
...
2016-01-13 01:34:21 +0100: rdd-copy -S --md5 -l server.log
2016-01-13 01:34:21 +0100: ========== Parameter settings ==========
2016-01-13 01:34:21 +0100: mode: server
2016-01-13 01:34:21 +0100: verbose: no
2016-01-13 01:34:21 +0100: quiet: no
2016-01-13 01:34:21 +0100: server port: 4832
2016-01-13 01:34:21 +0100: input file: <none>
2016-01-13 01:34:21 +0100: log file: server.log
...
2016-01-13 01:37:05 +0100: === done ***
2016-01-13 01:37:05 +0100: seconds: 147.787
2016-01-13 01:37:05 +0100: bytes written: 7918845952
2016-01-13 01:37:05 +0100: bytes lost: 0
2016-01-13 01:37:05 +0100: read errors: 0
2016-01-13 01:37:05 +0100: zero-block substitutions: 0
2016-01-13 01:37:05 +0100: MD5: a3fa962816227e35f954bb0b5be893ea
...
```

On the remote subject PC, run the client mode of rdd-copy using -C. Specify the input device using -I. The input device can be any locally attached storage device (it was a remote USB stick in this example). The output file, -O, has an additional option to indicate a network destination. The client tells the server which file to use for the acquired image, using the traditional Unix convention of *hostname:/path/to/filename*:

```
# rdd-copy -C --md5 -l client.log -I /dev/sde -O -N lab-pc:/evi/image.raw
# cat client.log
2016-01-13 01:34:37 +0100:
2016-01-13 01:34:37 +0100: 2016-01-13 01:34:37 CET
2016-01-13 01:34:37 +0100: rdd version 3.0.4
```

```
...
2016-01-13 01:34:37 +0100: rdd-copy -C --md5 -l client.log -I /dev/sde -O -N
    lab-pc:/evi/image.raw
2016-01-13 01:34:37 +0100: ========== Parameter settings ==========
2016-01-13 01:34:37 +0100: mode: client
2016-01-13 01:34:37 +0100: verbose: no
2016-01-13 01:34:37 +0100: quiet: no
2016-01-13 01:34:37 +0100: server port: 4832
2016-01-13 01:34:37 +0100: input file: /dev/sde
2016-01-13 01:34:37 +0100: log file: client.log
2016-01-13 01:34:37 +0100: output #0
2016-01-13 01:34:37 +0100:      output file: /evi/image.raw
2016-01-13 01:34:37 +0100:      segment size: 0
2016-01-13 01:34:37 +0100:      output as ewf compression: no ewf
2016-01-13 01:34:37 +0100:      output host: lab-pc
2016-01-13 01:34:37 +0100:      output port: 4832
...
2016-01-13 01:37:05 +0100: === done ***
2016-01-13 01:37:05 +0100: seconds: 147.787
2016-01-13 01:37:05 +0100: bytes written: 7918845952
2016-01-13 01:37:05 +0100: bytes lost: 0
2016-01-13 01:37:05 +0100: read errors: 0
2016-01-13 01:37:05 +0100: zero-block substitutions: 0
2016-01-13 01:37:05 +0100: MD5: a3fa962816227e35f954bb0b5be893ea
...
```

Both client and server specify log files using -l and a hash algorithm that can be verified at the end of the transfer. You can monitor the progress of the client and the server by adding -P 1 to either side (or both).

Secure Remote Imaging with ssh

In situations where rdd is not available, you can perform a basic acquisition using a single ssh command either on the remote PC containing the subject drive or on the examiner PC. The following example shows imaging a disk (a USB stick plugged into the remote PC in this example) over the network using a secure shell session originating from the remote PC:

```
# dd if=/dev/sdb | ssh lab-pc "cat > sandisk-02028302BCA1D848.raw"
7856127+0 records in
7856127+0 records out
4022337024 bytes (4.0 GB) copied, 347.411 s, 11.6 MB/s
```

The dd command is run locally, and the output is piped into the ssh command. Secure shell will pipe this data stream into the cat program on the examiner PC. The output from the cat program is redirected into a file residing on the examiner PC. Upon completion, a raw image will be available to examine with other forensic tools.

You could also acquire the image with secure shell originating from the examiner workstation and connecting to the remote PC with the attached subject disk. The following example demonstrates this from the examiner PC, imaging the same USB again:

```
# ssh remote-pc "dd if=/dev/sdb" > sandisk-02028302BCA1D848.raw
7856127+0 records in
7856127+0 records out
4022337024 bytes (4.0 GB) copied, 343.991 s, 11.7 MB/s
```

Here secure shell is instructed to run the dd command on the remote (subject) machine. The output from the remote dd command becomes the output of the local ssh command and is redirected to a local file. On completion, a raw image file is available for analysis on the examiner's PC.

You can replace the basic dd commands shown in this section with dcfldd, dc3dd, or any of the other acquisition tools that image to stdout. You can use this method to collect other information about a remote (subject) machine. To illustrate, here are some examples of collecting data about a remote PC that has been started with the DEFT Linux boot CD. In this example, hdparm, smartctl, and lshw data are collected and saved on the examiner workstation:

```
# ssh remote-pc "hdparm --dco-identify /dev/sda" > dco.lenovo-W38237SJ.txt
# ssh remote-pc "hdparm -I /dev/sda" > hdparm.lenovo-W38237SJ.txt
# ssh remote-pc "smartctl -x /dev/sda" > smartctl.lenovo-W38237SJ.txt
# ssh remote-pc "lshw" > lshw.lenovo-W38237SJ.txt
```

As in the previous example, ssh executes various commands on the remote machine, and the output is redirected to files on the local (examiner) workstation. The serial number of the disk is included in the filename to ensure an obvious link between the physical disk and the data files collected.

Remote Acquisition to a SquashFS Evidence Container

As demonstrated previously, SquashFS can be used as a forensic evidence container, with sfsimage used to image local disks. The sfsimage script can also image a disk on a remote machine directly into a SquashFS evidence container. Two examples are shown here.

The remote dd output can be piped via ssh into a local sfsimage command, creating a SquashFS forensic evidence container with the raw image:

```
$ ssh root@remote-pc "dd if=/dev/mmcblk0" | sfsimage -i - remote-pc.sfs
Started: 2016-05-08T10:30:34
Sfsimage version: Sfsimage Version 0.8
Sfsimage command: /usr/bin/sfsimage -i -
Current working directory: /home/holmes
Forensic evidence source:
```

```
Destination squashfs container: remote-pc.sfs
Image filename inside container: image.raw
Aquisition command: sudo dc3dd    log=errorlog.txt hlog=hashlog.txt hash=md5
    2>/dev/null | pv -s 0
31116288+0 records inMiB/s] [     <=>      ]
31116288+0 records out
15931539456 bytes (16 GB, 15 GiB) copied, 597.913 s, 26.6 MB/s
14.8GiB 0:09:58 [25.4MiB/s] [  <=>     ]
Completed: 2016-05-08T10:40:32
```

In this example, the remote PC is accessed by the root user (root@remote-pc), and a remote media card (/dev/mmcblk0) is imaged to stdout with a dd command. The stdout stream is transported over the ssh connection to the local sfsimage command where - (stdin) is the input file.

A second method uses the same principle, but with variables for the sfsimage shell script. In the sfsimage config() block or in a separate *sfsimage.conf* file, you can specify variables and configuration settings that control sfsimage behavior. Setting the DD variable to an ssh command will cause mksquashfs to take input from a remote machine via ssh. A config file in the current working directory is shown here:

```
$ cat sfsimage.conf
DD="ssh root@remote-pc \"dd if=/dev/mmcblk0\""
SQSUDO=""
```

The double quotes in the DD variable need to be escaped. The SQSUDO variable is set to an empty string, because no local root privileges are needed. When you run sfsimage with this config file in your local working directory, your configuration settings will override the default sfsimage settings.

It is important to note, that the input file should still be specified as a dash (-), because input is piped to stdin internally by the ssh command in the DD variable. The remote acquisition using sfsimage in this way looks like this:

```
$ sfsimage -i - remote-pc.sfs
Started: 2016-05-08T10:56:30
Sfsimage version: Sfsimage Version 0.8
Sfsimage command: /usr/bin/sfsimage -i -
Current working directory: /home/holmes
Forensic evidence source:
Destination squashfs container: remote-pc.sfs
Image filename inside container: image.raw
Aquisition command:  ssh root@remote-pc "dd if=/dev/mmcblk0" 2>/dev/null | pv -s 0
14.8GiB 0:09:03 [ 28MiB/s] [           <=>          ]
Completed: 2016-05-08T11:05:33
```

I showed this DD configuration example primarily to illustrate the possibility of embedding remote network-imaging commands into sfsimage. The embedding of complex acquisition commands into config files can generally be used to change the operation of the sfsimage script.

Acquire a Remote Disk to EnCase or FTK Format

You can also pipe remote ssh commands into other programs to perform tasks or conversions to other formats. A useful example is to remotely acquire a raw image and convert it to Encase/EWF as it's being written to disk. This example shows a remote PC being remotely imaged to an examiner workstation and saved as *.ewf files:

```
# ssh remote-pc "dd if=/dev/sda" | ewfacquirestream -D 16048539022588504422 -t
    eepc-16048539022588504422
ewfacquirestream 20140608

Using the following acquiry parameters:
Image path and filename:             eepc-16048539022588504422.E01
Case number:                         case_number
Description:                         16048539022588504422
Evidence number:                     evidence_number
Examiner name:                       examiner_name
Notes:                               notes
Media type:                          fixed disk
Is physical:                         yes
EWF file format:                     EnCase 6 (.E01)
Compression method:                  deflate
Compression level:                   none
Acquiry start offset:                0
Number of bytes to acquire:          0 (until end of input)
Evidence segment file size:          1.4 GiB (1572864000 bytes)
Bytes per sector:                    512
Block size:                          64 sectors
Error granularity:                   64 sectors
Retries on read error:               2
Zero sectors on read error:          no

Acquiry started at: Jun 22, 2015 21:22:47
This could take a while.

...
Status: acquired 3.7 GiB (3999301632 bytes)
        in 7 minute(s) and 38 second(s) with 8.3 MiB/s (8732099 bytes/second).

7815024+0 records in
7815024+0 records out
4001292288 bytes (4.0 GB) copied, 451.948 s, 8.9 MB/s
Acquiry completed at: Jun 22, 2015 21:30:25
```

```
Written: 3.7 GiB (4001526432 bytes) in 7 minute(s) and 38 second(s) with 8.3 MiB/s
    (8736957 bytes/second).
MD5 hash calculated over data:         e86d952a68546fbdab55d0b205cd1c6e
ewfacquirestream: SUCCESS
```

In this example, a description of the PC (eepc) and the serial number
(16048539022588504422) are embedded into the filename of the image.
The final output from the dd command is shown on completion, directly
followed by the ewfacquirestream completion message.

You can use EnCase, Sleuth Kit, or any other tool that supports EWF to
forensically analyze the resulting acquired image.

```
# ls -l eepc-16048539022588504422.*
-rw-r----- 1 root root 1572852270 Jun 22 21:30 eepc-16048539022588504422.E01
-rw-r----- 1 root root 1572851461 Jun 22 21:30 eepc-16048539022588504422.E02
-rw-r----- 1 root root  857059301 Jun 22 21:30 eepc-16048539022588504422.E03
```

Using additional flags with ewfacquirestream can provide more case
metadata details, increase the compression, and provide other features. See
the ewfacquirestream(1) manual page for more information.

Live Imaging with Copy-On-Write Snapshots

In general, it doesn't make sense to create a forensic image of a live system
when the disks you need to acquire contain the running OS. Blocks are
constantly changing on a live system. During the time needed to acquire a
sector-by-sector image, the filesystem will change significantly, causing the
imaged filesystem copy to be corrupt and inconsistent.

Sometimes it may not be feasible to boot a system with a forensic boot
CD to remotely acquire an image. On live servers that cannot be shut down,
the same method used to freeze the filesystem for backups might be lever-
aged in some situations. On systems that have Copy-on-Write (CoW) filesystems, you might be able to do a certain amount of forensic imaging if
filesystem snapshots have associated block devices (Logical Volume Manager [LVM] for example). This will provide a consistent snapshot of the
filesystem blocks at a certain point in time. If a CoW filesystem has no associated block device for a snapshot, the files will at least be frozen for a file-level
acquisition.

If the subject system is a cloud-based virtual machine, imaging the live
system over a network might be your only option, unless the cloud provider
can provide snapshot images.

Acquire Removable Media

Removable media are unique in that the drive device can be attached to a
system and operate without any media. Block devices that can be forensically

acquired only become available upon insertion of the media. USB thumb drives can be described as removable devices but not removable media. The medium is not removed from the USB thumb drive unless it is a memory card adapter or card reader.

This section covers basic removable media types, including memory cards, optical discs, and magnetic tapes.

Memory Cards

Most memory cards behave similarly to regular drives. Their storage is represented as a linear sequence of blocks, giving the appearance of a regular drive with sectors that you can access using any tool that operates on block devices.

In Figure 6-1, a Micro SD card is inserted into an SD card adapter, which is inserted into an SD card reader, which is inserted into a PC. Here, several items of removable media are stacked and still appear as a block device that you can image normally.

Figure 6-1: Removable memory card adapters

In this example, all three items were inserted and attached to the acquisition host. The kernel detected them and created a */dev/sdg* block device:

```
# dmesg
...
[65396.394080] usb-storage 3-2:1.0: USB Mass Storage device detected
[65396.394211] scsi host21: usb-storage 3-2:1.0
[65397.392652] scsi 21:0:0:0: Direct-Access     SanDisk  SDDR-113       1.00 PQ:
   0 ANSI: 0
```

```
[65397.393098] sd 21:0:0:0: Attached scsi generic sg5 type 0
[65398.073649] sd 21:0:0:0: [sdf] 3911680 512-byte logical blocks: (2.00 GB/1.87
    GiB)
[65398.074060] sd 21:0:0:0: [sdf] Write Protect is on
...
```

The SD adapter has a write-protect tab enabled, which is visible in the dmesg output.

In this example, the Micro SD card is imaged into a SquashFS evidence container using the sfsimage script:

```
$ sfsimage -i /dev/sdf MicroSD.sfs
Started: 2016-05-08T11:19:35
Sfsimage version: Sfsimage Version 0.8
Sfsimage command: /usr/bin/sfsimage -i /dev/sdf
Current working directory: /home/holmes
Forensic evidence source: if=/dev/sdf
Destination squashfs container: MicroSD.sfs
Image filename inside container: image.raw
Aquisition command: sudo dc3dd if=/dev/sdf log=errorlog.txt hlog=hashlog.txt hash=md5
    2>/dev/null | pv -s 2002780160
1.87GiB 0:02:34 [12.3MiB/s] [=================================================>] 100%
Completed: 2016-05-08T11:22:10
```

After imaging, a memory card can be safely removed from the card reader (assuming it has not been mounted).

Optical Discs

The different types of optical media vary in their physical and chemical properties; however, once you insert them into an attached optical drive, they have more similarities than differences. The three most common discs (DVD, CD-ROM, and Blu-ray) have a 2048-byte sector size and appear as a linear sequence of sectors (similar to a tape, but in a spiral). The primary difference is the density of the data bits (which is abstracted by the device hardware) and the disc capacity.

Imaging data discs is straightforward and similar to imaging hard disks or flash media. An example of an optical disc being imaged with dc3dd is shown here:

```
# dc3dd if=/dev/cdrom of=datacd.raw

dc3dd 7.2.641 started at 2016-01-13 23:04:31 +0100
compiled options:
command line: dc3dd if=/dev/cdrom of=datacd.raw
device size: 331414 sectors (probed),    678,735,872 bytes
sector size: 2048 bytes (probed)
  678735872 bytes ( 647 M ) copied ( 100% ),  142 s, 4.5 M/s
```

```
input results for device `/dev/cdrom':
   331414 sectors in
   0 bad sectors replaced by zeros

output results for file `datacd.raw':
   331414 sectors out

dc3dd completed at 2016-01-13 23:06:53 +0100
```

Using common forensic tools, you can then analyze the *datacd.raw* image file.

The recovery of Compact Disc Digital Audio (CDDA), or music CDs, is different from that of data discs. They contain a set of music tracks that are linear streams of pulse-code modulation (PCM) encoded bits. Unlike with data CDs, there is some tolerance for errors. For this reason, tools have been created to attempt the recovery of CDDA and manage drive issues such as misalignment and frame jitter.[7] Most CDDA tools are simple music CD *rippers* that convert the CD tracks into audio files (reencoded into some other audio format). In this example, cdparanoia performs a raw extraction of the PCM data:

```
# cdparanoia --output-raw --log-summary 1- cdda.raw
cdparanoia III release 10.2 (September 11, 2008)


Ripping from sector        0 (track  1 [0:00.00])
          to sector   251487 (track 15 [4:58.72])

outputting to cdda.raw

 (== PROGRESS == [                              | 251487 00 ] == :^D * ==)

Done.
```

This command rips the entire music CD into a single raw PCM audio image file containing all the audio tracks. You can then import this file into audio analysis software. Because the audio data has not been modified or reencoded, there is no audio quality loss or degradation.

DVD and Blu-ray discs with digital rights management (DRM) and region protection are a challenge to recover. Linux tools and instructions to recover encrypted content exist but have been deliberately left outside the scope of this book.

---

7. cdparanoia was developed when CD drives had more quality issues than today's drives.

Magnetic Tapes

Tapes have essentially disappeared from home environments. But they are still used in small, medium, and enterprise environments for backup and archiving. On rare occasions, you might receive a request to recover data from tapes. In corporate forensic labs for example, old tapes are sometimes found when company departments are reorganizing or moving locations.

Historically, popular tapes used have been 4mm DAT, 8mm Exabyte, and DLT tapes. Today, the most common types used are LTO and 8mm DAT. The maximum native/compressed capacities of these tapes is 160GB/320GB for DAT-320 and 6TB/15TB for LTO-7. Modern LTO drives also support encrypted tapes.

Modern tape drives are attached to host systems using a SAS or Fibre Channel interface. Historically, nearly all tape drives followed the SCSI Stream Command (SSC) standards (SSC-5 is the latest).

Tape technologies use their own concept of "files," which are placed in sequential order on a tape. Typically, a tape file consists of a backup archive created by backup or archiving software. Tape files are not randomly accessible like disk drives and optical discs. Instead, you access them by moving or *spacing* forward or backward to the beginning of a file number and then reading logical blocks until the end of the file.

Tapes have different markers that tell the tape drive information about the position of the head on the tape (see Figure 6-2). The interesting markers to understand here are as follows:

BOT or BOM (Beginning of Tape or Media)   Tells the drive where it can start reading or writing data.

EOF (End of File)   Tells the drive that the end of a tape file has been reached.

EOD (End of Data)   Tells the drive that the end of the written data has been reached (found immediately after the last tape file). This is the logical end of the tape.

PEOT, EOT, or EOM ([Physical] End of Tape or Media)   Tells the drive that the end of the physical tape length has been reached.

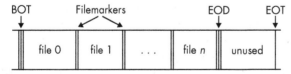

Figure 6-2: Files and markers on a tape

When you're acquiring tapes for forensic purposes, it's essential to copy every file on the tape up to the EOD marker (the last readable file on the tape). It's impossible to read past the EOD on a tape using standard SCSI commands. Some forensic firms offer specialized hardware and services which are able to recover data beyond the EOD.

You can extract files from a tape using dd variants. In the example that follows, three tape files are recovered from a tape. The nonrewinding device for tape access is chosen, typically */dev/nst0* on Linux, to prevent the drive from rewinding before all the files have been copied. The command is run repeatedly, always using the same input device (it takes the next file on the tape), until it reaches "0+0 records in," indicating that all files have been extracted:

```
# dcfldd if=/dev/nst0 of=file0.tape hashlog=hash0.log
0+46 records in
14+1 records out
# dcfldd if=/dev/nst0 of=file1.tape hashlog=hash1.log
22016 blocks (688Mb) written.
0+70736 records in
22105+0 records out
# dcfldd if=/dev/nst0 of=file2.tape hashlog=hash2.log
256 blocks (8Mb) written.
0+1442 records in
450+1 records out
# dcfldd if=/dev/nst0 of=file3.tape hashlog=hash3.log
0+0 records in
0+0 records out
```

After the tape files have been recovered, you can analyze the file type. Often, you can just use a basic file type program to determine which archive or backup format was used. In this example, two *.tar* files and one *.dump* file were extracted:

```
# ls -l
total 722260
-rw-r----- 1 root root     471040 Jan 14 01:46 file0.tape
-rw-r----- 1 root root 724336640 Jan 14 01:46 file1.tape
-rw-r----- 1 root root   14766080 Jan 14 01:47 file2.tape
-rw-r----- 1 root root          0 Jan 14 01:47 file3.tape
-rw-r----- 1 root root         46 Jan 14 01:46 hash0.log
-rw-r----- 1 root root         46 Jan 14 01:46 hash1.log
-rw-r----- 1 root root         46 Jan 14 01:47 hash2.log
-rw-r----- 1 root root         46 Jan 14 01:47 hash3.log
# file *.tape
file0.tape: POSIX tar archive (GNU)
file1.tape: POSIX tar archive (GNU)
file2.tape: new-fs dump file (little endian),  Previous dump Thu Jan 14 01:39:29
    2016, This dump Thu Jan  1 01:00:00 1970, Volume 1, Level zero, type: tape
    header, Label none, Filesystem / (dir etc), Device /dev/sdf1, Host lab-pc,
    Flags 3
file3.tape: empty
```

Each of the *hash*.log* files contains a separate MD5 hash for each tape file extracted. In this example, *file3.tape* is empty and can be ignored.

RAID and Multidisk Systems

The forensic acquisition of Redundant Array of Independent Disks (RAID) systems brings a number of challenges and might require additional steps to complete. Capacity planning is important, because it may involve imaging a large number of disks.

This section assumes the individual disks in a RAID have been imaged separately and exist on the acquisition workstation. The goal here is to assemble the imaged disks and make the meta device layer accessible as a file or block device, allowing you to use forensic analysis tools.

Typically, RAID systems create their own header information at the beginning of a disk (and sometimes at the end of a disk). The header is for unique identifiers (UUIDs), array names, timestamps, RAID configuration details, and other housekeeping information.

Proprietary RAID Acquisition

In situations where a hardware RAID controller was used and no software exists to assemble the RAID offline, you may need to clone the RAID disks and boot an examination system with the controller physically installed.

The examples in this section focus on Linux software RAID, but a number of open source tools are available that can support acquiring and analyzing proprietary RAID systems.

For example, the following packages contain such tools and are available from the Debian software repository:

dpt-i2o-raidutils   Adaptec I2O hardware RAID management utilities

array-info   A command line tool for reporting RAID status for several RAID types

cciss-vol-status   HP SmartArray RAID Volume Status Checker

cpqarrayd   A monitoring tool for HP (Compaq) SmartArray controllers

dpt-i2o-raidutils   Adaptec I2O hardware RAID management utilities

mpt-status   A tool to get RAID status out of mpt (and other) HW RAID controllers

varmon   VA RAID monitor

In addition to these software packages, the dmraid tool is able to identify RAID metadata for a number of proprietary formats. You can find a list of supported formats by using the -l flag, as follows:

```
# dmraid -l
asr    : Adaptec HostRAID ASR (0,1,10)
ddf1   : SNIA DDF1 (0,1,4,5,linear)
```

```
hpt37x  : Highpoint HPT37X (S,0,1,10,01)
hpt45x  : Highpoint HPT45X (S,0,1,10)
isw     : Intel Software RAID (0,1,5,01)
jmicron : JMicron ATARAID (S,0,1)
lsi     : LSI Logic MegaRAID (0,1,10)
nvidia  : NVidia RAID (S,0,1,10,5)
pdc     : Promise FastTrack (S,0,1,10)
sil     : Silicon Image(tm) Medley(tm) (0,1,10)
via     : VIA Software RAID (S,0,1,10)
dos     : DOS partitions on SW RAIDs
```

The dmraid tool uses the same device mapper facility shown in "Manage Drive Failure and Errors" on page 159 (where the dmsetup tool was used to simulate errors). The dmraid(8) manual page provides a number of examples for reassembling various proprietary RAID configurations.[8]

JBOD and RAID-0 Striped Disks

Just a Bunch Of Disks (JBOD) is the term used to indicate that a number of disks have been concatenated into one logical drive (without any RAID configuration for performance or redundancy). To assemble a group of disks into a single JBOD device, you can use the dmsetup command.

When you're building devices from multiple disks, it's useful to have a separate table file to define the device, offsets, and mappings. In this simple text file, you can also include comments with information about the disks.

The following example has a JBOD with three disks of different sizes (a charactaristic of JBOD systems is that any combination of drive sizes can be used). The JBOD device mapper table file (*jbod-table.txt* in this example) defines how they are concatenated. Run the **dmsetup** command with the table file as input to create the device in */dev/mapper*:

```
# cat jbod-table.txt
0        15589376 linear /dev/sdm 0
15589376 15466496 linear /dev/sdn 0
31055872 15728640 linear /dev/sdo 0
# dmsetup create jbod < jbod-table.txt
```

This table defines three mappings that construct the device file, which will appear in */dev/mapper*. Each line defines the offset in the mapper device, the number of sectors to map, the target type (linear), and the target device with an offset (sector zero here, because we want the whole device). Getting the offsets right can be tricky and may require some calculation. Double-check the offsets first if there are problems.

---

8. Heinz Mauelshagen, "dmraid - Device-Mapper RAID Tool: Supporting ATARAID Devices via the Generic Linux Device-Mapper." Paper presented at the Linux Symposium, Ottawa, Ontario, July 20–23, 2005.

The table is piped into the dmsetup create command, specifying the name of the mapper device. After the device is created, you can use regular forensic tools to operate on it. The following example shows the Sleuth Kit fsstat command being used on the newly created device:

```
# fsstat /dev/mapper/jbod
FILE SYSTEM INFORMATION
--------------------------------------------
File System Type: Ext4
Volume Name:
Volume ID: cfd74d32abd105b18043840bfd2743b3
...
```

When you no longer need the mapper device, remove it by using the dmsetup command, as follows:

```
# dmsetup remove /dev/mapper/jbod
```

See the dmsetup(8) manual page for more information about the different device mapper types the dmsetup tool uses. You can use device mappings for encryption, snapshots, RAID systems, and even simulating errors and failing devices (which is useful for testing the behavior of forensic tools).

RAID-0 striped disks are created for performance, not redundancy. A group of disks in a RAID-0 configuration has the combined capacity of all the drives, and disk access is distributed across the array (performance increases as disks are added).

If you know the offsets and chunk size of a striped RAID-0 array, the dmsetup tool can create a mapper device to represent the assembled array.

In the following example, a RAID-0 consisting of two striped disks is attached to the acquisition host. It is known that the subject RAID system has 2048 initial sectors containing metadata and that the chunk size is 128 sectors. You can then assemble the RAID as follows:

```
# dmsetup create striped --table '0 117243904 striped 2 128 /dev/sda 2048 /dev/sdb
    2048'
```

You can analyze this */dev/mapper* device using regular filesystem forensic tools. An example using Sleuth Kit's fls command on the newly created device is shown here:

```
# fls /dev/mapper/striped
r/r 4-128-4:    $AttrDef
r/r 8-128-2:    $BadClus
r/r 8-128-1:    $BadClus:$Bad
```

Don't forget to remove the device when the tasks are completed.

Microsoft Dynamic Disks

Microsoft created the Logical Disk Manager (LDM) to manage logical volumes, and you can use the Linux-based tool ldmtool to analyze Microsoft dynamic disks. The goal here is to make the volume available for block-level access by forensic tools.

In this example, two subject disks with a volume created by Microsoft LDM are attached to the acquisition host. An LDM disk group is identified by its *Globally Unique Identifier (GUID)*. You can scan the disks for the disk group GUID, which will lead to more information about the disk group when the ldmtool show command is used:

```
# ldmtool scan /dev/sda /dev/sdb
[
  "04729fd9-bac0-11e5-ae3c-c03fd5eafb47"
]
# ldmtool show diskgroup 04729fd9-bac0-11e5-ae3c-c03fd5eafb47
{
  "name" : "LENNY-Dg0",
  "guid" : "04729fd9-bac0-11e5-ae3c-c03fd5eafb47",
  "volumes" : [
    "Volume1"
  ],
  "disks" : [
    "Disk1",
    "Disk2"
  ]
}
```

The show command provides the disk group name and GUID, the volume names, and the names of disks. This is enough information to create a mapper device.

Knowing the GUID and the volume name, you can create a volume device:

```
# ldmtool create volume 04729fd9-bac0-11e5-ae3c-c03fd5eafb47 Volume1
[
  "ldm_vol_LENNY-Dg0_Volume1"
]
```

This creates a device in */dev/mapper* that corresponds to the filesystem on the dynamic disk (this is equivalent to a partition device like */dev/sda1*). Then you can use regular forensic analysis tools to operate on this device. An example using the Sleuth Kit fsstat command is shown as follows:

```
# fsstat /dev/mapper/ldm_vol_LENNY-Dg0_Volume1
FILE SYSTEM INFORMATION
--------------------------------------------
File System Type: NTFS
```

```
Volume Serial Number: 0CD28FC0D28FAD10
OEM Name: NTFS
Version: Windows XP

METADATA INFORMATION
--------------------------------------------
First Cluster of MFT: 786432
First Cluster of MFT Mirror: 2
Size of MFT Entries: 1024 bytes
Size of Index Records: 4096 bytes
...
```

When you no longer need the device, remove it using the `dmsetup` command, as shown in "JBOD and RAID-0 Striped Disks" on page 179.

RAID-1 Mirrored Disks

Mirrored disks are simple and consist of two identical disks (or should be if they were synchronized). Image both disks into separate image files. Depending on the mirroring software or hardware, a header might be in the beginning sectors of the disk that you need to skip when you're performing analysis work.

The following example shows mirrored disks containing an EXT4 partition. The mirroring software (Linux Software RAID) used the first 32,768 sectors, and the mirrored filesystem starts at that offset on the physical disks and without an offset for the multiple device,[9] md0:

```
# fsstat /dev/md0
FILE SYSTEM INFORMATION
--------------------------------------------
File System Type: Ext4
Volume Name:
Volume ID: f45d47511e6a2db2db4a5e9778c60685
...
# fsstat -o 32768 /dev/sde
FILE SYSTEM INFORMATION
--------------------------------------------
File System Type: Ext4
Volume Name:
Volume ID: f45d47511e6a2db2db4a5e9778c60685
...
# fsstat -o 32768 /dev/sdg
FILE SYSTEM INFORMATION
--------------------------------------------
```

---

9. The Linux md driver orginally meant *mirror device*, and some OSes call them *meta devices*.

```
File System Type: Ext4
Volume Name:
Volume ID: f45d47511e6a2db2db4a5e9778c60685
```

In this example, the same filesystem on md0 is also found at the 32k off-set of the two physical devices (sde and sdg). The cryptographic checksums of mirrored disks will probably not match each other, because the RAID header information might be different (unique disk UUIDs and so on) and the disks might not be perfectly synchronized.

Linux RAID-5

If multiple disks are part of a Linux RAID array, you can acquire them individually and then assemble them using several methods. The dmsetup tool provides an interface to mdadm using tables. The mdadm tool can operate on devices that have been mapped or looped. In the following example, three acquired drive images from a Linux MD RAID-5 setup are used.

An mmls analysis of the individual partition tables reveals a Linux RAID partition at sector 2048 of each disk image (*sda.raw*, *sdb.raw*, and *sdc.raw*). This sector offset is converted (using Bash math expansion) to a byte offset for the losetup command:

```
# mmls sda.raw
DOS Partition Table
Offset Sector: 0
Units are in 512-byte sectors

      Slot    Start         End           Length        Description
00:   Meta    0000000000    0000000000    0000000001    Primary Table (#0)
01:   -----   0000000000    0000002047    0000002048    Unallocated
02:   00:00   0000002048    0312580095    0312578048    Linux RAID (0xfd)
03:   -----   0312580096    0312581807    0000001712    Unallocated
# echo $((2048*512))
1048576
```

A read-only loop device is created for each of the disks in the array using the calculated byte offset (2048 sectors, which is 1048576 bytes):

```
# losetup --read-only --find --show -o 1048576 sda.raw
/dev/loop0
# losetup --read-only --find --show -o 1048576 sdb.raw
/dev/loop1
# losetup --read-only --find --show -o 1048576 sdc.raw
/dev/loop2
```

The preceding commands create loop devices corresponding to the three acquired image files. You can assemble an array using mdadm, as follows:

```
# mdadm -A --readonly /dev/md0 /dev/loop0 /dev/loop1 /dev/loop2
mdadm: /dev/md0 has been started with 3 drives.
```

Now you can access and analyze the RAID meta disk device using regular forensic tools on the */dev/md0* device. An example using Sleuth Kit's fsstat command is shown here:

```
# fsstat /dev/md0
FILE SYSTEM INFORMATION
-------------------------------------------
File System Type: Ext4
Volume Name:
Volume ID: 37b9d96d8ba240b446894383764412
...
```

You can also mount the newly created device and access it using regular file tools. The normal Linux mount command can be used as follows:

```
# mkdir mnt
# mount /dev/md0 mnt
mount: /dev/md0 is write-protected, mounting read-only
```

When you've completed the analysis, reverse the steps for the cleanup process, including using the stop command with the mdadm system:

```
# umount mnt
# rmdir mnt
# mdadm --stop /dev/md0
# losetup -d /dev/loop2
# losetup -d /dev/loop1
# losetup -d /dev/loop0
```

Depending on the system configuration, the Linux kernel may automatically attempt to reassemble attached RAID devices if they're detected, possibly starting a rebuild operation that could destroy evidence. It's important to use write blocking with live devices and ensure that read-only loop devices and arrays are created.

Many of the techniques described in this chapter apply to loop devices mapping to image files. More examples of creating and using loop devices are shown in Chapter 8.

Closing Thoughts

In this chapter, I covered the main topic of the book—forensic acquisition. You learned how to use the different dd-based tools, create images with forensic formats, and use SquashFS as a forensic evidence container. Various aspects of evidence preservation using cryptography were shown, including hashing, hash windows, signing, and timestamping. You now have a deeper understanding of error management and recovery when imaging problematic media. You are able to image over a network and image removable media and multi-disk (RAID) systems. This is the core of the forensic acquisition process.

7

FORENSIC IMAGE MANAGEMENT

This chapter covers various aspects of managing forensic image files after acquisition. Disk images are enormous compared to typical files on a disk, and moving, copying, and converting large image files can be cumbersome and time-consuming. You'll learn a number of techniques for managing large image files to help overcome various challenges. These techniques include compressing and splitting images for easier handling, securing images with encryption, and converting images between formats. In addition, I describe procedures for read-only mounting of an image for safe local browsing and demonstrate forensic cloning (or disk duplication). I also discuss the secure, reliable storage and network transfer of large image files. The chapter ends with a description of secure wiping and disposal of images and files. I'll begin with the topic of managing image compression.

Manage Image Compression

Raw disk images are always the same size as the total number of sectors they contain. The number of files or amount of data on the drive is irrelevant and does not affect the size of an uncompressed raw image. With the current widespread use of multiterabyte disks, maneuvering images within time and disk capacity constraints can be a challenge. Even simply copying an image can take many hours to complete. You can reduce this problem somewhat by keeping images compressed.

Compressing images in a forensic context involves sector-by-sector compression of the entire drive (as opposed to compressing each file on the disk). Disks with many gigabytes or terabytes of space that have never been written to over the life of the drive will compress better, because much of the drive still consists of untouched sectors filled with zeros. Well-used disks won't compress as well if most sectors on the drive have been allocated over the lifetime of the drive and still contain residual data. Disk images with large numbers of audio and video files will compress poorly as well, because these files are already compressed with their own algorithms.

It's important to choose the most appropriate and efficient compression tool and technique. Some tools might have file size limitations, either for the original source file or the compressed destination file. Other tools may be inefficient or use temporary files during compression, causing memory exhaustion or creating disk space issues. To solve some of these problems when you're performing compression activity, you can use piping and redirection.

One of the most useful features of working with a compressed forensic image is the ability to use forensic tools against it without having to uncompress the entire image. But this is problematic with some compression tools, because they're not able to seek within a compressed file. *Seeking* allows a program to randomly access any point in a file. Forensic formats are designed to allow analysis programs on-the-fly, random access to compressed images. The popular forensic formats all support image compression, which usually occurs during acquisition, although not all tools compress by default.

Standard Linux Compression Tools

Commonly used compression tools in the open source world today are zip, gzip, and bzip (version 1 or 2). The examples in this section use gzip, but you can use other compression tools as well. To attempt better compression at the expense of time and CPU cycles, you can adjust the level of compression.

Given enough disk space, you can simply compress a disk image file in place, like this:

```
$ gzip image.raw
```

This command creates the file *image.raw.gz* and deletes the original file on completion. Enough space needs to be available for the compressed and uncompressed files to coexist during the compression process. The same applies for uncompressing files using gunzip.

You can also compress images on the fly during acquisition using piping and redirection. For example:

```
# dcfldd if=/dev/sde | gzip > image.raw.gz
```

Here the input file is a raw disk device. Not specifying an output file for dcfldd sends the image data stream to stdout, which is piped into gzip, which is finally redirected into a compressed file.

The compressed file can be uncompressed to a raw image file, where you can use forensic tools to directly operate on it. Alternatively, you can pipe an uncompressed stream into some programs using stdout and stdin. For example:

```
$ zcat image.raw.gz | sha256sum
1b52ab6c1ff8f292ca88404acfc9f576ff9db3c1bbeb73e50697a4f3bbf42dd0  -
```

Here zcat uncompresses the image and pipes it into a program to produce a sha256 cryptographic hash. It's worth noting that the gzip file format contains additional metadata, such as a creation timestamp, original filename, and other information. The hash of a gzip container (*image.raw.gz*) will be different each time it's created, even though the hash of the compressed file inside will be the same.

EnCase EWF Compressed Format

The ewfacquire tool provides flags to control compression during the acquisition process. For example:

```
# ewfacquire -c bzip2:best -f encase7-v2 /dev/sdj
ewfacquire 20150126
...
EWF file format:                  EnCase 7 (.Ex01)
Compression method:               bzip2
Compression level:                best
...
MD5 hash calculated over data:    9749f1561dacd9ae85ac0e08f4e4272e
ewfacquire: SUCCESS
```

In this example, the -c flag can specify a compression algorithm together with a compression level. Here, the algorithm was bzip2 configured with the best possible compression level. Because only EWFv2 formats support bzip2, the format version encase7-v2 was specified as a parameter. Note that ewftools needs to be compiled with bzip2 support.[1]

---

1. As of this writing, the most recent version of ewfacquire had bzip2 support temporarily disabled (see section 20160404 in the *ChangeLog* file of the libewf software package).

FTK SMART Compressed Format

The command line ftkimager tool supports compressed images during acquisition, as the following example shows:

```
# ftkimager --compress 9 --s01 /dev/sdj image
AccessData FTK Imager v3.1.1 CLI (Aug 24 2012)
Copyright 2006-2012 AccessData Corp., 384 South 400 West, Lindon, UT 84042
All rights reserved.


Creating image...
Image creation complete.
```

Here the --s01 flag specifies the creation of a SMART ew-compressed image, and the --compress flag sets the highest compression level. You can use the --help flag to get more information about compression options for ftkimager.

AFFlib Built-In Compression

Although AFFv3 has been deprecated (*http://forensicswiki.org/wiki/AFF*) and the use of aimage is discouraged (*http://forensicswiki.org/wiki/Aimage*), aimage's use of AFFv3 compression is mentioned here for illustration purposes.

The following example demonstrates imaging a disk using aimage and specifying the LZMA compression algorithm (rather than the zlib default):

```
# aimage --lzma_compress --compression=9 /dev/sdj image.aff
im->outfile=image.aff
image.aff***************************** IMAGING REPORT *****************************
Input: /dev/sdj
  Model: Nano  S/N: 07A40C03C895171A
  Output file: image.aff
  Bytes read: 2,003,828,736
  Bytes written: 628,991,770

raw image md5:   9749 F156 1DAC D9AE 85AC 0E08 F4E4 272E
raw image sha1: 9871 0FB5 531E F390 2ED0 47A7 5BE4 747E 6BC1 BDB0
raw image sha256: 85B7 6D38 D60A 91F6 A0B6 9F65 B2C5 3BD9 F7E7 D944 639C 6F40 B3C4
     0B06 83D8 A7E5
Free space remaining on capture drive:  527,524 MB
```

The Sleuth Kit forensics software provides integrated support for AFFlib compressed images. AFFv4 introduces the aff4imager tool, which adds additional features. This can be fournd at *https://github.com/google/aff4/*.

SquashFS Compressed Evidence Containers

Recall that using SquashFS as a forensic evidence container was described in Chapter 6. When you're creating a SquashFS file, you can tune several compression parameters. Three compression algorithms (gzip, lzo, xz) are available, various metadata from SquashFS can be compressed (inode table, extended attributes), and other tweaks can be made as well. See the squashfs(1) manual page for more information.

In this example, a raw image file was converted to a compressed SquashFS file:

```
# mksquashfs image.raw image.sfs -comp lzo -noI
Parallel mksquashfs: Using 8 processors
Creating 4.0 filesystem on image.sfs, block size 131072.
...
Exportable Squashfs 4.0 filesystem, lzo compressed, data block size 131072
        compressed data, uncompressed metadata, compressed fragments, compressed
    xattrs
        duplicates are removed
Filesystem size 615435.77 Kbytes (601.01 Mbytes)
        31.45% of uncompressed filesystem size (1956923.96 Kbytes)
Inode table size 61232 bytes (59.80 Kbytes)
        100.00% of uncompressed inode table size (61232 bytes)
Directory table size 31 bytes (0.03 Kbytes)
        100.00% of uncompressed directory table size (31 bytes)
...
```

Here, the -comp flag sets the compression algorithm to lzo (gzip is the default), and the -noI flag prevents compression of the inodes (of the SquashFS container, not the evidence image).

The sfsimage shell script manages the creation of SquashFS forensic evidence containers with a few added forensic features.

The use of compression is fundamental when you're working with large forensic images. However, even compressed images can still be very large to manage. There is another method that makes this process easier: you can split forensic images into multiple smaller pieces.

Manage Split Images

Managing acquired disk images can be problematic due to their large file sizes. Breaking an image into smaller, easier-to-handle pieces can help solve this problem. Consider the following examples in which a split image can be beneficial:

- Network transfers over unstable connections can be done with multiple smaller downloads using split images.

- A large image might exceed the maximum file size for a software tool. Splitting the image offers a workaround.

- Storage media, such as tapes, CDs, or DVDs, have a fixed maximum capacity. Split images allow you to use a set of these media.

- Some filesystems (notably FAT) have a relatively small maximum file size.

The most common use of split images in digital forensics is for the transfer and storage of evidence. Historically, this has been done by burning the image to a set of CDs or DVDs.

The GNU split Command

Standard Unix and Linux systems have the split tool for breaking a large file into several smaller files. The following example uses the split command to break an existing image into DVD-sized chunks:

```
$ split -d -b 4G image.raw image.raw.
$ ls
image.raw.00  image.raw.01  image.raw.02  image.raw.03  image.raw.04
...
```

The -d flag specifies that a numeric extension should be added to *image.raw.* (note the trailing dot); the -b flag specifies the size of the chunks made from the *image.raw* file.

Using a combination of piping between several tools, you can combine compressing and splitting during acquisition to save time and space. Here's an example of a single command acquiring an image with dd, compressing it with gzip, and splitting it into CD-sized chunks:

```
# dd if=/dev/sdb | gzip | split -d -b 640m - image.raw.gz.
```

The split command's input file is -, which specifies stdin, and it splits the compressed byte stream into pieces. It's important to note that the parts are not individually gzipped and cannot be individually uncompressed. The split parts must be reassembled before they can be uncompressed.

Split Images During Acquisition

You can split an imaged hard disk into parts during the acquisition process rather than in a separate step at a later date. Before acquiring a large disk, consider whether you might need a split image in the future and what fragment size would make the most sense. Starting with the right split image could save you time and disk space during an investigation.

Split images are common in digital forensics and therefore are well supported by forensic acquisition and analysis tools. Typically, flags can set the fragment size and customize the extension of a split image.

The dcfldd tool provides built-in splitting functionality. For example, if you'll later transfer an image to a third party via a set of 16GB USB sticks, you can use dcfldd to acquire an image using the `split=16G` flag before the output file:

```
# dcfldd if=/dev/sdc split=16G of=image.raw
# ls
image.raw.000  image.raw.001  image.raw.002  image.raw.003  image.raw.004
...
```

The default extension is a three-digit number appended to the output filename.

Using the dc3dd tool, you can split images during acquisition by specifying the output size with `ofsz=`. The file extensions are numerical, as shown here:

```
# dc3dd if=/dev/sdh ofsz=640M ofs=image.raw.000
# ls -l
total 7733284
-rw-r----- 1 root root 671088640 Jan 14 10:59 image.raw.000
-rw-r----- 1 root root 671088640 Jan 14 10:59 image.raw.001
-rw-r----- 1 root root 671088640 Jan 14 10:59 image.raw.002
...
-rw-r----- 1 root root 671088640 Jan 14 11:00 image.raw.009
-rw-r----- 1 root root 671088640 Jan 14 11:00 image.raw.010
-rw-r----- 1 root root 536870912 Jan 14 11:00 image.raw.011
```

Be sure the file extension has enough zeros, or else dc3dd will fail to complete and generate an error message, such as `[!!] file extensions exhausted for image.raw.0`. The last file in the set will usually be smaller than the others (unless the image size is perfectly divisible by the split file size).

EnCase tools typically default to splitting images during acquisition. You can acquire a disk to a split EnCase image using ewfacquire by specifying a maximum segment file size using the `-S` flag:

```
# ewfacquire -S 2G /dev/sdc
...
# ls
image.E01  image.E02  image.E03  image.E04  image.E05  image.E06
...
```

The commercial EnCase forensic suite can then use these images directly.

The ftkimager tool provides the `--frag` flag to save an image into parts during acquisition, as shown in this example:

```
# ftkimager /dev/sdk image --frag 20GB --s01
AccessData FTK Imager v3.1.1 CLI (Aug 24 2012)
Copyright 2006-2012 AccessData Corp., 384 South 400 West, Lindon, UT 84042
All rights reserved.
...
```

```
# ls -l
total 53771524
-rw-r----- 1 holmes root 2147442006 Jul  2 08:01 image.s01
-rw-r----- 1 holmes root       1038 Jul  2 08:43 image.s01.txt
-rw-r----- 1 holmes root 2147412323 Jul  2 08:01 image.s02
-rw-r----- 1 holmes root 2147423595 Jul  2 08:02 image.s03
-rw-r----- 1 holmes root 2147420805 Jul  2 08:02 image.s04
...
```

Here the disk is acquired with a maximum fragment size set at 20GB, and the format is a SMART compressed image. Notice the addition of the *.txt* file containing the metadata. Unlike some forensic formats, this is not embedded into FTK split files created by ftkimager.

Access a Set of Split Image Files

Forensic tools, such as Sleuth Kit, provide support for operating directly on a set of split images without needing to reassemble them first. To list the supported images in Sleuth Kit, use the -i list flag with any Sleuth Kit image-processing tool:

```
$ mmls -i list
Supported image format types:
        raw (Single raw file (dd))
        aff (Advanced Forensic Format)
        afd (AFF Multiple File)
        afm (AFF with external metadata)
        afflib (All AFFLIB image formats (including beta ones))
        ewf (Expert Witness format (encase))
        split (Split raw files)
```

In this example, there is support for split raw images (including Unix split files), split AFF images, and split EnCase files (though this is not explicitly stated, split EnCase files are supported). Some of these image format types might need to be explicitly included when compiling the Sleuth Kit software.

In the following example, an EWF image is split into 54 pieces. Running the img_stat command on the first file provides information about the complete set of files:

```
$ img_stat image.E01
IMAGE FILE INFORMATION
--------------------------------------------
Image Type:            ewf

Size of data in bytes: 121332826112
MD5 hash of data:      ce85c1dffc2807a205f49355f4f5a029
```

Using various tools, you can operate on split images directly. Most Sleuth Kit commands will work with a set of split raw files when you specify the first file of the split image type.

Recent versions of Sleuth Kit will automatically check for sets of split files:

```
$ mmls image.raw.000
```

Earlier versions of Sleuth Kit may require that you specify a split image type:

```
$ fls -o 63 -i split image.000 image.001 image.002
```

To check whether a set of split files is recognized, the img_stat command will show the total bytes recognized, and for raw types, the byte offset ranges for each piece:

```
$ img_stat image.raw.000
IMAGE FILE INFORMATION
--------------------------------------------
Image Type: raw

Size in bytes: 2003828736


--------------------------------------------
Split Information:
image.raw.000   (0 to 16777215)
image.raw.001   (16777216 to 33554431)
image.raw.002   (33554432 to 50331647)
image.raw.003   (50331648 to 67108863)
image.raw.004   (67108864 to 83886079)
...
```

An alternative method for determining whether split files are supported is to run the command or tool with strace -e open and see if it opens each of the split file pieces.

Splitting files and working with a set of split files are useful, but sometimes you need to reassemble them into a single image. This is shown in the next section.

Reassemble a Split Image

Reassembling split forensic formats is generally not needed, because tools that are compatible with a particular forensic format (EWF, SMART, or AFF) should support split files.

Because no header or meta information is contained in a raw image, reassembly is simply a matter of concatenating the set of image fragments into a single image. Doing this carefully should be a two-step process, as shown here:

```
$ ls -1 image.raw.*
image.raw.000
image.raw.001
image.raw.002
image.raw.003
...
$ cat image.raw.* > image.raw
```

The ls -1 flag will list the files recognized by the shell-globbing pattern. Be sure to confirm that this is a complete and ordered list before using it to concatenate the files into a single image. If split pieces are missing or the file order is wrong, the assembled parts will not create the correct forensic image.

If you've received a stack of DVDs, each containing a fragment of a compressed raw image, you can reassemble them as follows:

```
$ cat /dvd/image.raw.gz.00 > image.raw.gz
$ cat /dvd/image.raw.gz.01 >> image.raw.gz
$ cat /dvd/image.raw.gz.02 >> image.raw.gz
$ cat /dvd/image.raw.gz.03 >> image.raw.gz
...
```

Here, DVDs are repeatedly inserted and mounted on /dvd, and split parts are added until the image file is restored. Note that > in the initial cat command creates the image file, and >> in the subsequent commands appends the data (not overwriting it). After all parts have been appended to the destination file, the cryptographic hash of the uncompressed image should match the one taken during acquisition.

You can also uncompress and assemble a set of split files from a compressed image by piping all the split files into zcat and redirecting the output to a file:

```
# cat image.raw.gz.* | zcat > image.raw
```

A useful method provided by AFFlib allows for the *virtual reassembly* of a set of fragments using a FUSE filesystem. The affuse tool can present a set of split files as a fully assembled raw image file, as follows:

```
# ls
image.raw.000  image.raw.011  image.raw.022  image.raw.033  image.raw.044
image.raw.001  image.raw.012  image.raw.023  image.raw.034  image.raw.045
...
#
```

```
# affuse image.raw.000 /mnt
# ls -l /mnt
total 0
-r--r--r-- 1 root root 8011120640 1970-01-01 01:00 image.raw.000.raw
```

Here, a directory full of raw files is represented as a single disk image file and is found in the */mnt* virtual filesystem. You can directly operate on this raw file using forensic tools.

Verify the Integrity of a Forensic Image

Verifying the cryptographic hash of an image is fundamental to performing digital forensics, and it's the basis of preserving digital evidence. This section provides examples of verifying an image's cryptographic hashes and signatures.

Verifying the preservation of evidence involves confirming that a current cryptographic hash of an image is identical to a hash taken at an earlier point in time. You can use hashing to verify a successful operation on a disk or image (acquisition, conversion, transfer, backup, and so on). You can also use it to verify that a disk or image file has not been tampered with over a longer period of time (months or even years).

The requirements for hashing (procedures and algorithms) depend on the legal jurisdiction where they are used and on the organizational policies governing a forensic lab. Thus, no hashing recommendations are provided here.

Verify the Hash Taken During Acquisition

After acquiring a disk, if you need to validate the acquisition hash, it's a simple (but possibly time-consuming) task of piping the contents of the disk into a cryptographic hashing program. Using a different program to validate a disk's hash provides an independent verification at the tool level. For example:

```
# img_stat image.E01
IMAGE FILE INFORMATION
--------------------------------------------
Image Type:           ewf

Size of data in bytes: 2003828736
MD5 hash of data:      9749f1561dacd9ae85ac0e08f4e4272e
# dd if=/dev/sdj | md5sum
3913728+0 records in
3913728+0 records out
9749f1561dacd9ae85ac0e08f4e4272e  -
2003828736 bytes (2.0 GB) copied, 126.639 s, 15.8 MB/s
```

Here, the img_stat output indicates the MD5 acquisition hash recorded by an EnCase imaging tool. A second tool, regular dd, is then used to recalculate the hash from the raw disk device. In this example, the two MD5 hashes match, confirming that the evidence integrity has been preserved.

Recalculate the Hash of a Forensic Image

Each of the forensic formats and the dd-based forensic tools can record or log a hash value of a disk image. To validate the recorded hash, you can recalculate the disk image's hash. In the following example, the hash was recorded during acquisition with dc3dd and stored in the *hashlog.txt*. The hash can be verified as follows:

```
# grep "(md5)" hashlog.txt
    5dfe68597f8ad9f20600a453101f2c57 (md5)
# md5sum image.raw
5dfe68597f8ad9f20600a453101f2c57  image.raw
```

The hashes match, confirming that the evidence file and the hash log are consistent and thus indicating that the evidence integrity has been preserved.

The following example validates the image stored in the metadata of the EnCase format. In this example, a dedicated tool, ewfverify, is used to validate the hash:

```
# ewfverify image.Ex01
ewfverify 20160424

Verify started at: May 14, 2016 14:47:32
This could take a while.
...
MD5 hash stored in file:          5dfe68597f8ad9f20600a453101f2c57
MD5 hash calculated over data:    5dfe68597f8ad9f20600a453101f2c57

ewfverify: SUCCESS
```

Here, the recalculated hash matches, confirming the consistency of the EWF image file. This tool will automatically validate the hash of a set of split files in the EnCase forensic format.

The affinfo tool performs similar validity checking for AFF files. In this example, the SHA1 hash is validated:

```
$ affinfo -S image.aff
image.aff is a AFF file
...
Validating SHA1 hash codes.
computed sha1: 9871 0FB5 531E F390 2ED0 47A7 5BE4 747E 6BC1 BDB0
   stored sha1: 9871 0FB5 531E F390 2ED0 47A7 5BE4 747E 6BC1 BDB0    MATCH
```

This output confirms that the hash of the image contained inside the AFF file is the same as the hash recorded in the AFF metadata.

Cryptographic Hashes of Split Raw Images

Calculating the cryptographic hash of a set of raw split files is straightforward, and you can do this by piping the concatenated parts into a hashing program. This example calculates the sha256 hash of a set of split raw files:

```
$ cat image.raw.* | sha256sum
12ef4b26e01eb306d732a314753fd86de099b02105ba534d1b365a232c2fd36a  -
```

This example assumes the filenames of the parts can be sorted in the correct order (can be verified in this example with ls -1 image.raw.*). The cat command is necessary here, as it is concatenating (assembling) all of the pieces before they are piped into sha256sum.

You can verify the cryptographic hash of an image that has been compressed and split into pieces by forming a command pipeline of several programs. In the following example, cat assembles the image and pipes it into zcat for uncompression. The output of zcat is sent to the hashing program, which produces a hash value upon completion:

```
$ cat image.raw.gz.* | zcat | md5sum
9749f1561dacd9ae85ac0e08f4e4272e  -
```

Here, the cat command is necessary because it is concatenating all the split pieces before passing to zcat. Using zcat image.raw.gz.* will fail because it will try to uncompress each piece rather than the assembled image.

In the Unix community, *useless use of cat (UUOC)* describes using the cat command to send a file to command when < could be used instead. Traditional Unix communities have given out UUOC awards to encourage more efficient use of shell command redirection. However, the examples in this section do need cat because they perform a concatenation function.

Identify Mismatched Hash Windows

As disks age, or as they are transported and handled, there's a risk of damage, possibly introducing bad sectors. If an original evidence disk produces unreadable sector errors since it was first imaged, the cryptographic checksum for the disk will fail to match. Hash windows become valuable in this case, because you can use them to identify more precisely which part of the disk failed to match. More important, hash windows can show which areas of a disk are still preserved, even though the hash for the entire disk has failed to match.

The specified size of a hash window determines how often a new hash is written during the acquisition of a disk or when you're verifying disk hash windows. When you're comparing two lists of hashes for verification, both lists must use the same size of hash window. To find the mismatching areas, you can compare the two hash logs using the Unix diff tool.

In the following example, a disk was imaged with dcfldd and a hash log with a 10M hash window size was saved. A subsequent verification failed to match the MD5 for the entire disk and provided a new hash log, also with a 10M hash window size:

```
$ diff hash1.log hash2.log
3c3
< 20971520 - 31457280: b587779d76eac5711e92334922f5649e
---
> 20971520 - 31457280: cf6453e4453210a3fd8383ff8ad1511d
193c193
< Total (md5): 9749f1561dacd9ae85ac0e08f4e4272e
---
> Total (md5): fde1aa944dd8027c7b874a400a56dde1
```

This output reveals mismatched hashes for the full image and also for the range of bytes between 20971520 and 31457280. Dividing by the 512-byte sector size identifies the sector range between 40960 and 61440 where the hash mismatch occurred. The hashes on the rest of the disk are still good; only the sectors with mismatched hashes have not been forensically preserved. Content (blocks, files, portions of files, and so on) residing on a hash-mismatched sector range can be excluded from the presented evidence at a later stage. If two cryptographic hashes of a full image are a match, you can assume that all the hash windows also match.

The cryptographic hashes of forensic images preserve the integrity of collected evidence. However, the hash values themselves are not protected against malicious or accidental modification. Confirming the integrity of the calculated hashes can be preserved using cryptographic signing and time-stamping. Confirming the validity of signatures and timestamps is shown in the next section.

Verify Signature and Timestamp

The previous chapter demonstrated the use of GnuPG to sign a disk's hashes. You can verify the signature without having the signing private key. The original person who signed the evidence is not needed; only their public key is needed. This example verifies the gpg signature of the person who signed the acquired disk image:

```
$ gpg < hash.log.asc

dc3dd 7.2.641 started at 2016-05-07 17:23:49 +0200
compiled options:
command line: dc3dd if=/dev/sda hof=image.raw ofs=image.000 ofsz=1G hlog=hash.log
    hash=md5
```

```
input results for device `/dev/sda':
    5dfe68597f8ad9f20600a453101f2c57 (md5)
...
dc3dd completed at 2016-05-07 17:25:40 +0200

gpg: Signature made Sat 07 May 2016 17:29:44 CEST using RSA key ID CF87856B
gpg: Good signature from "Sherlock Holmes <holmes@digitalforensics.ch>"
```

Here, the contents of the signed message (the acquisition output and hash) are displayed together with a gpg message indicating that the signature is valid.

For S/MIME signed messages, a similar command will validate (or invalidate) the signature from a PEM file and looks like this:

```
$ gpgsm --verify image.log.pem
gpgsm: Signature made 2016-01-25 19:49:42 using certificate ID 0xFFFFFFFFABCD1234
...
gpgsm: Good signature from "/CN=holmes@digitalforensics.ch/EMail=holmes@
    digitalforensics.ch"
gpgsm:                      aka "holmes@digitalforensics.ch"
```

Chapter 6 discussed using timestamping services to generate RFC-3161 timestamps from a timestamp authority. Validating a timestamp is similar to validating a signature with S/MIME and requires the correct chain of certificate authority (CA) certificates to be installed for verification to be successful. This example verifies the previous timestamp created with FreeTSA (*http://freetsa.org/*).

If the timestamping service's CA certificate is not installed on your system, it can be manually fetched. The TSA certificate should have been returned as part of the timestamp when the request was made (because of the -cert flag). For this example, the CA cert is fetched from FreeTSA as follows:

```
$ curl http://freetsa.org/files/cacert.pem > cacert.pem
```

Assuming CA and TSA certificates are available to OpenSSL and valid, you can validate the timestamp as follows:

```
$ openssl ts -verify -in hash.log.tsr -queryfile hash.log.tsq -CAfile cacert.pem
Verification: OK
```

The openssl ts command is used to verify the timestamp. The timestamp query (tsq) and timestamp reponse (tsr) are provided, and in this example, the file containing the timestamp server's CA certificate is specified. The third-party timestamp is valid (Verification: OK), indicating that the file (and the forensic acquisition hashes it contains) has not been modified since the specified time. If a particular timestamp authority is expected to be used permanently, you can add the CA certificates to the OS's trusted CA store.

AFFlib also has provisions for signing and validating signatures for acquired images using X.509 certificates.

This section did not discuss the web-of-trust or the public key infrastructure (PKI) needed to trust the keys being used to sign images and verify timestamps. The examples assume this trust is already established.

Convert Between Image Formats

Converting between forensic image formats can be advantageous for various reasons. If a lab has new software or infrastructure and the current format is unsupported or less efficient, converting to another format could be an option. If you'll be transferring an image to a third party, they might have a preferred image format. If you are receiving an image from a third party, you might want to convert it to your preferred format. This section provides examples of converting between formats on the command line. Conversion from a few source formats is shown, including EnCase, FTK, AFF, and raw images. In addition, the examples demonstrate converting various formats into SquashFS evidence containers.

When you're converting between image formats, it's preferable to use pipes and redirection. Avoid tools that use temporary files. During the conversion process, two copies of an image might coexist (one or both might be compressed). To prepare for the conversion process, do some capacity planning.

After conversion, check the hash values from the original image and the destination to ensure a match.

Convert from Raw Images

Converting a raw image to another format is usually straightforward, because you can use regular disk-imaging functionality. Instead of a raw device name, the filename of the raw image is used.

The following examples show a raw image file being converted into EnCase and FTK formats. The first example uses ewfacquire to convert *image.raw* to EnCase Expert Witness format:

```
$ ewfacquire image.raw -t image -f encase7
ewfacquire 20160424

Storage media information:
Type:                            RAW image
Media size:                      7.9 GB (7918845952 bytes)
Bytes per sector:                512

Acquiry parameters required, please provide the necessary input
Case number: 42
```

```
Description: The case of the missing red stapler
Evidence number: 1
Examiner name: S. Holmes
Notes: This red USB stick was found at the scene
...
Acquiry completed at: May 14, 2016 15:03:40

Written: 7.3 GiB (7918846140 bytes) in 54 second(s) with 139 MiB/s
    (146645298 bytes/second)
MD5 hash calculated over data:        5dfe68597f8ad9f20600a453101f2c57
ewfacquire: SUCCESS
```

Here, the specified source file is the raw image; -t is the base name of
the EnCase target *.e01* files. EnCase version 7 was specified, and when the
command is executed, a series of questions is asked. Because the raw file has
no case metadata, you need to enter it manually.

Converting from a raw image to FTK SMART is similar: you specify
the raw image as a source and manually add the case metadata. Using
ftkimage, you specify the case metadata on the command line, as shown
in this example:

```
$ ftkimager image.raw image --s01 --case-number 1 --evidence-number 1 --description
    "The case of the missing red stapler" --examiner "S. Holmes" --notes "This USB
    stick was found at the scene"
AccessData FTK Imager v3.1.1 CLI (Aug 24 2012)
Copyright 2006-2012 AccessData Corp., 384 South 400 West, Lindon, UT 84042
All rights reserved.

Creating image...
Image creation complete.
```

The --s01 flag specifies that a SMART compressed image will be created.
The base filename is specified simply as image, and appropriate file extensions will be automatically added.

Converting an image to a SquashFS forensic evidence container is also
just a simple command if you use the sfsimage script, like this:

```
$ sfsimage -i image.raw image.sfs
Started: 2016-05-14T15:14:13
Sfsimage version: Sfsimage Version 0.8
Sfsimage command: /usr/bin/sfsimage -i image.raw
Current working directory: /exam
Forensic evidence source: if=/exam/image.raw
Destination squashfs container: image.sfs
Image filename inside container: image.raw
Aquisition command: sudo dc3dd if=/exam/image.raw log=errorlog.txt hlog=hashlog.txt
    hash=md5 2>/dev/null | pv -s 7918845952
```

```
7.38GiB 0:00:22 [ 339MiB/s] [===================================>] 100%
Completed: 2016-05-14T15:14:37
```

Here, the raw image file was specified together with the destination SquashFS container filename. The sfsimage script builds the required SquashFS pseudo device and adds the log and hash information as regular text files. You can append additional case metadata to the evidence container manually (with sfsimage -a).

You can't directly access a gzip compressed raw image using typical forensic tools because of the inability to seek (randomly access any block within the file) within a gzip file. It's best to convert such files into compressed formats that are seekable. Then you can operate on them directly using forensic analysis tools. In this example, a gzipped raw image file is converted into a SquashFS compressed file using sfsimage:

```
$ zcat image.raw.gz | sfsimage -i - image.sfs
Started: 2016-05-14T15:20:39
Sfsimage version: Sfsimage Version 0.8
Sfsimage command: /usr/bin/sfsimage -i -
Current working directory: /exam
Forensic evidence source:
Destination squashfs container: image.sfs
Image filename inside container: image.raw
Aquisition command: sudo dc3dd    log=errorlog.txt hlog=hashlog.txt hash=md5
    2>/dev/null | pv -s 0
7.38GiB 0:00:38 [ 195MiB/s] [      <=>                              ]
Completed: 2016-05-14T15:21:18
```

The original file remains in raw form, but it's now inside a compressed filesystem. You can mount the resulting *.sfs file to access the raw image, as shown here:

```
$ sfsimage -m image.sfs
image.sfs.d mount created
$ ls image.sfs.d/
errorlog.txt  hashlog.txt  image.raw  sfsimagelog.txt
```

You can convert a raw image file into an AFF file by using a simple affconvert command:

```
$ affconvert image.raw
convert image.raw --> image.aff
Converting page 119 of 119
md5: 9749f1561dacd9ae85ac0e08f4e4272e
sha1: 98710fb5531ef3902ed047a75be4747e6bc1bdb0
bytes converted: 2003828736
Total pages: 120  (117 compressed)
Conversion finished.
```

Then you can add the case metadata with a separate tool, such as affsegment. The affconvert tool provides sensible defaults for compression, and the resulting file has the *.aff* extension with the basename of the raw file.

The following and final example shows the conversion of a raw image inside a SquashFS forensic evidence container to an AFF file using the affconvert command:

```
# affconvert -Oaff image.sfs.d/image.raw
convert image.sfs.d/image.raw --> aff/image.aff
Converting page 953 of 953
md5: d469842a3233cc4e7d4e77fd81e21035
sha1: 9ad205b1c7889d0e4ccc9185efce2c4b9a1a8ec6
bytes converted: 16001269760
Total pages: 954  (954 compressed)
Conversion finished.
```

Because SquashFS is read-only, you need to tell affconvert to write the output file to a different directory that is writable.

Convert from EnCase/E01 Format

The libewf package contains the ewfexport tool for converting EnCase EWF (*.E0*) files to other formats. This includes the ability to read one or more files and pipe them into other programs.

NOTE   *There is a bug in some older versions of ewfexport that appends the line* ewfexport: SUCCESS *to the end of an image after an export to stdout. This added string will cause a mismatch in the image MD5 hashes. The string is a fixed length of 19 bytes, so you can suppress it by piping it through* tail -c 19.

Manual Creation of a SquashFS Container

Throughout the book, you've seen examples of the sfsimage shell script. But it's useful to see one example of creating a SquashFS file without the script. This next example will make it easier to understand how sfsimage works internally.

The following EnCase acquisition contains 54 *.E0* files that will be assembled into a single raw image and placed into a SquashFS evidence container:

```
# ls
image.E01  image.E10  image.E19  image.E28  image.E37  image.E46
image.E02  image.E11  image.E20  image.E29  image.E38  image.E47
image.E03  image.E12  image.E21  image.E30  image.E39  image.E48
image.E04  image.E13  image.E22  image.E31  image.E40  image.E49
image.E05  image.E14  image.E23  image.E32  image.E41  image.E50
image.E06  image.E15  image.E24  image.E33  image.E42  image.E51
```

```
image.E07   image.E16   image.E25   image.E34   image.E43   image.E52
image.E08   image.E17   image.E26   image.E35   image.E44   image.E53
image.E09   image.E18   image.E27   image.E36   image.E45   image.E54
```

To begin, you need a mksquashfs pseudo definition file to define the commands that will create files inside the SquashFS container. The pseudo definition file contains the target filename, file type, permissions, ownership, and command to be executed. The output of that command will become the contents of the defined filename inside the SquashFS filesystem.

In the following example, a file named *pseudo_files.txt* has been created that contains two definitions. The first extracts the EnCase metadata with ewfinfo and places it into *image.txt* (this metadata would otherwise be lost). The second definition exports a raw image from the **.E0* files into *image.raw*:

```
# cat pseudo_files.txt
image.txt f 444 root root ewfinfo image.E01
image.raw f 444 root root ewfexport -u -t - image.E01
```

The ewfexport flag -u allows the conversion to execute unattended (otherwise it prompts the user with questions). The -t flag specifies the target, which in this example is stdout or the dash -.

With this definition file, you can create the compressed filesystem containing the generated files as follows:

```
# mksquashfs pseudo_files.txt image.sfs -pf pseudo_files.txt
Parallel mksquashfs: Using 12 processors
Creating 4.0 filesystem on image.sfs, block size 131072.
ewfexport 20160424


Export started at: May 12, 2016 19:09:42
This could take a while.
...
Export completed at: May 12, 2016 19:28:56

Written: 113 GiB (121332826112 bytes) in 19 minute(s) and 14 second(s) with
    100 MiB/s (105141097 bytes/second)
MD5 hash calculated over data:        083e2131d0a59a9e3b59d48dbc451591
ewfexport: SUCCESS
...
Filesystem size 62068754.40 Kbytes (60614.02 Mbytes)
        52.38% of uncompressed filesystem size (118492706.13 Kbytes)
...
```

The resulting SquashFS filesystem *image.sfs* will contain three files: the raw image file *image.raw*, *image.txt* containing the metadata, and the *pseudo_files.txt* file containing the definitions with the executed commands.

The mksquashfs(1) manual page has more information about the flags and options for creating SquashFS file systems.

You can view the contents of a SquashFS file with the unsquashfs command as follows:

```
# unsquashfs -lls image.sfs
...
-r--r--r-- root/root       121332826112 2016-05-12 19:09 squashfs-root/image.raw
-r--r--r-- root/root                770 2016-05-12 19:09 squashfs-root/image.txt
-rw-r----- root/root                 98 2016-05-12 16:58 squashfs-root/
    pseudo_files.txt
```

The final step is to verify the preservation of evidence by comparing MD5 hash values. The ewfinfo command provides the MD5 hash calculated during the original EnCase acquisition. A second MD5 checksum can be calculated with md5sum on the newly converted raw image inside the SquashFS container. To do this, you need to mount the SquashFS filesystem first. The following example shows each of these steps:

```
# ewfinfo image.E01
ewfinfo 20160424
...
Digest hash information
        MD5:                    083e2131d0a59a9e3b59d48dbc451591

# mkdir image.sfs.d; mount image.sfs image.sfs.d
# md5sum image.sfs.d/image.raw
083e2131d0a59a9e3b59d48dbc451591  image.sfs.d/image.raw
```

The result shows that the two MD5 hashes match, indicating a successfully preserved evidence conversion from EnCase to a raw image inside a SquashFS container. A third matching MD5 hash can be seen in the ewfexport output that was calculated during the conversion process. The ewfexport tool can also convert, or export, to other EnCase formats.

When the mounted SquashFS filesystem *image.sfs.d* is no longer needed, it can be unmounted with umount image.sfs.d. The sfsimage script manages these steps for you.

Convert Files from EnCase to FTK

The ftkimager tool can convert from EnCase to FTK. In this example, a set of EnCase *.e01* files are converted to SMART ew-compressed files with the same name but with the *.s01* extension:

```
# ftkimager image.E01 image --s01
AccessData FTK Imager v3.1.1 CLI (Aug 24 2012)
Copyright 2006-2012 AccessData Corp., 384 South 400 West, Lindon, UT 84042
All rights reserved.
```

```
Creating image...
Image creation complete.
```

Hashes are checked and added to the new FTK file. The original case metadata is not added to the newly converted files. Instead, it's extracted from the original format and saved as a separate file with the same name but with a *.txt* extension (*image.s01.txt* in this example).

Convert from FTK Format

The command line ftkimager tool converts between EnCase and FTK formats, and it allows you to use stdin and stdout for conversion with raw image files.

In the following example, a set of compressed FTK SMART *.s01* files are converted to the EnCase EWF *E01 format:

```
# ftkimager image.s01 image --e01
AccessData FTK Imager v3.1.1 CLI (Aug 24 2012)
Copyright 2006-2012 AccessData Corp., 384 South 400 West, Lindon, UT 84042
All rights reserved.

Creating image...
Image creation complete.
```

The case metadata is not transferred to the new format but is automatically saved to a separate file (*image.E01.txt*).

The ftkimager can convert SMART *.s01* files to stdout, where you can redirect them to raw image files or pipe them into other programs. In the following example, a set of FTK SMART files are converted into a SquashFS forensic evidence container using ftkimager output piped into sfsimage:

```
# ftkimager sandisk.s01 - | sfsimage -i - sandisk.sfs
Started: 2016-05-12T19:59:13
Sfsimage version: Sfsimage Version 0.8
Sfsimage command: /usr/bin/sfsimage -i -
Current working directory: /exam
Forensic evidence source:
Destination squashfs container: sandisk.sfs
Image filename inside container: image.raw
Aquisition command: sudo dc3dd    log=errorlog.txt hlog=hashlog.txt hash=md5
    2>/dev/null | pv -s 0
AccessData FTK Imager v3.1.1 CLI (Aug 24 2012)
Copyright 2006-2012 AccessData Corp., 384 South 400 West, Lindon, UT 84042
All rights reserved.

14.5GiB 0:01:37 [ 151MiB/s] [    <=>      ]
Completed: 2016-05-12T20:00:51
```

```
# sfsimage -a sandisk.s01.txt sandisk.sfs
Appending to existing 4.0 filesystem on sandisk.sfs, block size 131072
```

When you're converting from an FTK format into a raw disk image, the case metadata is not transferred. You need to manually save the case metadata, which is usually found in a separate text file. You can add this to the SquashFS container as shown in the previous example with the `sfsimage -a` command.

After performing a format conversion of any kind, you should verify the hash value separately on the destination format to ensure the evidence integrity has been preserved.

Convert from AFF Format

The affconvert tool can convert AFF images to a raw image (and from a raw image to the AFF format). The affconvert tool does not use stdin or stdout; instead, it reads or creates stand-alone files. The following simple example shows converting an AFF file to a raw image:

```
$ affconvert -r image.aff
convert image.aff --> image.raw
Converting page 96 of 96
bytes converted: 1625702400
Conversion finished.
```

To convert a raw image to an AFF format, simply use `affconvert` image.raw, and the corresponding *image.aff* file will be created.

To use piping and redirection with AFF files, you can use the affcat tool. The previous example can be also be done with `affcat` and redirected to a file (without any status or completion information, which is useful for scripts) as follows:

```
$ affcat image.aff > image.raw
```

To convert an AFF image to EnCase or FTK, the affcat tool can pipe an image via stdout or stdin into the appropriate tool, creating a new image in the desired format. For example, you can convert from AFF to a compressed FTK SMART image like this:

```
$ affcat image.aff | ftkimager - image --s01
AccessData FTK Imager v3.1.1 CLI (Aug 24 2012)
Copyright 2006-2012 AccessData Corp., 384 South 400 West, Lindon, UT 84042
All rights reserved.

Creating image...
Image creation complete.
```

Here, the - represents the stdin file descriptor receiving the raw image data, image is the base filename, and the final flag --s01 specifies the compressed format.

Similarly, you can convert to various EnCase formats using efwacquire-stream. For example:

```
$ affcat image.aff | ewfacquirestream -C 42 -E 1 -e "S. Holmes" -D "Data theft
    case" image
ewfacquirestream 20160424

Using the following acquiry parameters:
Image path and filename:          image.E01
Case number:                      42
Description:                      Data theft case
Evidence number:                  1
Examiner name:                    S. Holmes
...
Acquiry completed at: May 14, 2016 15:41:42

Written: 1.8 GiB (2003934492 bytes) in 10 second(s) with 191 MiB/s (200393449
    bytes/second)
MD5 hash calculated over data:         9749f1561dacd9ae85ac0e08f4e4272e
ewfacquirestream: SUCCESS
```

In the previous AFF conversion examples, the case metadata (case name, examiner name, acquisition times, hashes, and so on) is not preserved in the conversion from AFF to other formats. But you can export this information using affinfo and then add or save it manually to the destination format. Depending on the tool, you can also include metadata as command line flags as seen in the previous example with -C 42 -E 1 -e "S. Holmes" -D "Data theft case".

This final example demonstrates converting an AFF file to a compressed SquashFS forensic evidence container using sfsimage:

```
$ affcat image.aff | sfsimage -i - image.sfs
Started: 2016-05-14T15:47:19
Sfsimage version: Sfsimage Version 0.8
Sfsimage command: /usr/bin/sfsimage -i -
Current working directory: /exam
Forensic evidence source:
Destination squashfs container: image.sfs
Image filename inside container: image.raw
Aquisition command: sudo dc3dd    log=errorlog.txt hlog=hashlog.txt hash=md5
    2>/dev/null | pv -s 0
1.87GiB 0:00:06 [ 276MiB/s] [          <=>          ]
Completed: 2016-05-14T15:47:26
```

You can extract the metadata from AFF files using affinfo and then add it to the SquashFS forensic evidence container as follows:

```
$ affinfo image.aff > affinfo.txt
$ sfsimage -a affinfo.txt image.sfs
Appending to existing 4.0 filesystem on image.sfs, block size 131072
```

Once the image is converted, compare the hash values of the original image and the destination to ensure a match.

Secure an Image with Encryption

An important but often neglected component of digital forensics is information security. You should consider the information you acquire and extract during an investigation as sensitive and adequately protect its security.

The loss of data confidentiality may have undesired consequences. For example, it may violate organizational policy requirements, jeopardize legal and regulatory compliance, raise victim privacy issues, and do damage to the reputation of the investigating organization. Failing to adequately protect acquired evidence could result in damage to any of the parties involved, including the investigators and their employer, the victim, the defendant, and other participating parties. Leaked information could also interfere with or compromise an ongoing investigation.

This section focuses on methods for ensuring that information is protected, in particular, maintaining security during data transfer and storage (both long- and short-term storage). Adding security to images increases the complexity and the time needed to encrypt and then later decrypt the images, but the examples you'll see here attempt to keep this process as simple and efficient as possible. Basic symmetric encryption is used instead of more complex PKI or web-of-trust systems.

In addition to the methods shown in this section, the ZIP archive format could be used for encryption. Newer versions with the ZIP64 extensions support file sizes larger than 4GB. ZIP has the advantage of high compatability with other platforms such as Windows.

GPG Encryption

Using symmetric encryption, you can easily encrypt disk images for protection during network transfer or storage. GNU Privacy Guard (GPG) encryption provides a free implementation of the OpenPGP standard defined by RFC-4880. It's an alternative to the traditional PGP encryption created by Phil Zimmerman in the early 1990s.

It's useful to start the agent when you're using GPG. (The agent is started automatically when using gpg2.) This is typically done at login with the following command:

```
$ eval $(gpg-agent --daemon)
```

For all the examples that follow, the -v flag is used to increase verbosity. This makes the output more useful for documentation purposes (both in this book and for creating formal forensic reports describing the steps taken).

Using GPG to encrypt an existing image is very simple, as shown here:

```
$ gpg -cv image.raw
gpg: using cipher AES
gpg: writing to `image.raw.gpg'
Enter passphrase:
```

A passphrase is requested, and the image is encrypted with the default symmetric encryption algorithm, creating a new file with the extension *.gpg*. The size of the image is smaller because GPG compresses as it encrypts. This can be seen here:

```
$ ls -lh
total 1.2G
-r--r----- 1 holmes holmes 1.9G May 14 15:56 image.raw
-rw-r----- 1 holmes holmes 603M May 14 15:57 image.raw.gpg
```

The previous example showed encrypting a file in place. But you can also encrypt on the fly during acquisition:

```
$ sudo dcfldd if=/dev/sde | gpg -cv > image.raw.gpg
Enter passphrase:
gpg: using cipher AES
gpg: writing to stdout
241664 blocks (7552Mb) written.
241664+0 records in
241664+0 records out
```

Here, dcfldd acquires the attached disk via */dev/sde* and pipes it directly into the GPG program. The encrypted output of GPG is then redirected to a file. The sudo command escalates privileges to root in order to read the raw device.

Decrypting a GPG-encrypted image is just as simple as encrypting one. The only differences are the use of the decryption flag and the requirement to specify an output file (by default, it outputs to stdout). In the following example, a GPG-encrypted image file is decrypted to a regular (unprotected) file:

```
$ gpg -dv -o image.raw image.raw.gpg
gpg: AES encrypted data
Enter passphrase:
gpg: encrypted with 1 passphrase
gpg: original file name='image.raw'
```

This example demonstrates symmetric encryption without signing. You can also use GPG public and private keys to encrypt, decrypt, and sign images. The integrity is verified by comparing the hash of the GPG-encrypted image with the hash of the raw image file, as follows:

```
$ gpg -dv image.raw.gpg | md5sum
gpg: AES encrypted data
Enter passphrase:
gpg: encrypted with 1 passphrase
gpg: original file name='image.raw'
5dfe68597f8ad9f20600a453101f2c57  -
$ md5sum image.raw
5dfe68597f8ad9f20600a453101f2c57  image.raw
```

When you're decrypting an image, you need to do some capacity planning. After decryption, two copies of the image will exist (one or both will be compressed).

A GPG-encrypted file is not seekable, so you cannot operate on its contents directly with forensic analysis tools.

OpenSSL Encryption

Other cryptographic systems can also provide security for disk images. The OpenSSL toolkit (*http://www.openssl.org/*) provides a number of algorithms you can use to encrypt files. For example, to password encrypt an image with 256-bit AES using cipher block chaining mode, use this command:

```
# openssl enc -aes-256-cbc -in image.raw -out image.raw.aes
enter aes-256-cbc encryption password:
Verifying - enter aes-256-cbc encryption password:
```

OpenSSL is flexible regarding cipher types and modes, providing dozens of choices. Also supported are piping and redirection, and you can easily perform encryption during acquisition, for example:

```
# dcfldd if=/dev/sdg | openssl enc -aes-256-cbc > image.raw.aes
enter aes-256-cbc encryption password:
Verifying - enter aes-256-cbc encryption password:
241664 blocks (7552Mb) written.
241664+0 records in
241664+0 records out
```

Decrypting an OpenSSL-encrypted file is also relatively straightforward, provided you know the encryption algorithm, as shown here:

```
# openssl enc -d -aes-256-cbc -in image.raw.aes -out image.raw
enter aes-256-cbc decryption password:
```

The addition of the -d flag signifies this is a decryption operation (enc specifies that symmetric ciphers are being used). Because OpenSSL doesn't provide an automatic method to detect which symmetric encryption was used, it's important to document how the file was encrypted.

Unless specifically compiled with zlib, OpenSSL doesn't compress files. To add compression on the fly during an acquisition, add gzip to the pipeline, like this:

```
# dcfldd if=/dev/sdg | gzip | openssl enc -aes-256-cbc > image.raw.gz.aes
enter aes-256-cbc encryption password:
Verifying - enter aes-256-cbc encryption password:
241664 blocks (7552Mb) written.
241664+0 records in
241664+0 records out
```

To verify the cryptographic hash of the image, you can run a similar command pipe, as follows:

```
$ openssl enc -d -aes-256-cbc < image.raw.gz.aes | gunzip | md5sum
enter aes-256-cbc decryption password:
4f9f576113d981ad420bbc9c251bea0c  -
```

Here, the decryption command takes the compressed and encrypted file as input and pipes the decrypted output to gunzip, which outputs the raw image to the hashing program.

Some implementations of ZIP also support built-in encryption and can be used to secure images and other evidence files.

Forensic Format Built-In Encryption

GPG and OpenSSL are well-known tools for performing various encryption tasks, providing compatibility and interoperability with other tools. However, they're not designed for digital forensics, and encrypted image files cannot be used directly by standard forensic tools (they must be decrypted first). Some versions of the popular forensic formats discussed throughout this book support randomly accessible encrypted images.

The ftkimager program can protect image files using a password or a certificate. An example of encrypting with a password (*monkey99*) during acquisition is shown here:

```
# ftkimager --outpass monkey99 --e01  /dev/sdg image
AccessData FTK Imager v3.1.1 CLI (Aug 24 2012)
Copyright 2006-2012 AccessData Corp., 384 South 400 West, Lindon, UT 84042
All rights reserved.

Creating image...
Image creation complete.
```

NOTE *Including a password in command parameters is generally bad practice. The password is visible in the shell history, and anyone can view the password in the process table.*

Attempting to access an encrypted image without a password, or with the incorrect password, will generate the following error messages:

```
** Source is encrypted; please provide credentials for decryption.
** AD Decryption setup failed.
```

Operating on an encrypted image requires including the password on the command line, as follows:

```
# ftkimager --inpass monkey99 image.E01 - > image.raw
AccessData FTK Imager v3.1.1 CLI (Aug 24 2012)
Copyright 2006-2012 AccessData Corp., 384 South 400 West, Lindon, UT 84042
All rights reserved.
```

Some versions of the EWF format support encryption, and as of this writing, libewf support was at various stages of development. Refer to the latest source code for current encrypted-format support.

The AFFlib suite allows you to directly access encrypted images via the Advanced Forensics Format (AFF) library. From the start, AFFlib was developed with information security in mind. It has a number of encryption possibilities for protecting forensic images, including password-based (symmetric) and certificate-based (X.509) encryption. You can add the protection to an existing acquired image using the affcrypto tool. Here is an example:

```
# affcrypto -e -N monkey99 image.aff
image.aff:    967 segments;     0 signed;    967 encrypted;     0 pages;
       0 encrypted pages
```

Recent versions of dd_rescue implement a plugin interface and (at the time of this writing) had plugins for LZO compression, cryptographic hashing, and symmetric encryption (AES). The following example shows imaging a disk (*/dev/sdc*) and saving the output in encrypted form using the AES plugin:

```
# dd_rescue -L crypt=enc:passfd=0:pbkdf2 /dev/sdc samsung.raw.aes
dd_rescue: (info): Using softbs=128.0kiB, hardbs=4.0kiB
dd_rescue: (input): crypt(0): Enter passphrase:
dd_rescue: (warning): some plugins don't handle sparse, enabled -A/--nosparse!
dd_rescue: (info): expect to copy 156290904.0kiB from /dev/sdc
dd_rescue: (info): crypt(0): Derived salt from samsung.raw.aes=00000025433d6000
dd_rescue: (info): crypt(0): Generate KEY and IV from same passwd/salt
dd_rescue: (info): ipos: 156286976.0k, opos: 156286976.0k, xferd: 156286976.0k
                        errs:      0, errxfer:      0.0k, succxfer: 156286976.0k
              +curr.rate:    38650kB/s, avg.rate:    56830kB/s, avg.load: 14.9%
```

```
                    >------------------------------------.< 99% ETA: 0:00:00
dd_rescue: (info): read /dev/sdc (156290904.0kiB): EOF
dd_rescue: (info): Summary for /dev/sdc -> samsung.raw.aes
dd_rescue: (info): ipos: 156290904.0k, opos: 156290904.0k, xferd: 156290904.0k
                 errs:      0, errxfer:        0.0k, succxfer: 156290904.0k
            +curr.rate:    29345kB/s, avg.rate:    56775kB/s, avg.load: 14.9%
                    >-------------------------------------< 100% TOT: 0:45:53
```

If examiners in a forensics lab expect high volumes of encryption, signing, and timestamping of images and evidence, it's worth investing the use of a PKI. This could be an in-house PKI system or an external commercial PKI provider.

General Purpose Disk Encryption

The examples in the previous sections focused on protecting individual files or file containers. An alternative is to protect the entire drive where the image files reside. You can do this with filesystem encryption, in hardware, in user space, or in the kernel. You'll see several examples in this section.

There are high-capacity secure external drives on the market that can be used to safely transport image files, such as Lenovo's ThinkPad Secure Hard Drives, one of which is shown in Figure 7-1. These drives are OS independent and encrypt drive contents with a pin entered in a physical keypad on the device.

Figure 7-1: ThinkPad Secure Hard Drive

TrueCrypt was once the most popular free and cross-platform filesystem software available. But in May 2014, an unexpected and unexplained announcement from the developers recommended people find alternatives to TrueCrypt because development was stopped. A number of forks and compatible projects resulted, several of which are listed here:

- VeraCrypt: *https://veracrypt.codeplex.com/*
- tc-play: *https://github.com/bwalex/tc-play/*
- CipherShed: *https://ciphershed.org/*
- zuluCrypt: *http://mhogomchungu.github.io/zuluCrypt/* (not an implementation of TrueCrypt but a TrueCrypt manager worth mentioning)

The rest of the examples in this section use VeraCrypt. As of this writing, VeraCrypt was under active development and gaining in popularity as an alternative to TrueCrypt.

The following example encrypts an empty external drive in its entirety. You can then use the encrypted container for secure transfer or storage of evidence data. The veracrypt tool asks a number of questions regarding the setup of the encrypted container. Note that in this example, */dev/sda* is an examiner's drive, not a subject drive.

```
# veracrypt -c /dev/sda
Volume type:
 1) Normal
 2) Hidden
Select [1]:

Encryption Algorithm:
 1) AES
 2) Serpent
 3) Twofish
 4) AES(Twofish)
 5) AES(Twofish(Serpent))
 6) Serpent(AES)
 7) Serpent(Twofish(AES))
 8) Twofish(Serpent)
Select [1]:

Hash algorithm:
 1) SHA-512
 2) Whirlpool
 3) SHA-256
Select [1]:

Filesystem:
 1) None
 2) FAT
 3) Linux Ext2
 4) Linux Ext3
 5) Linux Ext4
 6) NTFS
```

```
Select [2]: 5

Enter password:
Re-enter password:

Enter PIM:

Enter keyfile path [none]:

Please type at least 320 randomly chosen characters and then press Enter:

The VeraCrypt volume has been successfully created.
```

The drive has now been initialized as a VeraCrypt container (this can take a long time, depending on the speed of the PC and the size of the drive). To mount a VeraCrypt volume, you use a simple command that includes the source device and the mount point:

```
# veracrypt /dev/sda /mnt
Enter password for /dev/sda:
Enter PIM for /dev/sda:
Enter keyfile [none]:
Protect hidden volume (if any)? (y=Yes/n=No) [No]:
# veracrypt -l
1: /dev/sda /dev/mapper/veracrypt1 /mnt
```

Safely removing the device requires "dismounting" the VeraCrypt volume and is also done using a simple command that specifies the mount point:

```
# veracrypt --dismount /mnt
```

At this point, you can physically detach the drive from the system. The encrypted drive in this example is an entire raw device, but it's also possible to use a VeraCrypt container file. The mount point in this example is */mnt*, but it can be anywhere in the filesystem.

There are other full-disk encryption systems that can be used to secure forensic image files and other data. You can use self-encrypting drives (SEDs), discussed in detail in "Identify and Unlock Opal Self-Encrypting Drives" on page 128, with the sedutil-cli command to create an encrypted drive for storage and transport. Filesystem encryption, such as Linux LUKS and dm-crypt, offers similar levels of protection. Although these encryption systems will secure evidence data on a drive, they might not be interoperable with other OSes (Windows or OS X, for example).

Disk Cloning and Duplication

In some situations, a clone or duplicate copy of a disk is preferred to an image file. Each duplicate is an exact sector-by-sector copy of the original disk. A newly cloned disk will have a cryptographic checksum that matches the original. A cloned disk can be useful for several reasons:

- To use analysis tools and methods that require writing to disk
- To boot a PC with the disk clone
- To reconstruct RAID arrays using proprietary controllers

Cloning disks is a straightforward process; it is basically acquisition in reverse. Be sure to exercise caution during the duplication process, because you could destroy data if the wrong device is mistakenly used as the destination.

Prepare a Clone Disk

The size (number of sectors) of the destination, or clone, disk must be equal to or larger than the original disk. Because cloning involves a sector-by-sector copy, the destination disk must have the capacity to hold all sectors of the original disk. In some cases, having a larger destination disk is not a problem, because the PC and OS will be limited to what was defined in the partition table and ignore the rest of the disk. In other cases, duplicating the exact number of sectors of the disk is important, as software and tools may have certain sector number expectations. Some examples include the analysis of GPT partitions (where a backup is stored at the end of a disk) and RAID systems, and the analysis of certain strains of malware that partly reside in the final sectors of the disk.

Securely wiping (with zeroed sectors) the destination disk before cloning is critical to remove traces of previous data and reduce the risk of contaminating the clone.

Use HPA to Replicate Sector Size

The HPA can be used to simulate the same number of sectors on the cloned disk as on the original.[2] Setting the HPA on a cloned disk is beneficial if there is an expectation of the exact same number of sectors as the original. This is especially important when you're reconstructing a RAID system with a proprietary controller or duplicating a disk with data expected in the final sectors of the disk.

NOTE *You should know the exact sector count of the original drive (this was determined when the drive was attached to the examination host) before setting the HPA with the hdparm tool.*

---

2. The sector size could also be replicated using a DCO.

In this example, the HPA on a 500GB disk is set to duplicate a 120GB drive. The original disk reports 234441648 512-byte sectors, which you can use to set the *maximum visible sectors* on the clone drive. Use the following commands:

```
# hdparm -N /dev/sdk

/dev/sdk:
 max sectors    = 976773168/976773168, HPA is disabled
# hdparm --yes-i-know-what-i-am-doing -N p234441648 /dev/sdk

/dev/sdk:
 setting max visible sectors to 234441648 (permanent)
 max sectors    = 234441648/976773168, HPA is enabled
# hdparm -I /dev/sdk
...
        LBA    user addressable sectors:  234441648
...
        device size with M = 1000*1000:    120034 MBytes (120 GB)
...
```

The first hdparm -N command shows the initial state with 500GB of accessible sectors and a disabled HPA. The second hdparm command requires the --yes-i-know-what-i-am-doing flag to configure dangerous settings, such as changing the sector size. The -N p234441648 specifies the number of sectors. It is prefixed with the letter p so the change is permanent across drive restarts. The final hdparm command checks whether the drive is now reporting the new sector size, which is now the same as that of the clone (120GB).

Write an Image File to a Clone Disk

To write an image to a new disk, use the same tools as when you acquire a disk but in reverse.

You can create a disk clone directly from the original suspect disk or from a previously acquired image file using the standard dd utilities. This example shows writing a raw image file to a clone disk using dc3dd:

```
# dc3dd if=image.raw of=/dev/sdk log=clone.log

dc3dd 7.2.641 started at 2016-01-16 01:41:44 +0100
compiled options:
command line: dc3dd if=image.raw of=/dev/sdk log=clone.log
sector size: 512 bytes (assumed)
120034123776 bytes ( 112 G ) copied ( 100% ),  663 s, 173 M/s

input results for file `image.raw':
   234441648 sectors in
```

```
output results for device `/dev/sdk':
    234441648 sectors out

dc3dd completed at 2016-01-16 01:52:48 +0100
```

Now you can verify the cryptographic hash against the original. If the sector count of the original and clone disks don't match, either an error is generated (if the clone doesn't have enough sectors to complete the duplication activity) or the hash values won't match.

You can write a set of split images, compressed images, or encrypted images back to a clone disk without creating a regular image file first.

You can also use non-raw formats, such as AFF, EnCase EWF, or FTK SMART, to create clone disks. If a particular forensic tool cannot write an image back to a device, it might be able to pipe a raw image into a dd program, which can.

Image Transfer and Storage

Managing the transfer and long-term storage of forensic images safely and successfully requires some thought and planning. Often, situations occur in which you need to transfer an image to another party, such as another department within a large organization, an independent third-party forensics firm, or a law enforcement agency.

Several factors influence how transfers are completed, primarily the size of the data and the security of that data. In addition, depending on the organization, you might have to consider legal and regulatory requirements, as well as organizational policy requirements. For example, a global bank might not be able to transfer some disk images across national borders due to banking regulations prohibiting the transfer of client data outside the country.

Storing images for the long term also requires some thought and planning. If an image will be reopened several years later, different staff, tools, and infrastructure could be in place. It is important to document what has been stored and maintain backward compatibility with the software used in the past.

Write to Removable Media

In the past, a stack of CDs or DVDs were used in the transfer of acquired drive images. With compression and splitting, using these media was a cheap and feasible transfer method. Today, 4TB and 6TB disks are common, and 10TB disks are already on the consumer market. Optical discs are no longer a practical transfer medium for today's larger image sizes, even with compression. However, for completeness, several examples are shown here.

The following simple example shows burning a SquashFS file to CD-ROM. The mkisofs command is a symlink to genisoimage and is used to create the filesystem to be burned to a disk with the wodim tool.

```
# mkisofs -r -J maxtor-2gb-L905T60S.sfs | wodim dev=/dev/cdrom -
...
Starting to write CD/DVD at speed  48.0 in real TAO mode for single session.
...
 97.45% done, estimate finish Sat Jan 16 02:36:16 2016
 98.88% done, estimate finish Sat Jan 16 02:36:15 2016
...
348929 extents written (681 MB)
Track 01: Total bytes read/written: 714606592/714606592 (348929 sectors).
```

Here is a simple example of burning an image to a DVD. The growisofs tool began as a frontend to genisoimage and developed into a general-purpose DVD and Blu-ray burning tool.

```
# growisofs -Z /dev/dvd -R -J ibm-4gb-J30J30K5215.sfs
Executing 'genisoimage -R -J ibm-4gb-J30J30K5215.sfs | builtin_dd of=/dev/dvd
    obs=32k seek=0'
...
 99.58% done, estimate finish Sat Jan 16 02:30:07 2016
 99.98% done, estimate finish Sat Jan 16 02:30:07 2016
1240225 extents written (2422 MB)
...
```

The following example shows burning an image to a Blu-ray disc using the growisofs command:

```
# growisofs -allow-limited-size  -Z /dev/dvd -R -J atlas-18gb.sfs
Executing 'genisoimage -allow-limited-size -R -J atlas-18gb.sfs | builtin_dd
    of=/dev/dvd obs=32k seek=0'
...
This size can only be represented in the UDF filesystem.
...
/dev/dvd: pre-formatting blank BD-R for 24.8GB...
...
 99.79% done, estimate finish Sat Jan 16 02:20:10 2016
 99.98% done, estimate finish Sat Jan 16 02:20:10 2016
2525420 extents written (4932 MB)
...
```

Burning large images to optical discs under Linux can be quirky. Depending on the drive and the media used, unexpected or inconsistent behavior might be observed. Be sure to test the compatibility of drives and media before using them in a production environment.

Inexpensive Disks for Storage and Transfer

Creating a stack of optical discs from a set of split and compressed images requires a systematic process that can be time-consuming and error prone. The maximum capacity of Blu-ray discs is currently 100GB (BD-R XL). The cost per gigabyte of Blu-ray discs is more than the cost per gigabyte for cheap hard disks.

When you factor in human effort, risk of error, time required to burn data to optical discs, and cost per gigabtye, simply buying and using cheap hard disks becomes an attractive possibility for offline storage and transfer of forensic images.

Perform Large Network Transfers

Some of the issues concerning acquiring images via a network were already discussed in Chapter 6.

Large network transfers of acquired images may take long periods of time to complete and might saturate a corporate internal network or internet link. Dropped connections and timeouts might also occur during such long network transfers.

Transferring large forensic images between hosts on a network is not nearly as fast as transferring them between disks on a local machine. To put network bandwidth speeds into perspective, it helpful to compare them to common disk speeds. Table 7-1 compares two fast drive interfaces to two fast network interfaces.

Table 7-1: Transfer Speeds of Common Interfaces

Interface	Speed
NVME	4000MB/s
SATA III	600MB/s
Gigibit Ethernet	125MB/s
Fast Ethernet	12.5MB/s

For a more detailed comparison of different bandwidths, see the Wikipedia page at *https://en.wikipedia.org/wiki/List_of_device_bit_rates*.

Depending on the network bandwidth and the image size, the physical delivery of a storage container with the acquired subject image(s) could be faster than a network transfer.

But in some situations, secure network data transfer is necessary. Ensuring security during a transfer may have certain side effects, such as increased complexity or performance penalties. For network data transfer over untrusted or unknown networks, you can use several standard secure protocols, including SSL/TLS, ssh/sftp, or IPSEC.

The following simple example shows the transfer of a forensic image file using scp (secure copy) from the OpenSSH software package:

```
$ scp image.raw server1.company.com:/data/image.raw
image.raw                    11% 1955MB  37.8MB/s   06:51 ETA
...
```

Here, an image file (*image.raw*) is copied over an insecure network to a specific data directory on a remote server. Using scp has several advantages, including strong encryption algorithms, built-in compression, real-time progress status, estimated completion time, and strong authentication possibilities. Most important for forensic investigators, scp allows for very large file sizes (assuming the software binary was compiled with 64-bit large file size support) and is easily capable of transferring large disk images.

If an image file is already encrypted, the underlying security might be less of a concern, and you can use traditional file transfer protocols, such as File Transfer Protocol (FTP) or Windows Server Message Block (SMB). However, when you're using insecure and weakly authenticated protocols to transfer encrypted files, you should confirm the file integrity by verifying the cryptographic hash after the transfer is complete.

Secure Wiping and Data Disposal

Whenever you discard or reuse a disk, or you no longer need temporary files, take diligent steps to properly erase the contents. Several command line wiping and secure deletion methods are available for this purpose.

Dispose of Individual Files

In some situations, you'll need to securely erase individual files but not the entire disk. For example, you might need to dispose of temporary acquired images on the acquisition host. In this scenario, using a file shredder/wiper is sensible because it reduces the risk of destroying other data on the examiner's workstation.

The standard Linux coreutils package includes the shred tool, which attempts to securely delete files, as shown here:

```
$ shred -v confidential-case-notes.txt
shred: confidential-case-notes.txt: pass 1/3 (random)...
shred: confidential-case-notes.txt: pass 2/3 (random)...
shred: confidential-case-notes.txt: pass 3/3 (random)...
```

A software package called the secure_deletion toolkit provides a suite of tools that attempts to erase swap, cache, memory, inodes, and files. In particular, srm will wipe an individual file. Another command line tool called wipe also will erase files.

Wiping individual files is a complex process and depends on many variables related to the OS and filesystem used. There are no guarantees that all fragments of a wiped or shredded file have been completely destroyed.

Secure Wipe a Storage Device

Wiping entire physical drives involves writing zeros or random bytes to every user-accessible sector on the drive. This does not guarantee that all hidden or user-inaccessible areas of a physical drive are wiped. Sectors protected by an HPA or DCO (which can be removed), remapped bad sectors, overprovisioned areas of flash drives, and inaccessible system areas of a drive are not user accessible and therefore cannot be wiped with normal Linux tools. In spite of this, wiping all user-accessible sectors still provides a reasonable level of assurance, so this is a diligent method of data disposal for reusing drives within a lab.

Depending on a particular organization's risk appetite and policies, data disposal might require one or more of the following:

- No wiping at all, just common reformatting
- Wiping all visible sectors with one pass of zeros
- Wiping all visible sectors with multiple passes of random data
- Physically degaussing drives
- Physically shredding drives

The disposal method required is a risk-based decision that depends on the sensitivity of the data on the drive, who might have an interest in recovering the data, cost and effort for recovery, and other factors.

This first example uses dc3dd to write zeros to each visible sector on the disk. The dc3dd tool has built-in wiping functionality, and you can use it as follows:

```
# dc3dd wipe=/dev/sdi

dc3dd 7.2.641 started at 2016-01-16 00:03:16 +0100
compiled options:
command line: dc3dd wipe=/dev/sdi
device size: 29305206 sectors (probed),    120,034,123,776 bytes
sector size: 4096 bytes (probed)
120034123776 bytes ( 112 G ) copied ( 100% ), 3619 s, 32 M/s

input results for pattern `00':
   29305206 sectors in

output results for device `/dev/sdi':
   29305206 sectors out

dc3dd completed at 2016-01-16 01:03:35 +0100
```

You could also complete this task using dd with */dev/zero* as the input file, but dc3dd is faster.

To confirm the disk has been wiped with zeros, you can use dd to read the disk into a hexdump program:

```
# dd if=/dev/sda | hd
```

If the entire disk is full of zeros, the hexdump (hd) tool will display one line of zeros followed by an asterisk (*), indicating a repeated pattern across the entire disk.

```
0000000 000000 000000 000000 000000 000000 000000 000000 000000
*
```

If the result shows only zeros, the user-accessible sectors of the drive have been successfully wiped.

The following example uses the nwipe tool, a fork of Darik's Boot and Nuke (dban) tool. The nwipe tool can specify different wiping standards, randomicity, and number of rounds, and it will provide a log file of the activity. The Canadian RCMP TSSIT OPS-II wipe version is shown here:[3]

```
# nwipe --autonuke --nogui --method=ops2 /dev/sdj
[2016/01/15 23:14:56] nwipe: notice: Opened entropy source '/dev/urandom'.
[2016/01/15 23:14:56] nwipe: info: Device '/dev/sdj' has sector size 512.
[2016/01/15 23:14:56] nwipe: warning: Changing '/dev/sdj' block size from 4096 to
    512.
[2016/01/15 23:14:56] nwipe: info: Device '/dev/sdj' is size 160041885696.
[2016/01/15 23:14:56] nwipe: notice: Invoking method 'RCMP TSSIT OPS-II' on device
    '/dev/sdj'.
[2016/01/15 23:14:56] nwipe: notice: Starting round 1 of 1 on device '/dev/sdj'.
[2016/01/15 23:14:56] nwipe: notice: Starting pass 1 of 8, round 1 of 1, on device
    '/dev/sdj'.
[2016/01/15 23:57:00] nwipe: notice: 160041885696 bytes written to device
    '/dev/sdj'.
[2016/01/15 23:57:00] nwipe: notice: Finished pass 1 of 8, round 1 of 1, on device
    '/dev/sdj'.
...
```

When you're wiping drives, ensure the DCO and HPA have been removed. With NVME drives, make sure each individual namespace has been wiped (most consumer NVME drives have only a single namespace).

Issue ATA Security Erase Unit Commands

The ATA standard specifies a security erase command that you can issue directly to a drive to wipe a disk. The ATA SECURITY ERASE UNIT command will

---

3. I am Canadian; hence the favoritism for the RCMP method. :-)

write zeros to all user accessible sectors of the disk. The EXTENDED SECURITY ERASE command will write a predefined pattern (defined by the drive manufacturer) instead of zeros.

Running hdparm displays the capabilities and status of security on the drive. Also provided is the estimated time needed to securely erase the drive, as shown here:

```
# hdparm -I /dev/sdh
...
        device size with M = 1000*1000:        500107 MBytes (500 GB)
...
Security:
        Master password revision code = 7
                supported
                enabled
        not     locked
        not     frozen
        not     expired: security count
                supported: enhanced erase
        Security level high
        60min for SECURITY ERASE UNIT. 60min for ENHANCED SECURITY ERASE UNIT.
```

Some drives will reject the erase command if you don't explicitly set a password first. In the following example, a Western Digital drive was used, and the password was first set to *dummy* before the --security-erase command was accepted:

```
# hdparm --security-erase dummy /dev/sdh
security_password="dummy"

/dev/sdh:
 Issuing SECURITY_ERASE command, password="dummy", user=user
```

The drive has now been securely wiped and can be reused. If a drive requires setting a password, don't forget to disable the password after the security erase has completed.

Destroy Encrypted Disk Keys

You can securely destroy encrypted disks and filesystems by destroying all known copies of the encryption key. If the key was generated on a secure device such as a smartcard, a TPM, or an Opal drive, then only one copy of the key will exist. If a drive or filesystem was provisioned in an enterprise environment, there might be backup or escrow copies of the key for recovery purposes.

Key-wiping procedures for OS-based encrypted drives, such as Microsoft BitLocker, Apple FileVault, Linux LUKS/dm-crypt, or TrueCrypt variants, require detailed knowledge of where the keys are stored. Keys might be password/passphrase protected and stored in a file or in a certain block on the drive. They might also be stored in a key file elsewhere. If it's not possible to locate and securely destroy all copies of a private key, the alternative is to wipe the disk with the full drive-wiping method described in a previous section.

Typically, secure external USB thumb drives have a factory reset function for lost passwords. This can be used to destroy the key and hence the contents of the drive. For example, you can reset the Corsair Padlock2 thumb drive by holding down both the KEY and 0/1 buttons for three seconds, followed by entering **911** to reset the key and destroy the drive contents. On iStorage datashur drives, hold down both the KEY and 2 buttons for three seconds and then enter **999** to reset the key.

Destroying the contents of Opal SED drives is also instantaneous and simply involves destroying the encryption key on the drive by entering the *Physical Security ID (PSID)*. The PSID usually has a QR code on the physical cover of the drive that you can scan instead of typing it in by hand. You cannot get the PSID by querying the drive with ATA commands; it's only visible on the cover of the physical drive.

The sedutil-cli command has a special option for irrevocably resetting the drive key using the PSID:

```
# time sedutil-cli --yesIreallywanttoERASEALLmydatausingthePSID
    3HTEWZBOTVOLH2MZU8F7LCFD28U7GJPG /dev/sdi
- 22:21:13.738 INFO: revertTper completed successfully

real    0m0.541s
user    0m0.000s
sys     0m0.000s
```

The encryption key in the drive is now reset, and the data is effectively destroyed. The disk is factory reset, unlocked, and can be reused. The time needed to destroy the data on this 120GB drive was half a second.

Closing Thoughts

In this chapter, you learned a variety of techniques for managing forensic images, including the use of compression with common Linux tools and built-in compression with forensic formats. You saw more examples of the SquashFS compressed filesystem and the sfsimage script for managing forensic evidence containers. I demonstrated splitting and reassembling images, duplicating drives, and converting between image formats. You also learned how to verify hashes, signatures, and timestamps and how to protect images with encryption during network transfer and storage. Finally, I showed the secure disposal of forensic image files and drives.

8

SPECIAL IMAGE ACCESS TOPICS

This chapter demonstrates techniques for getting information about disk image files and making them accessible as block devices and as mounted directories. You'll learn to set up loop devices and create logical devices with device mapper tools. You'll also explore methods to map or convert software-encrypted disk images, making them accessible by forensic tools. These methods are useful in situations in which the contents of an image cannot be accessed directly and a layer of active translation or decryption is needed. Examples of such images include encrypted filesystems, virtual machine (VM) images, and other image file formats that forensic tools do not directly support.

Each section also includes examples of safely mounting (read-only) image files as regular filesystems on the forensic acquisition host. Then you can easily browse and access the filesystem using common programs, such as file managers, office suites, file viewers, media players, and so on.

Forensically Acquired Image Files

The basis for many of the methods and examples you'll see in this section is the Linux loop device (not to be confused with a loopback device, which is a network interface). A *loop device* is a pseudo device that can be associated with a regular file, making the file accessible as a block device in */dev*.

Linux systems typically create eight loop devices by default, which might not be enough for a forensic acquisition host, but you can increase that number, either manually or automatically, on boot up. To create 32 loop devices during boot up, add `max_loop=32` to the `GRUB_CMDLINE_LINUX_DEFAULT=` line in the */etc/default/grub* file; after reboot, 32 unused loop devices should be available. The sfsimage script uses loop devices to mount SquashFS forensic evidence containers.

This chapter will cover different VM images from common VM systems from QEMU, VirtualBox, VMWare, and Microsoft Virtual PC. I also describe access to OS-encrypted filesystems, including Microsoft's BitLocker, Apple's FileVault, Linux LUKS, and VeraCrypt (a fork of TrueCrypt). But let's begin the with the simplest form of image: a raw disk image acquired using a dd-style acquisition tool.

Raw Image Files with Loop Devices

The simplest demonstration of a loop device can be shown using a raw image file (possibly acquired from a simple `dd` command). The `losetup` command attaches and detaches loop devices from a Linux system. This example creates a block device for an *image.raw* file:

```
# losetup --read-only --find --show image.raw
/dev/loop0
```

Here, the flags specify that the loop should be read-only (`--read-only`) and the next available loop device should be used (`--find`) and displayed on completion (`--show`). The filename specified (*image.raw*) will then become available as an attached block device.

Running the `losetup` command without parameters displays the status of all configured loop devices. Here we can see the one just created:

```
# losetup
NAME       SIZELIMIT OFFSET AUTOCLEAR RO BACK-FILE
/dev/loop0         0      0         0  1 /exam/image.raw
```

The */dev/loop0* device now points to */exam/image.raw*, and you can access it with any tools that operate on block devices. For example, here the Sleuth Kit `mmls` command is able to see the partition table on the *image.raw* file using the loop device:

```
# mmls /dev/loop0
DOS Partition Table
```

```
Offset Sector: 0
Units are in 512-byte sectors

     Slot    Start        End          Length       Description
00:  Meta    0000000000   0000000000   0000000001   Primary Table (#0)
01:  -----   0000000000   0000002047   0000002048   Unallocated
02:  00:00   0000002048   0058597375   0058595328   Linux (0x83)
03:  00:01   0058597376   0078129151   0019531776   Linux Swap / Solaris x86 (0x82)
04:  00:02   0078129152   0078231551   0000102400   NTFS (0x07)
05:  00:03   0078231552   0234441647   0156210096   Mac OS X HFS (0xaf)
```

When you no longer need a loop device, simply detach it as follows:

```
# losetup --detach /dev/loop0
```

Loop devices are flexible and configurable. In the previous mmls example, a filesystem starts at sector 2048. It's possible to specify an offset each time you run a forensic tool, but it's easier to have a separate device for each partition (similar to */dev/sda1* for example). You can create a separate loop device with the losetup command just for that partition by specifying the correct offset flag (--offset) and size flag (--sizelimit). However, a more commonly accepted way is to use the device mapper.

You could do this manually using dmsetup and mapping tables as described in "RAID and Multidisk Systems" on page 178. However, the kpartx tool automates the creation of partition devices for a particular image file. A forensically acquired image with four partitions is used in the following example to demonstrate the kpartx tool making mapper devices for each partition:

```
# kpartx -r -a -v image.raw
add map loop0p1 (252:0): 0 58595328 linear /dev/loop0 2048
add map loop0p2 (252:1): 0 19531776 linear /dev/loop0 58597376
add map loop0p3 (252:2): 0 102400 linear /dev/loop0 78129152
add map loop0p4 (252:3): 0 156210096 linear /dev/loop0 78231552
```

Here, the kpartx tool reads the partition table on a disk or image file, creates a loop device for the whole image, and then creates mapper devices for each partition. The -r flag ensures the drive loop and partition mappings are read-only, and -a flag instructs kpartx to map everything it finds. Use the verbose flag -v to document the command output and to indicate what was just mapped.

In this example, a loop device is created (*/dev/loop0*) for the whole image file and is accessible as a raw block device. In addition, partition devices are now available in the */dev/mapper* directory, and you can access them using forensic tools that operate on partitions, without specifying any offsets. Here are a few example Sleuth Kit commands for some of the partitions:

```
# fsstat /dev/mapper/loop0p1
FILE SYSTEM INFORMATION
--------------------------------------------
File System Type: Ext4
Volume Name:
Volume ID: d4605b95ec13fcb43646de38f7f49680
...
# fls /dev/mapper/loop0p3
r/r 4-128-1:    $AttrDef
r/r 8-128-2:    $BadClus
r/r 8-128-1:    $BadClus:$Bad
r/r 6-128-1:    $Bitmap
r/r 7-128-1:    $Boot
d/d 11-144-2:   $Extend
r/r 2-128-1:    $LogFile
r/r 0-128-1:    $MFT
...
# fsstat /dev/mapper/loop0p4
FILE SYSTEM INFORMATION
--------------------------------------------
File System Type: HFS+
File System Version: HFS+
...
```

A filesystem mapped to a device from an image file can be safely mounted as read-only. This will allow you access it with a standard file manager, applications, and other file-analysis tools. You can mount and unmount loop partitions, as shown in this example:

```
# mkdir p3
# mount --read-only /dev/mapper/loop0p3 p3
# mc ./p3
...
# umount p3
# rmdir p3
```

Here, a directory, *p3*, representing the partition was created in the same directory as the raw image. Then *p3* was used as the mount point (the chosen mount point can be anywhere on the examiner host filesystem). Midnight Commander (mc) is a text-based file manager (a Norton Commander clone) and is used in this example to review the files on the mounted partition. When the mount point is no longer needed, the umount command (this command is spelled correctly with only one *n*) unmounts the filesystem, and rmdir removes the mount point directory. This is the traditional Unix way to mount and unmount a filesystem on a host system.

When you no longer need the drive loop and partition mappings, you can remove them all by using the kpartx delete (-d) flag and the name of the image file, like this:

```
# kpartx -d image.raw
loop deleted : /dev/loop0
```

Note that this "delete" has no effect on the disk image's contents. The loop and mappings are deleted, not the drive image, and the drive image is not modified.

If a raw image has a corrupt or overwritten partition table, you can scan the image for filesystems and use dmsetup to manually map filesystems as devices (using dmsetup tables).

When you create, mount, unmount, or detach a loop device, root privileges are required. They're also required for operating on the */dev/loopX* device with forensic tools. The examples shown in this section were run as the root user to reduce the complexity of the command lines, making them easier to understand. Prefixing the commands with sudo can be used to run privileged commands as a non-root user.

Forensic Format Image Files

The ewflib software package includes a tool called ewfmount to "mount" the contents of a forensic image, making it accessible as a regular raw image file.

The following example shows a group of *.e01* files. A mount point, raw in this example, is created with mkdir and will contain the raw image file:

```
# ls
image.E01  image.E02  image.E03  image.E04  image.E05
# mkdir raw
```

The ewfmount tool creates a FUSE filesystem containing a virtual raw image from one or more EWF files. You can run ewfmount command with the first of the EnCase EWF files and the mount point to access a raw image file like this:

```
# ewfmount image.E01 raw
ewfmount 20160424

# ls -l raw
total 0
-r--r--r-- 1 root root 16001269760 May 17 21:20 ewf1
```

You can then operate on this virtual raw image file using tools that don't support EWF formats directly. In the following example, a hex editor (without EWF support) is used in sector mode to analyze the raw image:

```
# hexedit -s raw/ewf1
...
```

The kpartx tool is again useful to identify partitions and create corresponding loop devices, enabling the use of tools that can operate on block devices and allowing the mounting of the filesystems for regular browsing. The kpartx output of the *.e01 files mounted with ewfmount is shown here:

```
# kpartx -r -a -v raw/ewf1
add map loop0p1 (252:0): 0 29848707 linear /dev/loop0 63
add map loop0p2 (252:1): 0 2 linear /dev/loop0 29848770
add map loop0p5 : 0 1397592 linear /dev/loop0 29848833
```

Let's continue using this example to create a mount point for a partition and mount and access a filesystem:

```
# mkdir p1
# mount --read-only /dev/mapper/loop0p1 p1
# ls p1
cdrom  home/      lib32/      media/      proc/  selinux/  tmp/  vmlinuz
bin/   dev/       initrd.img  lib64       mnt/   root/     srv/  usr/
boot/  etc/       lib/        lost+found/ opt/   sbin/     sys/  var/
...
```

In this example, a mount point corresponding to the partition is created in the local directory, the partition device is mounted on it, and the filesystem is accessed with ls. If possible, avoid the use of /mnt or other shared mount directories when mounting evidence files and containers. It is easier to perform forensic work when the mount points for an image are in the same working directory as other related case files.

As before, when the work is completed, you need to clean up the mounts and virtual files. Again, this is done in the reverse order:

```
# umount p1
# kpartx -d raw/ewf1
loop deleted : /dev/loop0
# fusermount -u raw
# rmdir p1 raw
```

The fusermount command is shown in this example, but the standard Linux umount command would also work. Make sure your current working directory is not inside the mount point and that no programs have open files inside the mount points. Both conditions will cause these cleanup steps to fail.

When using SquashFS forensic evidence containers, you can access the raw image by mounting the *.sfs* file with sfsimage -m, creating the partition devices, and then mounting the desired partition. You can then execute regular commands on the subject image's filesystem. A complete example is shown here:

```
# sfsimage -m image.sfs
image.sfs.d mount created
# kpartx -r -a -v image.sfs.d/image.raw
add map loop1p1 (252:0): 0 29848707 linear /dev/loop1 63
add map loop1p2 (252:1): 0 2 linear /dev/loop1 29848770
add map loop1p5 : 0 1397592 linear /dev/loop1 29848833
# mkdir p1
# mount /dev/mapper/loop1p1 p1
mount: /dev/mapper/loop1p1 is write-protected, mounting read-only
# ls -l
...
```

Once you are finished accessing the raw image and its filesystems, clean up with SquashFS forensic evidence containers is also done in reverse. The sfsimage -u command unmounts a SquashFS filesytem as shown in this example:

```
# umount p1
# kpartx -d image.sfs.d/image.raw
loop deleted : /dev/loop1
# sfsimage -u image.sfs.d/
image.sfs.d unmounted
```

This section has demonstrated several methods for accessing the contents of forensic formats, both as block devices and as regular filesystems. The ewfmount tool also works with FTK SMART files. Afflib has a similar tool called affuse for mounting *.aff* files. Both ewfmount and affuse can operate on single or split files of their respective formats.

Note that many forensic tools (Sleuth Kit, for example) are able to operate directly on forensic formats without the need for a raw block device or raw file.

Prepare Boot Images with xmount

Forensic investigators often want to examine a subject drive image with non-forensic tools, such file managers, office suites, applications, or other file viewer tools. This can be done by making the drive contents safely available over a read-only mount for the local examiner machine to access.

In some cases, it is useful to boot a subject drive in a VM to observe and interact directly with the live subject environment. This allows you to view the subject's desktop and use the installed programs of the subject PC. To do this, you can use a number of tools described in this section.

The xmount (pronounced "crossmount") tool creates a virtual disk image that you can boot using VM software, such as VirtualBox or kvm-qemu. The xmount tool allows you to simulate a read-write drive, making the VM think the disk is writable, but it continues to protect the image in a read-only state. Multiple VM output formats are available, including raw, DMG, VDI, VHD, VMDK, and VMDKS.

The input formats include forensically acquired image files, such as *.raw, EnCase *.ewf, and AFFlib *.aff files.

Here is an example of a raw image (*image.raw*) set up with xmount as a VirtualBox *.vdi* file:

```
$ mkdir virtual
$ xmount --cache xmount.cache --in raw image.raw --out vdi virtual
$ ls virtual/
image.info  image.vdi
$ cat virtual/image.info
------> The following values are supplied by the used input library(ies) <------

--> image.raw <--
RAW image assembled of 1 piece(s)
30016659456 bytes in total (27.955 GiB)

------> The following values are supplied by the used morphing library <------

None
$ virtualbox
```

In this example, the directory *virtual* is created to hold the virtual image file (it will be FUSE mounted). From an existing *image.raw* file, the xmount command creates a write-cached VirtualBox VDI image in the *./virtual* directory. This is just a virtual representation of the image file; it is not copied or converted (thus not wasting disk space on the examiner machine). The --in and --out flags specify the image format used. The input formats must be raw, AFF, or EWF. Multiple output formats are possible.

Booting an OS image in a VM can be challenging when the installed OS is expecting a different hardware configuration than provided by the VM. Typically, this is less of an issue with Linux installations but can be problematic with Windows and OS X. To solve this problem, two tools, opengates and openjobs, were created to prepare Windows and OS X images for safely booting subject disks in a virtual environment. I won't cover how to use opengates and openjobs, but you can find more information about them at *https://www.pinguin.lu/openjobs/* and *https://www.pinguin.lu/opengates/*.

When you no longer need the VM image, you can clean up by unmounting the virtual image and removing the mount point directory:

```
$ fusermount -u virtual
$ ls virtual/
$ rmdir virtual
```

A *xmount.cache* file containing data written during the use of the VM might exist. You can save the file if you need to continue the previous VM session, or you can remove it.

VM Images

With the increasing performance of home computers, hardware virtualization in most modern CPUs, and the availability of inexpensive or free virtualization software, there is an increased need to analyze the contents of VM images. In some cases, you might find many VM images on subject PCs. This section focuses on accessing common VM image file types such as QCOW2, VDI, VMDK, and VHD.

QEMU QCOW2

The QCOW2 format is a common VM image type found on Linux and used by the QEMU emulator. In this section, I'll make a QCOW2 image available as a block device and safely mount it for browsing.

The libqcow-utils package (written by Joachim Metz, author of ewflib) contains the qcowinfo and qcowmount tools. You can use both tools in the same way as you used the ewfinfo and ewfmount tools in previous examples. But the following example shows an alternative method using the qemu-img command, the nbd kernel module, and the qemu-nbd tool. This method offers performance advantages because it operates in the kernel and saves you a few steps because you don't need to use kpartx.

Given a **.qcow2* file, the qemu-img command can provide a summary of the file:

```
# qemu-img info image.qcow2
image: image.qcow2
file format: qcow2
virtual size: 5.0G (5368709120 bytes)
disk size: 141M
cluster_size: 65536
Format specific information:
    compat: 1.1
    lazy refcounts: false
    refcount bits: 16
    corrupt: false
```

To access a QCOW image in a raw image representation with nbd, you need to load the nbd kernel module:

```
# modprobe nbd
# dmesg | grep nbd
[16771.003241] nbd: registered device at major 43
```

Unlike with the losetup command, the device is not automatically chosen. A */dev/nbd** device needs to be specified as follows:

```
# qemu-nbd --read-only --connect /dev/nbd0 image.qcow2
# dmesg | grep nbd0
[16997.777839]  nbd0: p1
```

Here, the QCOW2 image file was connected to the kernel module in read-only mode, and the partition device was automatically detected. You can use this raw device with forensic tools, as shown in this example:

```
# mmls /dev/nbd0
DOS Partition Table
Offset Sector: 0
Units are in 512-byte sectors

     Slot    Start       End         Length      Description
00:  Meta    0000000000  0000000000  0000000001  Primary Table (#0)
01:  -----   0000000000  0000002047  0000002048  Unallocated
02:  00:00   0000002048  0010485759  0010483712  Linux (0x83)
```

The partition devices (the raw device name with p1 in this example) are also ready for you to use directly with forensic tools. To illustrate, here's the fls command operating directly on a filesystem on the partition device:

```
# fls /dev/nbd0p1
d/d 11: lost+found
r/r 12: hosts
d/d 327681:     $OrphanFiles
...
```

Mounting the devices locally for browsing is trivial. A local mount point directory is created, and the filesystem is mounted normally, as follows:

```
# mkdir p1
# mount /dev/nbd0p1 p1
mount: /dev/nbd0p1 is write-protected, mounting read-only
# ls p1
hosts  lost+found/
```

The cleanup here is similar to the examples using loop devices, but with fewer steps. All processes should close files, and you should leave the mounted directory so it can be unmounted. A qemu-nbd disconnect command specifying the device name will unregister the device from the kernel, like so:

```
# umount p1
# qemu-nbd --read-only --disconnect /dev/nbd0
```

```
/dev/nbd0 disconnected
# rmdir p1
```

An optional step is to remove the kernel module using `rmmod nbd`. But there is no harm in leaving it in if you'll be doing more QCOW mounts. You can also autoload the nbd module at boot by adding it to the */etc/modules* file.

VirtualBox VDI

VirtualBox is an open source project maintained by Oracle (formerly Sun Microsystems). Although it supports multiple VM image formats, VirtualBox VDI images are used in the examples that follow. The same `qemu-nbd` command is used as before but with an OpenSolaris image.

The VirtualBox software package includes a number of utilities; the VBoxManage tool is shown here, providing information about the VDI image:

```
# VBoxManage showhdinfo OpenSolaris.vdi
UUID:           0e2e2466-afd7-49ba-8fe8-35d73d187704
Parent UUID:    base
State:          created
Type:           normal (base)
Location:       /exam/OpenSolaris.vdi
Storage format: VDI
Format variant: dynamic default
Capacity:       16384 MBytes
Size on disk:   2803 MBytes
Encryption:     disabled
```

You can mount VirtualBox images using `qemu-nbd` and the nbd kernel module (as you saw in the previous section using QCOW2). The Open-Solaris example shown here is slightly different from the partitioning scheme Windows and Linux use. Multiple disk slices[1] are also shown:

```
# qemu-nbd -c /dev/nbd0 OpenSolaris.vdi
# dmesg
...
[19646.708351]  nbd0: p1
                p1: <solaris: [s0] p5 [s1] p6 [s2] p7 [s8] p8 >
```

In this example, a single Solaris partition (`p1`) contains multiple slices (`p5`, `p6`, `p7`, and `p8`).

You can use the same methods as in the previous QEMU example to access the raw and partition devices, then mount the partitions as

---

1. The term *slices* originates from BSD UNIX, and it's a common partitioning scheme in the UNIX world.

read-only to a local mount point. Here again, you don't need to use kpartx to find the partitions, because the kernel does it automatically. Once you are finished accessing the partitions (or slices, here), perform the cleanup steps to unmount filesystems and disconnect the nbd device.

VMWare VMDK

The *Virtual Machine DisK (VMDK)* format is used by VMWare's VM software products. The following example uses the libvmdk-utils software package on an Apple Lion VMDK image split into multiple parts:

```
# ls
lion-000001-s001.vmdk    lion-000003-s007.vmdk    lion-s009.vmdk
lion-000001-s002.vmdk    lion-000003-s008.vmdk    lion-s010.vmdk
lion-000001-s003.vmdk    lion-000003-s009.vmdk    lion-s011.vmdk
lion-000001-s004.vmdk    lion-000003-s010.vmdk    lion-s012.vmdk
lion-000001-s005.vmdk    lion-000003-s011.vmdk    lion-s013.vmdk
lion-000001-s006.vmdk    lion-000003-s012.vmdk    lion-s014.vmdk
lion-000001-s007.vmdk    lion-000003-s013.vmdk    lion-s015.vmdk
lion-000001-s008.vmdk    lion-000003-s014.vmdk    lion-s016.vmdk
...
```

You can retrieve information about the assembled image and each of the "Extents" using vmdkinfo:

```
# vmdkinfo lion.vmdk
vmdkinfo 20160119

VMware Virtual Disk (VMDK) information:
        Disk type:                      2GB extent sparse
        Media size:                     42949672960 bytes
        Content identifier:             0xadba0513
        Parent content identifier:      0xffffffff
        Number of extents:              21

Extent: 1
        Filename:                       lion-s001.vmdk
        Type:                           Sparse
        Start offset:                   0
        Size:                           2146435072 bytes
...
```

Creating a mount point and mounting the image makes it accessible as a raw image file:

```
# mkdir lion
# vmdkmount lion.vmdk lion
vmdkmount 20160119
```

```
# ls -ls lion
total 0
0 -r--r--r-- 1 root root 42949672960 May 17 22:24 vmdk1
# mmls lion/vmdk1
GUID Partition Table (EFI)
Offset Sector: 0
Units are in 512-byte sectors
```

	Slot	Start	End	Length	Description
00:	Meta	0000000000	0000000000	0000000001	Safety Table
01:	-----	0000000000	0000000039	0000000040	Unallocated
02:	Meta	0000000001	0000000001	0000000001	GPT Header
03:	Meta	0000000002	0000000033	0000000032	Partition Table
04:	00	0000000040	0000409639	0000409600	EFI System Partition
05:	01	0000409640	0082616503	0082206864	Untitled
06:	02	0082616504	0083886039	0001269536	Recovery HD
07:	-----	0083886040	0083886079	0000000040	Unallocated

Using kpartx, as shown earlier in the chapter, will create the associated disk and partition block devices. You can then use forensic analysis tools on them directly or mount them on the local machine to browse the filesystem.

Microsoft VHD

A number of methods help you make the Microsoft VHD virtual image format accessible. For example, you can use the qemu-nbd method or use the libvhdi-utils with vhdiinfo and vhdimount.

A third method is available using the blktap-utils with the Xen blktap xapi interface. Similar to the nbd method, the blktap requires you to insert a kernel module and manually allocate a device. A tapdisk process is spawned, attached to the driver, and instructed to open a disk image. The manual pages for blktap-utils aren't very useful, but you can find a description on the Xen website at *http://wiki.xen.org/wiki/Mounting_a_.vhd_disk_image_using_blktap/tapdisk* and at *http://lists.xen.org/archives/html/xen-api/2012-05/msg00149.html*.

To complete this section, I'll repeat the process for setting up devices using the libvhdi tools. For simplicity, the previous examples used the privileged root user. But the following examples demonstrate a nonprivileged user authorized to use sudo.

To run the FUSE mount and unmount commands as a nonprivileged user, you need to set *user_allow_other* in */etc/fuse.conf*.

You can find information about the image using vhdiinfo, and no special privileges are required:

```
$ vhdiinfo windows.vhd
vhdiinfo 20160111
```

```
Virtual Hard Disk (VHD) image information:
        Format:             1.0
        Disk type:          Dynamic
        Media size:         136365211648 bytes
        Identifier:         c9f106a3-cf3f-6b42-a13f-60e349faccb5
```

You can FUSE mount the image without root privileges, but you need to explicitly instruct the vhdimount command to allow the root user access by adding the -X allow_root flag. This flag is also needed to allow root to perform further actions through sudo (like creating block devices with kpartx):

```
$ mkdir raw
$ vhdimount -X allow_root windows.vhd raw
vhdimount 20160111

$ ls -l raw/
total 0
-r--r--r-- 1 holmes holmes 136365211648 Jan 20 08:14 vhdi1
```

The raw image is now available in the *./raw* directory, and you can access it with standard tools. To create loop and mapper devices, run kpartx with the sudo command. Once the devices are created, you can access them with tools via the sudo command. The sudo command is required for all block device access. Examples with kpartx and fls are shown here:

```
$ sudo kpartx -r -a -v ./raw/vhdi1
add map loop0p1 (252:0): 0 266334018 linear /dev/loop0 63
$ sudo fls /dev/mapper/loop0p1
r/r 4-128-4:    $AttrDef
r/r 8-128-2:    $BadClus
r/r 8-128-1:    $BadClus:$Bad
r/r 6-128-1:    $Bitmap
r/r 7-128-1:    $Boot
d/d 11-144-4:   $Extend
r/r 2-128-1:    $LogFile
r/r 0-128-1:    $MFT
```

Mounting the filesystem also requires sudo, and explicitly specifying -o ro mounts it as read-only. An example of creating a mount point, mounting the filesystem from the previous example, and accessing it with ls is shown here:

```
$ mkdir p1
$ sudo mount -o ro /dev/mapper/loop0p1 p1
$ ls p1
AUTOEXEC.BAT            IO.SYS          $RECYCLE.BIN/
...
```

The cleanup of this session requires sudo for unmounting the raw image and removing the loop and mapper devices. You can remove the FUSE mount of the *.vhd file without root privileges. These steps are shown here:

```
$ sudo umount p1
$ sudo kpartx -d raw/vhdi1
loop deleted : /dev/loop0
$ fusermount -u raw
```

You configure the sudo command by editing the */etc/sudoers* file. Many of the examples in this book use the root user for simplicity's sake to reduce the number of commands on an already complex command line. It's good practice to work as a nonprivileged user with security mechanisms such as sudo.

OS-Encrypted Filesystems

Now let's look at accessing popular encrypted filesystems. The focus is not on key recovery (although I do provide a couple of suggestions) but on accessing the filesystems with a known key. It's assumed the keys or passwords are available from memory dumps, escrow/backup in enterprise organizations, individuals legally compelled to provide them, victims offering to help, commercial recovery services/software, or other sources.

You can determine the type of filesystem encryption with various partition-analysis tools that can identify headers, magic numbers, and other artifacts unique to a particular encrypted filesystem type. You'll find an overview of identifying filesystem encryption in a forensic context at *http://encase-forensic-blog.guidancesoftware.com/2014/04/version-7-tech-tip-spotting-full-disk.html*.

In this section, you'll find the information about a particular encrypted image needed to create an unencrypted block device or file that you can access using forensic tools or safely mount for local browsing.

Microsoft BitLocker

Microsoft's current default filesystem encryption is BitLocker. It encrypts at the block level, protecting entire volumes. A variant of BitLocker designed for removable media is called BitLocker-To-Go, which uses encrypted container files on a regular unencrypted filesystem. Two open source tools, dislocker and libbde, are shown in the examples in this section.

Written by Romain Coltel, you'll find the dislocker package at *https://github.com/Aorimn/dislocker/*. It provides various tools for handling BitLocker volumes, including viewing metadata, creating decrypted image files, and FUSE mounting volumes.

The dislocker-find tool scans all attached partition devices and specified files to identify the existence of any BitLocker volumes. Scanning for BitLocker devices might not be necessary if the subject device was already identified during the process of attaching it to the acquisition host.

The `dislocker-metadata` command provides an overview of a BitLocker drive. The next example is an image taken from a USB thumb drive. The entire drive is encrypted, and it doesn't have a partition table. The image file can be queried as follows:

```
# dislocker-metadata -V bitlocker-image.raw
...
Wed Jan 20 13:46:06 2016 [INFO] BitLocker metadata found and parsed.
Wed Jan 20 13:46:06 2016 [INFO] =====[ Volume header informations ]=====
Wed Jan 20 13:46:06 2016 [INFO]    Signature: 'MSWIN4.1'
Wed Jan 20 13:46:06 2016 [INFO]    Sector size: 0x0200 (512) bytes
...
Wed Jan 20 13:46:06 2016 [INFO]    Number of sectors (64 bits): 0x0000000200000000
   (8589934592) bytes
Wed Jan 20 13:46:06 2016 [INFO]    MFT start cluster: 0x0000000000060001 (393217)
   bytes
...
Wed Jan 20 13:46:06 2016 [INFO] ====================[ BitLocker information
   structure ]====================
Wed Jan 20 13:46:06 2016 [INFO]    Signature: '-FVE-FS-'
Wed Jan 20 13:46:06 2016 [INFO]    Total Size: 0x02f0 (752) bytes (including
   signature and data)
Wed Jan 20 13:46:06 2016 [INFO]    Version: 2
Wed Jan 20 13:46:06 2016 [INFO]    Current state: ENCRYPTED (4)
Wed Jan 20 13:46:06 2016 [INFO]    Next state: ENCRYPTED (4)
Wed Jan 20 13:46:06 2016 [INFO]    Encrypted volume size: 7918845952 bytes
   (0x1d8000000), ~7552 MB
...
```

The output of this command provides a lot of detailed cryptographic information not shown here. You can save the output of `dislocker-metadata` to a text file for documentation purposes. This command can also operate directly on attached devices.

As in previous password and encryption examples, it's assumed that you have the key. Some commercial tools are available to attempt password brute force to recover the key. In addition, you can use a volatility plug-in to extract the FVEK from a memory image (*https://github.com/elceef/bitlocker/*), and you could use this tool in conjunction with the inception memory-dumping tool. The use of these tools is not covered here.

You can create a virtual file or block device to operate on a decrypted view of the disk image "in place." The process to do so is similar to the examples in "VM Images" on page 237. The dislocker software package provides a tool to create a FUSE filesystem with virtual representation of the decrypted volume:

```
# mkdir clear
# dislocker-fuse -u -V bitlocker-image.raw clear
Enter the user password:
# ls -l clear/
total 0
-rw-rw-rw- 1 root root 7918845952 Jan  1  1970 dislocker-file
...
```

The file that appears in the *clear* directory is a decrypted representation of the encrypted filesystem, and you can operate on it using regular forensic tools. An example using Sleuth Kit's fsstat is shown here:

```
# fsstat clear/dislocker-file
FILE SYSTEM INFORMATION
--------------------------------------------
File System Type: FAT32

OEM Name: MSDOS5.0
Volume ID: 0x5a08a5ba
Volume Label (Boot Sector): NO NAME
Volume Label (Root Directory): MY SECRETS
File System Type Label: FAT32
Next Free Sector (FS Info): 34304
Free Sector Count (FS Info): 15418664
...
```

You can safely mount the decrypted filesystem image for normal browsing. The mount command has a loop option, which allows a partition image file to be directly mounted, as shown here:

```
# mkdir files
# mount -o loop,ro clear/dislocker-file files
# ls files
Penguins.jpg  private/  System Volume Information/
...
```

The cleanup in this example is a simple matter of unmounting the files' mount point, removing the FUSE mount, and deleting the mount directories:

```
# umount files
# rmdir files
# fusermount -u clear
# rmdir clear
```

Note that the preceding examples were done with root privileges to reduce complexity and make them easier to understand. You can perform the same commands as a nonprivileged user, as shown here:

```
$ dislocker-metadata -V bitlocker-image.raw
$ mkdir clear files
$ dislocker-fuse -u -V bitlocker-image.raw -- -o allow_root clear
$ sudo mount -o loop,ro,uid=holmes clear/dislocker-file files
...
$ sudo umount files
$ fusermount -u clear
$ rmdir clear files
```

Here dislocker-fuse passes -o allow_root to the FUSE driver, allowing sudo to be used for mounting and unmounting. The uid=holmes ensures that Mr. Holmes can access the mounted files without root privileges. It's assumed that Mr. Holmes is a member of the FUSE Unix group, and the */etc/fuse.conf* file contains the line *user_allow_other*.

Using dislocker, you can provide three possible credentials to unlock a BitLocker container. A -u flag (used in the previous example) specifies that the user's password be requested. A -p flag provides a recovery password (48 digits long). And an -f flag specifies a key file (BEK file).

Using a recovery password (-p) instead of a user password (-u) requires manually keying in the 48-digit recovery password, as follows:

```
# dislocker-fuse -p -V bitlocker-image.raw clear
Enter the recovery password: XXXXXX-XXXXXX-XXXXXX-XXXXXX-XXXXXX-XXXXXX-XXXXXX-XXXXXX
Valid password format, continuing.
```

The non-root version of this command passes flags to FUSE, which allows for mounting with sudo:

```
$ dislocker-fuse -p -V bitlocker-image.raw -- -o allow_root clear
```

You can also decrypt the BitLocker image and save it separately as a regular filesystem image (only the specified volume is saved, not the partition table or other partitions). This will take some time depending on the size of the BitLocker image, as the entire image is decrypted and written to a new image file on the disk. You'll need to do some capacity planning, because the two images, encrypted and decrypted, will take up space on the acquisition host. You can create a decrypted version of the volume as follows:

```
# dislocker-file -u -V bitlocker-image.raw bitlocker-image.clear
Enter the user password:
# ls -hs
total 15G
7.4G bitlocker-image.clear   7.4G bitlocker-image.raw
```

The resulting decrypted image file is the same size as the original because each BitLocker block was decrypted and the cleartext block written to the new image. This command does not need root privileges.

Now you can mount the decrypted BitLocker image file and access it as a partition using a mount command with a loop option:

```
# mkdir files
# mount -o loop,ro bitlocker-image.clear files
# ls files/
Penguins.jpg  private/  System Volume Information/
```

The only command that is different for non-root use is mount:

```
$ sudo mount -o loop,ro,uid=holmes bitlocker-image.clear files
```

Because BitLocker is the default filesystem encryption on the dominant OS platform, it's worth providing a second example using a different software package. The libbde package (written by Joachim Metz, the author of ewflib) also provides libraries and tools to access BitLocker images.

The example shown next is slightly more complex than the previous one, because it involves a notebook disk with a regular partition table (in contrast to a USB thumb drive without a partition table). After calculating the offsets from the mmls output, the bdeinfo tool is demonstrated to provide a compact overview of the BitLocker container.

Both dislocker and libbde can be given a byte offset for the start of the BitLocker-encrypted volume. But this is unnecessary when working with image files of volumes/partitions or devices without partitions. In this example, an acquired image has a partition table, and the BitLocker-encrypted volume offset (in bytes) must be calculated.

NOTE *Always be sure about the units used for a command. Some tools use sector offsets, and others use byte offsets. It is important to distinguish and convert between the two.*

The next example demonstrates how to determine the byte offset. The Sleuth Kit mmls command displays the partition table and the sector offsets for each partition. The sector offset must be converted into a byte offset, which can be used with the decryption tools:

```
# mmls image0.raw
DOS Partition Table
Offset Sector: 0
Units are in 512-byte sectors

      Slot    Start       End         Length      Description
00:   Meta    0000000000  0000000000  0000000001  Primary Table (#0)
01:   -----   0000000000  0000002047  0000002048  Unallocated
02:   00:00   0000002048  0004098047  0004096000  NTFS (0x07)
03:   00:01   0004098048  0625140399  0621042352  NTFS (0x07)
```

```
04:  -----   0625140400   0625142447   0000002048   Unallocated
# echo $((4098048*512))
2098200576
```

You can convert the sector offset shown by mmls to a byte offset by multi-plying by the sector size. On the command line it is convenient to use Bash math expansion. In this example, the sector offset is 4098048 and the sector size is 512. Multiplying these gives a byte offset of 2098200576. You can use this value for the bdeinfo command as follows:

```
# bdeinfo -o 2098200576 image0.raw
bdeinfo 20160119

BitLocker Drive Encryption information:
        Encryption method:          AES-CBC 128-bit with Diffuser
        Volume identifier:          5f61cbf2-75b5-32e5-caef-537fce3cf412
        Creation time:              Jan 10, 2014 17:43:50.838892200 UTC
        Description                 :Notebook System 15.01.2014
        Number of key protectors:   2

Key protector 0:
        Identifier:                 3cd1fd6c-2ecb-2dc7-c150-839ce9e710b6
        Type:                       TPM

Key protector 1:
        Identifier:                 837ef544-e1ca-65c1-a910-83acd492bc1a
        Type:                       Recovery password
...
```

The bdemount command operates similarly to the dislocker command and creates a virtual file that represents the decrypted image (the full key has been shortened here):

```
# mkdir raw
# bdemount -o 2098200576 -r 630641-...-154814 image.raw raw
```

The file will appear in the *./raw* directory, where you can analyze it directly or mount it to a loop device for regular browsing. The mount commands are the same as the previous BitLocker example, so they're not repeated here.

Apple FileVault

Apple's filesystem encryption built into OS X is FileVault. It is also a block-level encryption system, and several open source tools are available to decrypt it. Two tools I'll describe here are libfvde and VFDecrypt. (The libfvde software package was written by Omar Choudary and Joachim Metz, and you'll find it at *https://github.com/libyal/libfvde/*.)

Before you use the libfvde tools, you need to calculate the correct byte offset of the FileVault-encrypted volume. The `mmls` command provides the sector offset of the volume, which needs to be converted to bytes:

```
# mmls image.raw
GUID Partition Table (EFI)
Offset Sector: 0
Units are in 512-byte sectors

     Slot      Start         End           Length        Description
00:  Meta      0000000000    0000000000    0000000001    Safety Table
01:  -----     0000000000    0000000039    0000000040    Unallocated
02:  Meta      0000000001    0000000001    0000000001    GPT Header
03:  Meta      0000000002    0000000033    0000000032    Partition Table
04:  00        0000000040    0000409639    0000409600    EFI System Partition
05:  01        0000409640    0235708599    0235298960    HDD
06:  02        0235708600    0236978135    0001269536    Recovery HD
07:  -----     0236978136    0236978175    0000000040    Unallocated
# echo $((409640*512))
209735680
```

Multiplying the sector offset by the sector size using simple Bash math expansion provides a byte offset of 209735680, which you can use for the fvdeinfo and fvdemount tools.

The fvdeinfo tool provides an overview of the FileVault-encrypted volume:

```
# fvdeinfo -o 209735680 image.raw
fvdeinfo 20160108

Core Storage information:

Physical volume:
        Size:                     120473067520 bytes
        Encryption method:        AES XTS

Logical volume:
        Size:                     120137519104 bytes
```

To decrypt the FileVault volume, you need to recover the *EncryptedRoot .plist.wipekey* file and provide either a user password or recovery key. You can find and extract the *wipekey* file using Sleuth Kit tools, as shown here:

```
# fls -r -o 235708600 image.raw | grep EncryptedRoot.plist.wipekey
+++++ r/r 1036: EncryptedRoot.plist.wipekey
# icat -o 235708600 image.raw 1036 > EncryptedRoot.plist.wipekey
```

The recursive fls output of the Recovery HD partition uses the sector offset found with mmls. The output is grepped for the *EncryptedRoot .plist.wipekey* file. After it's found, the icat tool is used to extract it (using the inode, which is 1036 in this example). Notice how a sector offset was used with fls and icat, and not a byte offset.

The 24-character recovery key is used with the -r flag and the now-recovered *EncryptedRoot.plist.wipekey* file. You can then use this key to create a FUSE mount of a decrypted representation of the volume, as shown here (the recovery key has been shortened):

```
# mkdir clear
# fvdemount -o 209735680 -r FKZV-...-H4PD -e EncryptedRoot.plist.wipekey image.raw
    clear
fvdemount 20160108

# ls -l clear
total 0
-r--r--r-- 1 root root 120137519104 Jan 20 22:23 fvde1
...
```

You can provide a user password (-p) instead of a recovery key (-r), and also using the *EncryptedRoot.plist.wipekey* file, you can access the resulting volume image with regular forensic tools. An example using Sleuthkit's fsstat on the decrypted volume is shown here:

```
# fsstat clear/fvde1
FILE SYSTEM INFORMATION
--------------------------------------------
File System Type: HFS+
File System Version: HFS+

Volume Name: HDD
...
```

You can also mount this decrypted volume as a regular filesystem for browsing, as follows:

```
# mkdir files
# mount -o loop,ro clear/fvde1 files
# ls -l files
total 8212
drwxrwxr-x 1 root    80     50 Mar  2  2015 Applications/
drwxr-xr-x 1 root root     39 Jun  2  2015 bin/
drwxrwxr-t 1 root    80      2 Aug 25  2013 cores/
dr-xr-xr-x 1 root root      2 Aug 25  2013 dev/
...
```

When the analysis work is complete, you'll need to do some cleanup:

```
# umount files
# rmdir files
# fusermount -u clear
# rmdir clear
```

Note that the preceding examples were done with root privileges to reduce complexity and make them easier to understand. Most of the commands can be done as non-root with a few exceptions. Examples in which a command is different when run by a nonprivileged user are shown here:

```
$ fvdemount -o 209735680 -r FKZV-...-H4PD -e EncryptedRoot.plist.wipekey image.raw
    -X allow_root clear
$ sudo mount -o loop,ro clear/fvde1 files
$ sudo ls files/Users/somebody/private/directory
$ sudo umount files
```

The -X allow_root string in the fvdemount command allows root to access the FUSE mounted directory. The sudo command is needed to mount and unmount the hfsplus filesystem. When you're browsing the filesystem, you might also need the sudo command if filesystem permissions restrict access to files or directories.

Several other notable open source tools exist for operating on File-Vault images. The VFDecrypt tool also provides decryption of FileVault images. Originally written by Ralf-Philipp Weinmann, David Hulton, and Jacob Appelbaum, it is now maintained by Drake Allegrini. You'll find it at *https://github.com/andyvand/VFDecrypt/*. It can decrypt an image into an unencrypted volume image.

FileVault Cracking software was created by some of the same authors as VFDecrypt; you'll find it at *http://openciphers.sourceforge.net/oc/vfcrack.php*.

Linux LUKS

A number of file encryption systems are available in the open source world. Some, like eCryptfs or encfs, are directory based. Others, like GPG and various crypt tools, operate on individual files.

In this section, I mainly focus on the LUKS encryption system, but I'll also touch on plain dm-crypt and loop-AES. Using the cryptsetup tool, you can set up all three. (You can also use the cryptsetup tool to manage True-Crypt volumes, which I'll describe in the following section.)

The examples that follow operate on a forensically acquired image with a LUKS-encrypted filesystem. We'll create a block device representing the decrypted content of an encrypted filesystem and show methods to safely mount the filesystem structure for browsing with regular tools. The three goals are to get information about the encryption, create a device that can be accessed with forensic tools, and safely mount the filesystem for regular browsing.

The first step requires the byte offset of the LUKS-encrypted partition. The sector offset is shown by Sleuth Kit's mmls of the image file. The byte offset is the sector offset multiplied by the sector size, which is calculated to be 1048576 using simple Bash math expansion:

```
# mmls luks.raw
DOS Partition Table
Offset Sector: 0
Units are in 512-byte sectors

     Slot    Start       End         Length      Description
00:  Meta    0000000000  0000000000  0000000001  Primary Table (#0)
01:  -----   0000000000  0000002047  0000002048  Unallocated
02:  00:00   0000002048  0058626287  0058624240  Linux (0x83)
# echo $((2048*512))
1048576
```

You can use the byte offset to create a loop device of the encrypted partition by employing losetup as follows:

```
# losetup --read-only --find --show -o 1048576 luks.raw
/dev/loop0
```

The LUKS-encrypted partition is now accessible as a block device, which the cryptsetup tool can use. You can find information about the encrypted partition using cryptsetup's luksDump command:

```
# cryptsetup luksDump /dev/loop0
LUKS header information for /dev/loop0

Version:        1
Cipher name:    aes
Cipher mode:    xts-plain64
Hash spec:      sha1
Payload offset: 4096
MK bits:        256
MK digest:      8b 88 36 1e d1 a4 c9 04 0d 3f fd ba 0f be d8 4c 9b 96 fb 86
MK salt:        14 0f 0d fa 7b c3 a2 41 19 d4 6a e4 8a 16 fe 72
                88 78 a2 18 7b 0f 74 8e 26 6d 94 23 3d 11 2e aa
MK iterations:  172000
UUID:           10dae7db-f992-4ce4-89cb-61d126223f05

Key Slot 0: ENABLED
        Iterations:             680850
        Salt:                   8a 39 90 e1 f9 b6 59 e1 a6 73 30 ea 73 d6 98 5a
                                e1 d3 b6 94 a0 73 36 f7 00 68 a2 19 3f 09 62 b8
```

```
        Key material offset:    8
        AF stripes:             4000
Key Slot 1: DISABLED
Key Slot 2: DISABLED
Key Slot 3: DISABLED
Key Slot 4: DISABLED
Key Slot 5: DISABLED
Key Slot 6: DISABLED
Key Slot 7: DISABLED
```

The key slots can be of interest from a forensics perspective. A LUKS volume can have up to eight keys, meaning there are potentially eight different passwords where you can attempt recovery.

With the password to the LUKS-encrypted filesystem, you can use crypt-setup's open command on the loop0 device to create a mapper device. This device provides a decrypted representation of the encrypted image. The mapper device is named *clear* in this example:

```
# cryptsetup -v --readonly open /dev/loop0 clear
Enter passphrase for /hyb/luks/luks.raw:
Key slot 0 unlocked.
Command successful.
```

The encrypted loop device is opened with the --readonly flag. The verbose (-v) flag is also given to provide more information about the success of the decryption key. After a successful key has been entered, a new (decrypted) partition device will appear in the */dev/mapper* directory and can be operated on using standard forensic tools. For example, you can run the Sleuth Kit fsstat tool:

```
# fsstat /dev/mapper/clear
FILE SYSTEM INFORMATION
--------------------------------------------
File System Type: Ext4
Volume Name: My Secrets
Volume ID: ba673056efcc5785f046654c00943860
...
```

You can also mount this partition device on the local machine for regular browsing:

```
# mkdir clear
# mount --read-only /dev/mapper/clear clear
# ls clear
lost+found/  the plan.txt
```

Once the examination work is complete, the cleanup process can take place. Each step is done in reverse:

```
# umount clear
# rmdir clear
# cryptsetup close clear
# losetup --detach /dev/loop0
```

Note that this is a simplified example of a single partition on a single non-bootable data disk. A LUKS-encrypted disk with an bootable OS may have an additional Logical Volume Manager (LVM) layer. Such disks may have additional devices that appear in the */dev/mapper* directory (root, swap, and so on). You can access or mount each of these devices individually. During the cleanup process, you need to remove the partition devices with dmsetup before closing the LVM device with cryptsetup.

For simplicity, the steps shown in this section were performed as a root user. To run the examples as a non-root user, losetup, cryptsetup, mount, and umount need sudo to execute, as do any tools that access the */dev/mapper* partition device. Depending on the filesystem mounted, additional user options may be useful (uid=holmes for example).

Images encrypted with plain dm-crypt and loop-AES can also be decrypted using the cryptsetup tool. These follow a similar process as the preceding LUKS example. The cryptsetup open command needs to have either plain or loopaes specified using the --type flag. For example:

```
# cryptsetup -v --readonly open --type plain /dev/loop0 clear
Enter passphrase:
Command successful.
```

Using --type loopaes will also require a key file. Specifying --type luks is also possible, but unnecessary, because it's the default.

You'll find more information about cryptsetup and LUKS at *https://gitlab .com/cryptsetup/cryptsetup/wikis/home/*. And you'll find a compatible Windows implementation at *https://github.com/t-d-k/librecrypt/*.

TrueCrypt and VeraCrypt

After development of TrueCrypt was stopped, several forks emerged. The dominating fork at the moment is VeraCrypt. It offers backward compatibility as well as new extensions.

The two examples of VeraCrypt I'll provide are a normal encrypted container and a hidden container. I used the standard command line version of VeraCrypt in conjunction with familiar tools to make the containers available for further analysis.

The first example shows a simple encrypted TrueCrypt or VeraCrypt container file. The --file-system=none flag is important because it prevents VeraCrypt from mounting any filesystems:

```
$ veracrypt --mount-options=readonly --filesystem=none secrets.tc
Enter password for /exam/secrets.tc:
Enter PIM for /exam/secrets.tc:
Enter keyfile [none]:
```

Using the -l flag, you can list all the decrypted containers on the host system by slot number. The slot number is an important identifier to use in subsequent commands. In this example, the slot number is 1 and the familiar /dev/mapper/* directory is used:

```
$ veracrypt -l
1: /exam/secrets.tc /dev/mapper/veracrypt1 -
```

After providing the correct credentials, you can request more information about the container by specifying the slot number, as shown here:

```
$ veracrypt --volume-properties --slot=1
Slot: 1
Volume: /exam/secrets.tc
Virtual Device: /dev/mapper/veracrypt1
Mount Directory:
Size: 2.0 GB
Type: Normal
Read-Only: Yes
Hidden Volume Protected: No
Encryption Algorithm: AES
Primary Key Size: 256 bits
Secondary Key Size (XTS Mode): 256 bits
Block Size: 128 bits
Mode of Operation: XTS
PKCS-5 PRF: HMAC-SHA-512
Volume Format Version: 2
Embedded Backup Header: Yes
```

Two devices have been created. The device */dev/loop0* is encrypted as a raw image (the same as the file on the filesystem). The device shown in the volume properties, */dev/mapper/veracrypt1*, is the decrypted volume, which you can operate on directly using forensic tools. Here is an example of Sleuth Kit examining the filesystem:

```
$ sudo fls /dev/mapper/veracrypt1
r/r * 4:        photo.jpg
r/r 6:  spy-photo.jpg
```

```
v/v 66969091:    $MBR
v/v 66969092:    $FAT1
v/v 66969093:    $FAT2
d/d 66969094:    $OrphanFiles
```

You can also mount the mapper device on the local machine and browse the filesystem with regular tools, like this:

```
$ mkdir clear
$ sudo mount -o ro,uid=holmes /dev/mapper/veracrypt1 clear
$ ls -l clear
total 360
-rwxr-x--- 1 holmes root 366592 Jan 21 23:41 spy-photo.jpg
```

Obviously, deleted files will not be visible in the user-mounted area; they will only be visible when you use forensic tools via the */dev/mapper/veracrypt1* device.

Again, the cleanup process is the reverse of the setup process:

```
$ sudo umount clear
$ rmdir clear
$ veracrypt -d --slot=1
```

The second VeraCrypt example I'll provide shows how to access a hidden volume. One feature of TrueCrypt and VeraCrypt is that it's possible to have two passwords that reveal two separate volumes. The use of both passwords is compared in the two command outputs below.

Here, *hidden.raw* is a VeraCrypt drive containing a hidden volume. Providing the first password produces a functioning standard TrueCrypt container with files, claiming the full 1GB capacity of the drive and showing Type: Normal:

```
$ ls -l
total 3098104
-rw-r----- 1 holmes holmes 1024966656 Jan 22 00:07 hidden.raw
...
$ veracrypt --mount-options=readonly --filesystem=none hidden.raw
Enter password for /exam/hidden.raw: [XXXXXXXXXXX]
...
$ veracrypt --volume-properties --slot=1
Slot: 1
Volume: /exam/hidden.raw
Virtual Device: /dev/mapper/veracrypt1
Mount Directory:
```

```
Size: 977 MB
Type: Normal
Read-Only: Yes
...
$ sudo fls /dev/mapper/veracrypt1
...
r/r 20: fake secrets.pdf
...
```

If the volume is dismounted and then mounted again using the hidden volume's password, you'll see a completely different set of files. The time needed to mount the volume is also different. With the container in the preceding example, 3.5 seconds was needed to unlock it, whereas unlocking the hidden container in the same file needed 29 seconds. This is because the standard volume decryption is attempted first (with all supported algorithms), and upon failing, the decryption of a hidden volume is finally tried. In the volume properties, the real size is now shown together with Type: Hidden, as shown here:

```
$ veracrypt -d --slot=1
$ veracrypt --mount-options=readonly --filesystem=none hidden.raw
Enter password for /exam/hidden.raw: [YYYYYYYYYYY]
...
$ veracrypt --volume-properties --slot=1
Slot: 1
Volume: /exam/hidden.raw
Virtual Device: /dev/mapper/veracrypt1
Mount Directory:
Size: 499 MB
Type: Hidden
Read-Only: Yes
...
$ sudo fls /dev/mapper/veracrypt1
...
r/r 19: the real hidden secrets.pdf
...
```

The mapped device of a hidden volume produces a filesystem that you can directly analyze with forensic tools.

TrueCrypt and VeraCrypt volumes can also be managed by newer versions of cryptsetup (version 1.6.7 and later), providing you with similar mounting possibilities.

There are commercial and open source cracking tools for TrueCrypt/VeraCrypt containers, but their use is beyond the scope of this book.

Closing Thoughts

In this chapter, you learned to make acquired image files available as block devices, create partition devices, and safely make them available for use with regular filesystem tools. You also learned to use loop devices and became more familiar with */dev/mapper* devices. I showed tips for booting up suspect images and demonstrated methods for accessing VM images from various VM formats. Finally, you learned how to make a variety of encrypted filesystems available for access in decrypted form.

9

EXTRACTING SUBSETS OF FORENSIC IMAGES

This chapter covers the selective extraction of data regions from an attached drive or a forensically acquired image file. You'll learn to extract whole partitions, deleted or partially overwritten partitions, inter-partition gaps, and various volume and file slack areas. In addition, you'll see how to extract special areas such as Unified Extensible Firmware Interface (UEFI) partitions, the sectors hidden by a DCO or HPA, and hibernation partitions such as Intel Rapid Start Technology.

The final sections demonstrate extraction of data from allocated and unallocated (possibly deleted) areas of the disk for further examination and manual extraction of sectors using offsets. Let's begin with determining the partition layout of the drive.

Assess Partition Layout and Filesystems

Once you've attached a disk to your system or have acquired an image file, you can perform an analysis of the disk partition scheme. This section explains how to identify filesystems, partition tables, and commonly used disk partition schemes.

The disk layout, or *partition scheme*, refers to the method used to organize the *partitions* (or *slices*) on a hard disk. The most common partition schemes you'll find in consumer computing are DOS, GPT, BSD, and APM (Apple Partition Map, sometimes called *mac*). We'll start with identifying the partition scheme used on a disk.

Partition Scheme

Each partition or slice on a disk contains a separate filesystem or is used for some other special purpose. A small portion of the disk (often just the first sector) defines the layout of the disk by specifying the starting sector of each partition, the partition size, the partition type, labels, and so on.

To determine the disk partition scheme, you can examine the initial sectors of the disk for indicators. There is no official "Assigned Number" designation for partition schemes (there are only half a dozen or so). Don't confuse this with DOS MBR partition types or IDs, which list up to 255 possible filesystems and other formats that could reside inside a DOS partition. When you attach the subject disk to a workstation, the Linux kernel will attempt to detect and interpret the partition scheme used, and it will create the devices for each partition it finds.

You can use the Sleuth Kit mmstat command to identify the most common partition schemes. A list of supported partition schemes is shown here:

```
# mmstat -t list
Supported partition types:
        dos (DOS Partition Table)
        mac (MAC Partition Map)
        bsd (BSD Disk Label)
        sun (Sun Volume Table of Contents (Solaris))
        gpt (GUID Partition Table (EFI))
```

Running mmstat will output the name of the scheme used:

```
# mmstat image.raw
dos
```

Alternatively, you can use the disktype tool to identify the partition scheme. The disktype tool provides more verbose information and supports partitions, filesystems, and file and archive containers. The following example shows output from disktype:

```
$ sudo disktype /dev/sda

--- /dev/sda
Block device, size 27.96 GiB (30016659456 bytes)
DOS/MBR partition map
```

```
Partition 1: 27.95 GiB (30015610880 bytes, 58624240 sectors from 2048)
   Type 0x83 (Linux)
```

You'll find the original disktype software package at *http://disktype .sourceforge.net/*. Also, you'll find a fork and multiple patches for disktype at *https://github.com/kamwoods/disktype/*, *https://github.com/Pardus-Linux/ Packages/tree/master/system/base/disktype/files/*, and *https://github.com/ ericpaulbishop/gargoyle/tree/master/package/disktype/patches/*.

A storage medium does not require a partition table or even a filesystem. Binary data can be written directly to the raw disk and accessed by any program capable of understanding it (for example, some databases can directly use raw disks). It's possible to have disks without partition schemes. In such cases, the filesystem starts at sector zero and continues to the end of the disk (that is, the whole disk is the partition). This is common with some older USB sticks and floppy disks. In such cases, partition analysis tools will be ineffective and generally report a false or nonexistent partition table. If a tool cannot detect a partition type, it's worth checking whether a filesystem was written directly to a raw device. In this example, mmstat finds nothing, but fsstat does identify a filesystem:

```
# mmls /dev/sdj
Cannot determine partition type
# disktype /dev/sdj

--- /dev/sdj
Block device, size 1.406 MiB (1474560 bytes)
FAT12 file system (hints score 5 of 5)
  Volume size 1.390 MiB (1457664 bytes, 2847 clusters of 512 bytes)

# mmstat /dev/sdj
Cannot determine partition type
# fsstat /dev/sdj
FILE SYSTEM INFORMATION
--------------------------------------------
File System Type: FAT12
...
```

Some encrypted volumes attempt to hide their existence or information about the filesystem used, and they don't use a recognizable partition scheme.

Partition Tables

A partition scheme will have a disk block or set of blocks describing how it's organized. These are called *partition tables* (or *disklabels* for BSD systems), and you can query them using various tools.

You can use the Sleuth Kit `mmls` command to list the partition tables on a disk or a forensically acquired image. In this example, `mmls` finds a regular DOS partition scheme with a FAT32 partition:

```
# mmls image.raw
DOS Partition Table
Offset Sector: 0
Units are in 512-byte sectors

     Slot    Start         End           Length        Description
00:  Meta    0000000000    0000000000    0000000001    Primary Table (#0)
01:  -----   0000000000    0000000062    0000000063    Unallocated
02:  00:00   0000000063    0005028344    0005028282    Win95 FAT32 (0x0b)
03:  -----   0005028345    0005033951    0000005607    Unallocated
```

The traditional DOS partition scheme is not able to handle disks larger than 2TB. The GPT partition scheme was created to allow larger disks to be organized with a greater number of partitions. GPT supports 128 partitions compared to the 4 that DOS supports (not counting extended partitions). I have written a paper on the forensic analysis of GPT disks and GUID partition tables; you can find it here: *http://dx.doi.org/10.1016/j.diin.2009.07.001*.

Most new PC systems are being shipped with GPT partitions today. An example of a Windows 8 system's partition table is shown here:

```
# mmls lenovo.raw
GUID Partition Table (EFI)
Offset Sector: 0
Units are in 512-byte sectors

     Slot    Start         End           Length        Description
00:  Meta    0000000000    0000000000    0000000001    Safety Table
01:  -----   0000000000    0000002047    0000002048    Unallocated
02:  Meta    0000000001    0000000001    0000000001    GPT Header
03:  Meta    0000000002    0000000033    0000000032    Partition Table
04:  00      0000002048    0002050047    0002048000
05:  01      0002050048    0002582527    0000532480    EFI system partition
06:  02      0002582528    0003606527    0001024000
07:  03      0003606528    0003868671    0000262144    Microsoft reserved partition
08:  04      0003868672    1902323711    1898455040    Basic data partition
09:  05      1902323712    1953523711    0051200000
```

Gary Kessler provides several partition table–parsing tools that provide much greater detail. You'll find these tools at *http://www.garykessler.net/software/index.html*.

To illustrate the level of detail Kessler's parsing tools provide, here is partial output from the partition table from the preceding example generated using the gptparser.pl tool:

```
$ gptparser.pl -i lenovo.raw

GPT Parser V1.4 beta - Gary C. Kessler (14 March 2013)

Source file = /exam/lenovo.raw
Input file length = 17408 bytes.


***** LBA 0: Protective/Legacy MBR *****


000:  00 00 00 00 00 00 00 00 00 00 00 00 00 00 00 00   ...............
016:  00 00 00 00 00 00 00 00 00 00 00 00 00 00 00 00   ...............
...
=== Partition Table #5 (LBA 3, bytes 0:127) ===
000-015  Partition type GUID: 0xA2-A0-D0-EB-E5-B9-33-44-87-C0-68-B6-B7-26-99-C7
         GUID: EBD0A0A2-B9E5-4433-87C0-68B6B72699C7
         Type: Data partition (Linux *or* Windows)
016-031  Partition GUID: 0x64-12-FF-80-A7-F7-72-42-B6-46-25-33-6D-96-13-B5
         GUID: 80FF1264-F7A7-4272-B646-25336D9613B5
032-039  First LBA: 0x00-08-3B-00-00-00-00-00 [3,868,672]
040-047  Last LBA: 0xFF-27-63-71-00-00-00-00 [1,902,323,711]
048-055  Partition attributes: 0x00-00-00-00-00-00-00-00
056-127  Partition name --
056:  42 00 61 00 73 00 69 00 63 00 20 00 64 00 61 00   B.a.s.i.c. .d.a.
072:  74 00 61 00 20 00 70 00 61 00 72 00 74 00 69 00   t.a. .p.a.r.t.i.
088:  74 00 69 00 6F 00 6E 00 00 00 00 00 00 00 00 00   t.i.o.n.........
104:  00 00 00 00 00 00 00 00 00 00 00 00 00 00 00 00   ...............
120:  00 00 00 00 00 00 00 00                           ........
      Name: Basic data partition
...
```

The tool provides detailed information about each of the 128 GPT partitions.

Filesystem Identification

The disktype tool, already presented in "Partition Scheme" on page 260, allows you to identify partition schemes and filesystems within partitions. The Sleuth Kit fsstat tool provides more comprehensive information about a filesystem. The fsstat tool can operate directly on a partition device or on a forensically acquired image if you specify the sector offset.

In the previous examples, the sector offset of a Windows volume on the *lenovo.raw* image file was 3868672. You can provide this sector offset to the fsstat tool using the -o flag to analyze the filesystem metadata:

```
# fsstat -o 3868672 lenovo.raw
FILE SYSTEM INFORMATION
--------------------------------------------
File System Type: NTFS
Volume Serial Number: 4038B39F38B39300
OEM Name: NTFS
Volume Name: Windows8_OS
Version: Windows XP

METADATA INFORMATION
--------------------------------------------
First Cluster of MFT: 786432
...
```

If the drive is directly attached to your workstation, the Linux kernel will attempt to parse the partition table and make the disk and partition devices available in */dev*, where you can access them directly.

However, if you're examining a raw image file (*.raw*, *.ewf*, and so on), there will be no device files for the image. The kernel will not interpret the partition table and will not create the familiar partition devices (*/dev/sda1*, */dev/sda2*, and so on). You must specify an offset when accessing a partition within an image file.

It's better to rely on forensic tools to determine the partition details rather than to trust the kernel. If a disk is corrupt or damaged, the kernel might refuse to create the partition devices or create the wrong ones. The examples you saw in this section always specified an offset rather than using the kernel. In situations that involve malware, antiforensics, or other malicious misdirection, using forensic tools instead of the kernel should take precedence.

Partition Extraction

This section describes the extraction of individual partitions, inter-partition gaps, and other areas of the disk like the DCO and HPA. Let's begin with some basic examples of extracting regular partitions.

Extract Individual Partitions

To access and extract individual partitions rather than the entire hard disk, you can use several techniques. I'll demonstrate a few examples of partition extraction using a directly attached drive with a partition device, a partition mapper device, and image files operated on by Sleuth Kit's mmcat- and dd-style tools.

If a disk is accessible as an attached device, acquiring the partition is similar to performing a full acquisition with a raw drive device but uses the partition device instead. In the following example, the first partition of */dev/sda* is extracted to a file:

```
# dcfldd if=/dev/sda1 of=partition.raw
```

Extracting partitions requires some capacity planning, because the partition will consume disk space (possibly alongside the full drive image). If you need only temporary access to a partition from an acquired image file, you can attach it as a loop device and access it. The following steps demonstrate this method.

First, use the mmls tool to identify the partition to be attached as a loop, as follows:

```
# mmls lenovo.raw
GUID Partition Table (EFI)
Offset Sector: 0
Units are in 512-byte sectors
...
05:  01     0002050048  0002582527  0000532480  EFI system partition
...
```

Then use Bash math expansion to convert the sector offset and sector length into a byte offset and byte length:

```
# echo $((2050048*512))
1049624576
# echo $((532480*512))
272629760
```

The calculated byte offset and byte length are then passed to losetup to create a loop device, as follows:

```
# losetup --read-only --find --show --offset 1049624576 --sizelimit 272629760
    lenovo.raw
/dev/loop2
```

You can access this resulting loop device using forensic tools in the same way as you access the partition device of an attached disk. An example using Sleuth Kit fls is shown here:

```
# fls /dev/loop2
r/r 3:  SYSTEM_DRV  (Volume Label Entry)
d/d 4:  EFI
d/d 5:  BOOT
d/d * 7:        MSIa11f8.tmp
d/d * 8:         _SI2DBB4.TMP
```

```
d/d * 9:       _190875_
...
```

If you need to extract a partition from an existing acquired image into a separate file, you can use the dd tools or the Sleuth Kit mmcat command.

To extract a partition from an acquired image, the initial step is to identify the partition and sector details. In the following example, the partition table from an acquired disk image shows the partition to be extracted:

```
# mmls image.raw
DOS Partition Table
Offset Sector: 0
Units are in 512-byte sectors

     Slot    Start       End          Length       Description
...
02:  00:00   0000000063  0078124094   0078124032   Linux (0x83)
...
```

Extracting a partition from an already acquired image file using dcfldd or dd requires adding skip (dc3dd uses iskip) and count parameters, which cause the command to jump (skip) ahead to the start of the partition and acquire only the size of the partition:

```
$ dcfldd if=image.raw of=partition.raw bs=512 skip=63 count=78124032
```

In this command, the block size is set to 512 bytes to match the sector size, the start of the partition is at sector 63, and 78124032 sectors should be extracted. With a little additional calculation, you can improve the performance of this command by changing the 512-byte block size to something larger (but don't forget to adjust the skip and count parameters if you do this).

With Sleuth Kit version 3.0 and later, you can use the mmcat tool to easily extract partitions. To recover the first partition in the previous example using mmcat, you must specify the mmls slot number (not the DOS partition number). In this case, the first partition is located in the mmls slot number two and can be extracted as follows:

```
$ mmcat image.raw 2 > partition.raw
```

The mmcat tool simply pipes the output to stdout, so you must either redirect it to a file or pipe it into a program.

Find and Extract Deleted Partitions

To exhaustively search for partially overwritten or deleted partitions of a forensically acquired image, you can use several methods. Sleuth Kit provides a basic tool called sigfind to search for binary signature strings. Two useful tools for comprehensive partition searching are gpart and testdisk. These tools implement filesystem recognition algorithms with more intelligent guessing to identify lost partitions.

Running gpart without any options starts a scan for partitions, skipping over areas identified as allocated. For example:

```
# gpart lenovo.raw

Begin scan...
Possible partition(Windows NT/W2K FS), size(1000mb), offset(1mb)
Possible partition(Windows NT/W2K FS), size(3mb), offset(1030mb)
Possible partition(Windows NT/W2K FS), size(3mb), offset(1494mb)
Possible partition(Windows NT/W2K FS), size(926980mb), offset(1889mb)
Possible partition(Windows NT/W2K FS), size(25000mb), offset(928869mb)
End scan.

...
Guessed primary partition table:
Primary partition(1)
    type: 007(0x07)(OS/2 HPFS, NTFS, QNX or Advanced UNIX)
    size: 1000mb #s(2048000) s(2048-2050047)
    chs:  (0/32/33)-(406/60/28)d (0/32/33)-(406/60/28)r

...
```

Adding a -f flag tells gpart to be exhaustive, looking for partitions in every sector of the entire disk, even in areas where no partitions are expected to be found. This will take much longer than the default gpart scan without flags.

The testdisk tool (*http://www.cgsecurity.org/*, written by Christophe Grenier, who also wrote the photorec carving tool) provides several features in addition to partition searching. Testdisk provides an interactive interface, supports multiple disk layouts (DOS, GPT, BSD, and more), detects several dozen partition types, generates activity logs, and can extract discovered partitions to a file. You can use testdisk on devices, raw image files, and even *.e01* files.

Use the testdisk tool with caution. This tool was designed for repairing and recovering partitions, and it could easily modify evidence. Be sure to use a write blocker before running this tool on attached subject disks.

Also included with the tool is a comprehensive user interactive menu system to define options and activities. Shown here is a batch mode example operating on an attached disk:

```
# testdisk /list /dev/sdb
TestDisk 7.0, Data Recovery Utility, April 2015
Christophe GRENIER <grenier@cgsecurity.org>
http://www.cgsecurity.org
Please wait...
Disk /dev/sdb - 15 GB / 14 GiB - CHS 14663 64 32
Sector size:512
```

```
Model: SanDisk Ultra Fit, FW:1.00

Disk /dev/sdb - 15 GB / 14 GiB - CHS 14663 64 32
    Partition               Start       End    Size in sectors
 1 P FAT32 LBA              0  1  1 14663  44 18   30031218 [NO NAME]
    FAT32, blocksize=16384
```

You can perform a certain amount of manual analysis to search for deleted partitions. If the partition table shows a large area of unallocated space on a disk, check this area to determine whether a partition exists. In the following example, mmls shows nearly 2.5GB (4863378 sectors) of empty space at the end of a thumb drive:

```
# mmls /dev/sdb
DOS Partition Table
Offset Sector: 0
Units are in 512-byte sectors

     Slot      Start        End         Length      Description
000: Meta      0000000000   0000000000  0000000001  Primary Table (#0)
001: -------   0000000000   0000002047  0000002048  Unallocated
002: 000:000   0000002048   0025167871  0025165824  Win95 FAT32 (0x0c)
003: -------   0025167872   0030031249  0004863378  Unallocated
```

This unallocated space could be a deleted partition. In this example, running fsstat using the offset of the empty space discovers a valid filesystem:

```
# fsstat -o 25167872 /dev/sdb
FILE SYSTEM INFORMATION
--------------------------------------------
File System Type: Ext3
Volume Name:
Volume ID: 74a2f1b777ae52bc9748c3dbca837a80

Last Written at: 2016-05-21 15:42:54 (CEST)
Last Checked at: 2016-05-21 15:42:54 (CEST)
...
```

If you detect a valid filesystem, you can use the meta information about it to determine the probable size of the partition. Knowing the size and starting offset, you can extract the discovered partition or further analyze it. You can extract it using dd-style tools or more easily with mmcat, like this:

```
# mmcat /dev/sdb 3 > deleted_partition.raw
```

Here, the mmcat output of the deleted partition discovered in mmls slot 003 is sent to a file called *deleted_partition.raw*.

Identify and Extract Inter-Partition Gaps

In some cases, there may be gaps between partitions that were created accidentally or due to adjacent partitions meeting on cylinder or block boundaries. There could also be intentional gaps that were created for hiding data. You can identify and recover these inter-partition gaps in the same way as you extract a partition. Use mmls to determine the size and sector offset of the gap, and then use dd or mmcat to extract it.

The mmls output of a partition table is shown here. The disk contains two partitions, and there is a gap between them:

```
# mmls /dev/sdb
DOS Partition Table
Offset Sector: 0
Units are in 512-byte sectors

      Slot      Start       End         Length      Description
000:  Meta      0000000000  0000000000  0000000001  Primary Table (#0)
001:  -------   0000000000  0000002047  0000002048  Unallocated
002:  000:000   0000002048  0015626236  0015624189  Linux (0x83)
003:  -------   0015626237  0015626239  0000000003  Unallocated
004:  000:001   0015626240  0030031249  0014405010  Linux (0x83)
```

In this example, the first partition ends on sector 15626236, but the adjacent partition starts on sector 15626240, indicating a three-sector gap between them. Although you can extract this inter-partition gap using dd, using mmcat is simpler:

```
# mmcat /dev/sdb 3 > gap.raw
# ls -l gap.raw
-rw-r----- 1 root root 1536 May 21 16:11 gap.raw
```

The resulting file is three sectors in size with the contents of the gap between the two partitions. Larger gaps between partitions that contain partially overwritten, corrupted, or identifiable filesystem fragments can be analyzed with carving tools such as foremost.

The gap between the last partition and the end of a disk can also be of interest. It may contain artifacts such as content from previously overwritten partitions, backup copies of the GPT partition, or even malware attempting to hide segments of binary code.

Extract HPA and DCO Sector Ranges

You have already learned how to identify and remove HPA and DCO restrictions. Once removed, these areas of the disk can be extracted for separate analysis.

In this example, hdparm shows that an HPA exists, and the mmls output shows three slots, one of them being a Linux partition:

```
# hdparm -N /dev/sdh

/dev/sdh:
 max sectors   = 234441648/976773168, HPA is enabled
# mmls /dev/sdh
DOS Partition Table
Offset Sector: 0
Units are in 512-byte sectors

     Slot    Start       End         Length      Description
00:  Meta    0000000000  0000000000  0000000001  Primary Table (#0)
01:  -----   0000000000  0000002047  0000002048  Unallocated
02:  00:00   0000002048  0234441647  0234439600  Linux (0x83)
```

After you successfully remove the HPA (and tell the kernel to rescan the SCSI bus), running the same commands again produces different output, as shown here:

```
# hdparm -N p976773168  /dev/sdh

/dev/sdh:
 setting max visible sectors to 976773168 (permanent)
 max sectors   = 976773168/976773168, HPA is disabled
# mmls /dev/sdh
DOS Partition Table
Offset Sector: 0
Units are in 512-byte sectors

     Slot    Start       End         Length      Description
00:  Meta    0000000000  0000000000  0000000001  Primary Table (#0)
01:  -----   0000000000  0000002047  0000002048  Unallocated
02:  00:00   0000002048  0234441647  0234439600  Linux (0x83)
03:  -----   0234441648  0976773167  0742331520  Unallocated
```

Now, hdparm indicates the HPA is disabled, and the mmls output shows an additional line of output (slot 03) representing the sectors previously hidden by the HPA.

Using the mmcat command with partition slot 03 will extract the data from HPA, as follows:

```
# mmcat /dev/sdh 3 > hpa.raw
```

This example uses a live disk attached to an acquisition host. When an image file is acquired from a disk with the HPA removed, mmls will see this hidden region.

Extracting sectors hidden by a DCO is identical to the method shown here with the HPA. First use hdparm to expose the DCO-protected sectors, and then extract them using dd or mmcat. This procedure does not need to be repeated with additional examples specifically demonstrating sectors from a DCO.

Other Piecewise Data Extraction

In this final section, I describe various additional examples of piecewise data extraction. The contents of this section (in fact the contents of most of this chapter) blur together slightly with forensic filesystem analysis, which is not the intended scope of the book. For this reason, the examples are slightly less descriptive.

Extract Filesystem Slack Space

Slack space is a traditional digital forensics concept referring to allocated but unused data at the end of disk sectors, filesystem blocks, or filesystems (RAM slack, file slack, and partition slack, respectively).

To visualize slack space, imagine this book as a hard disk, where paragraphs are sectors, chapters are files, and body of the text is the partition. Notice that paragraphs don't finish exactly at the end of a line, chapters don't finish exactly at the end of a page, and the end of the book might have a couple of additional blank pages. These empty spaces are the book's "slack space." With storage media, if the OS or physical drive has not explicitly written zeros to these areas, they might still contain data from previously written files.

Historically, extracting and analyzing slack space has been useful in forensic investigations. However, the value of slack space is beginning to decrease due to several factors:

- SSDs are using TRIM commands to zero unallocated blocks.
- Modern OSes are writing back zeros to unused portions of sectors and blocks.
- Disks with native 4K sectors align with filesystem block sizes.
- OSes create partitions and filesystems aligned to block boundaries.

As part of the forensic process, acquiring and analyzing potential slack areas are still diligent steps to complete.

To extract all slack space on a given image, you can use the Sleuth Kit blkls command. Slack space is filesystem specific, so you must extract slack space on each filesystem separately (you can't just use the entire raw disk). In this example, the filesystem offsets of the acquired image are found with mmls, and the slack space of each one is extracted:

```
# mmls lenovo.raw
GUID Partition Table (EFI)
Offset Sector: 0
```

```
Units are in 512-byte sectors

      Slot    Start       End         Length      Description
04:   00      0000002048  0002050047  0002048000
05:   01      0002050048  0002582527  0000532480  EFI system partition
06:   02      0002582528  0003606527  0001024000
...
08:   04      0003868672  1902323711  1898455040  Basic data partition
...
# blkls -o 2048 -s lenovo.raw > slack.04
# blkls -o 2050048 -s lenovo.raw > slack.05
# blkls -o 2582528 -s lenovo.raw > slack.06
# blkls -o 3868672 -s lenovo.raw > slack.08
```

The slack space for each recognized filesystem is saved to a file. The blkls command's -s flag extracts all slack space (and only slack space). It is important to understand that slack space does not refer to unallocated blocks or sectors. Slack space is the unused area found within *allocated* blocks and sectors of a filesystem.

Extract Filesystem Unallocated Blocks

This next example will gather all unallocated blocks from filesystems on an acquired image. Unallocated blocks are filesystem specific, so you need to perform this operation separately on each recognized filesystem.

Here, the mmls command is again used to determine the offsets of each filesystem, and the blkls command is used to extract unallocated blocks:

```
# blkls -o 2048 lenovo.raw > unalloc.04
# blkls -o 2050048 lenovo.raw > unalloc.05
# blkls -o 2582528 lenovo.raw > unalloc.06
# blkls -o 3868672 lenovo.raw > unalloc.08
```

The correct blkls flag for extracting unallocated blocks is -A, but because it's the default command behavior, you can omit it.

You can also perform the inverse action of extracting all (and only) allocated blocks using the blkls -a command.

Manual Extraction Using Offsets

In certain situations, you might use a hex editor to browse, search, or manually analyze the contents of a disk or acquired disk image. The hex editor may provide a byte offset, a sector offset, or both.

This example uses the console-based hexedit tool to analyze a disk:

```
# hexedit -s /dev/sda
```

The hexedit tool allows you to directly edit block device files and edit very large image files (no loading in memory or temp files), and it provides a sector mode (entire sectors and sector offsets are shown).

In the following example, the sector offset is 2048 (the start of an NTFS partition), the byte offset is 0x100181, and the entire sector is shown (note: hexedit assumes 512-byte sectors):

```
00100000   EB 52 90 4E 54 46 53 20  20 20 20 00 02 08 00 00   .R.NTFS    .....
00100010   00 00 00 00 00 F8 00 00  3F 00 FF 00 00 08 00 00   ........?.......
00100020   00 00 00 00 80 00 80 00  01 48 00 00 00 00 00 00   .........H......
00100030   04 00 00 00 00 00 00 00  80 04 00 00 00 00 00 00   ................
00100040   F6 00 00 00 01 00 00 00  22 90 FD 7E 2E 42 12 09   ........"..~.B..
00100050   00 00 00 00 FA 33 C0 8E  D0 BC 00 7C FB 68 C0 07   .....3.....|.h..
00100060   1F 1E 68 66 00 CB 88 16  0E 00 66 81 3E 03 00 4E   ..hf......f.>..N
00100070   54 46 53 75 15 B4 41 BB  AA 55 CD 13 72 0C 81 FB   TFSu..A..U..r...
00100080   55 AA 75 06 F7 C1 01 00  75 03 E9 D2 00 1E 83 EC   U.u.....u.......
00100090   18 68 1A 00 B4 48 8A 16  0E 00 8B F4 16 1F CD 13   .h...H..........
001000A0   9F 83 C4 18 9E 58 1F 72  E1 3B 06 0B 00 75 DB A3   .....X.r.;...u..
001000B0   0F 00 C1 2E 0F 00 04 1E  5A 33 DB B9 00 20 2B C8   ........Z3... +.
001000C0   66 FF 06 11 00 03 16 0F  00 8E C2 FF 06 16 00 E8   f...............
001000D0   40 00 2B C8 77 EF B8 00  BB CD 1A 66 23 C0 75 2D   @.+.w......f#.u-
001000E0   66 81 FB 54 43 50 41 75  24 81 F9 02 01 72 1E 16   f..TCPAu$....r..
001000F0   68 07 BB 16 68 70 0E 16  68 09 00 66 53 66 53 66   h...hp..h..fSfSf
00100100   55 16 16 16 68 B8 01 66  61 0E 07 CD 1A E9 6A 01   U...h..fa.....j.
00100110   90 90 66 60 1E 06 66 A1  11 00 66 03 06 1C 00 1E   ..f`..f...f.....
00100120   66 68 00 00 00 00 66 50  06 53 68 01 00 68 10 00   fh....fP.Sh..h..
00100130   B4 42 8A 16 0E 00 16 1F  8B F4 CD 13 66 59 5B 5A   .B..........fY[Z
00100140   66 59 66 59 1F 0F 82 16  00 66 FF 06 11 00 03 16   fYfY.....f......
00100150   0F 00 8E C2 FF 0E 16 00  75 BC 07 1F 66 61 C3 A0   ........u...fa..
00100160   F8 01 E8 08 00 A0 FB 01  E8 02 00 EB FE B4 01 8B   ................
00100170   F0 AC 3C 00 74 09 B4 0E  BB 07 00 CD 10 EB F2 C3   ..<.t...........
00100180   0D 0A 41 20 64 69 73 6B  20 72 65 61 64 20 65 72   ..A disk read er
00100190   72 6F 72 20 6F 63 63 75  72 72 65 64 00 0D 0A 42   ror occurred...B
001001A0   4F 4F 54 4D 47 52 20 69  73 20 6D 69 73 73 69 6E   OOTMGR is missin
001001B0   67 00 0D 0A 42 4F 4F 54  4D 47 52 20 69 73 20 63   g...BOOTMGR is c
001001C0   6F 6D 70 72 65 73 73 65  64 00 0D 0A 50 72 65 73   ompressed...Pres
001001D0   73 20 43 74 72 6C 2B 41  6C 74 2B 44 65 6C 20 74   s Ctrl+Alt+Del t
001001E0   6F 20 72 65 73 74 61 72  74 0D 0A 00 00 00 00 00   o restart.......
001001F0   00 00 00 00 00 00 00 00  80 9D B2 CA 00 00 55 AA   ..............U.
```

```
---   sda     --0x100181/0x6FD21E000--sector 2048-------------------------
```

From the byte or sector offset, you can construct dd commands to extract what was found within the hex editor.

The following example uses a sector size of 512, a sector offset, and a sector count to extract a range of data (four 512-byte sectors) from an image:

```
# dd if=/dev/sda of=sectors.raw skip=2048 bs=512 count=4
```

The next example extracts the same range of data using byte offsets. The skip command uses Bash math expansion to convert hexadecimal into decimal, which is needed for dd; the block size is 1 byte; and the count is the number of bytes required.

```
# dd if=/dev/sda of=bytes.raw skip=$((0x100000)) bs=1 count=2048
```

The two previous examples extract the same block (four sectors or 2048 bytes) of data. Note that when extracting regions of a disk, it is sensible to ensure you have sector- or block-aligned offsets (that is, multiples of the sector size or block size).

In cases in which you need to extract a range of filesystem blocks, use the Sleuth Kit blkcat command. The following example extracts 25 blocks from a filesystem starting at block 100:

```
# blkcat /dev/sda1 100 25 > blocks.raw
```

The filesystem block size should be detected by the tool.

The examples in this final section showed how you can access images; use offsets; and extract a range of bytes, sectors, or blocks. You can also use other Sleuth Kit commands to map sectors to blocks and map blocks to inodes and filenames. These tasks are filesystem specific and move into the realm of filesystem forensic analysis.

Closing Thoughts

In this final chapter, you learned how to extract subsets of drives and forensic images. The chapter focused on extracting various portions of an image such as sectors hidden by an HPA or DCO, deleted partitions, and interpartition gaps. You also saw the manual extraction of specified sectors and blocks, including unallocated blocks and slack space. This chapter bordered on forensic analysis, as it looked at identifying partition schemes, understanding partition tables, and identifying filesystems. Since this book is about forensic acquisition and not forensic analysis, it is a fitting final chapter.

CLOSING REMARKS

I hope you have found this book a useful educational tool, and I hope that going forward you'll continue to find it a helpful reference. Whether you're a professional forensics practitioner or a student learning about forensics, this book aims to demonstrate fundamental concepts, show how things work, and provide a set of practical tool examples with the Linux command line.

Many new forensic books focus on application-layer analysis, cloud forensics, mobile forensics, big data analytics, and other new and exciting areas. Traditional digital forensic acquisition and evidence preservation of storage media might seem less exciting by comparison, but it is still a fundamental function that new forensic investigators need to learn.

The community must not be complacent when it comes to advancements in traditional storage media forensics. A lot of change continues to happen in this area, and we as a community need to keep up with the latest developments. This book is intended to be a resource that includes coverage of the latest changes in traditional storage media forensics.

Clearly, not all of the examples, tools, and methods shown here are suitable for every professional forensic lab setting. Many open source forensic tools are a small software development effort undertaken by volunteers (sometimes just a single developer), and some are even abandoned software projects. These cannot easily compete with the products of larger commercial software companies. Nonetheless, even tools that are in experimental stages of development will provide you with an understanding of the problems and how the solutions might look. In addition, I encourage you to explore other tools and methods that might not be covered in this book—open source tools are continuously and rapidly changing, and for every tool and method shown here, there are alternatives that could achieve the same result.

As a final word of encouragement to readers: Learn!

I was drawn into digital forensics and investigation because it's a field where you're always learning. The investigative process is learning—learning about how events in an incident transpired. The digital forensics process is learning—learning how technologies are interacting with each other and reconstructing a sequence of technological activity. Digital forensics research and development is learning—learning to develop new tools and methods to overcome challenges and to understand complex technology to advance the body of knowledge.

Digital forensics is a fascinating field. Enjoy it!

INDEX

E

EIDE (Enhanced Integrated Drive
  Electronics), 32
eject shell command, 133
*Electronic Crime Scene Investigation: A
  Guide for First Responders*
  (US DOJ), 3, 7
EnCase EWF
  built-in encryption, 215
  compressed format, 189
  converting AFF images to, 209–210
  converting FTK files to, 208
  converting raw images to, 202–203
  converting to another format,
    205–208
  forensic acquisition, 145–146
  hash windows, 153
  image access tasks, 233–234
  overview, 62
  recalculating hash of forensic
    image, 198
  remote forensic acquisition, 171–172
  splitting images during
    acquisition, 193
encrypted filesystems, accessing
  Apple FileVault, 248–251
  Linux LUKS, 251–254
  Microsoft BitLocker, 243–248
  overview, 243
  TrueCrypt, 254–257
  VeraCrypt, 254–257
EncryptedRoot.plist.wipekey file, 249–250
encryption. *See also* cryptography;
    encrypted filesystems,
    accessing
  flash drives, 17, 131, 131*f*, 228
  key-wiping procedures, 227–228
  Opal, 128–131
  securing disk image with, 211–218
Enhanced Integrated Drive Electronics
  (EIDE), 32
environmental factors, 91–93
EO1. *See* EnCase EWF
EOD (End of Data) marker, on tapes,
  14, 176
EOF (End of File) marker, on tapes, 176
EOM (End of Media) marker, on
  tapes, 176
EOT (End of Tape) marker, on tapes, 176
erasing forensic image data, 224–228
errors, drive, 159–165
estimated completion time, 87–88

evidence
  containers. *See* forensic file formats
  disk. *See* subject disk
  integrity of, 197–202. *See also*
    cryptography
  organizing, 76–83
EWF. *See* EnCase EWF
ewfacquirestream tool, 172, 210
ewfacquire tool
  compressing images, 189
  converting raw images to EWF,
    202–203
  cryptographic hashing algorithms,
    151, 151*t*
  error handling, 161
  forensic acquisition, 141, 145–147
  splitting images during
    acquisition, 193
ewfexport tool, 205, 206, 207
ewfinfo tool, 206, 207
ewfmount tool, 233, 234
ewfverify tool, 198
examination directory structure, 79–81
examination host. *See* acquisition host
Expert Witness Format. *See* EnCase EWF
EXTENDED SECURITY ERASE command, 227
Extensible Host Controller Interface
  (xHCI), 29–30
external drives, encrypting, 216, 217–218
extracted files, naming conventions for,
  77–78
extracting subsets of data. *See* data
  extraction

F

failure, drive, 159–165
FC (Fibre Channel) interface, 25–26, 26*f*
FDE (full-disk encryption), 128–131,
  216–218
fg command, 93
Fibre Channel (FC) interface, 25–26, 26*f*
file compression, 85
file formats. *See* forensic file formats
files, naming conventions for, 76–79
file shredder, 224–225
file sizes, reporting, 86–87
file slack, 43
filesystems. *See also* encrypted filesystems,
    accessing
  accessing forensic file format as,
    233–235
  data CD, 20

The Electronic Frontier Foundation (EFF) is the leading organization defending civil liberties in the digital world. We defend free speech on the Internet, fight illegal surveillance, promote the rights of innovators to develop new digital technologies, and work to ensure that the rights and freedoms we enjoy are enhanced — rather than eroded — as our use of technology grows.

EFF.ORG

ELECTRONIC FRONTIER FOUNDATION

Protecting Rights and Promoting Freedom on the Electronic Frontier

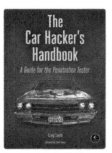

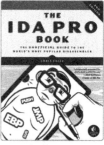